LEGO® Mindstorms® NXT
The Mayan Adventure

James Floyd Kelly

Apress®

LEGO® Mindstorms® NXT: The Mayan Adventure

Copyright © 2006 by James Floyd Kelly

ISBN-13 (pbk): 978-159059-763-7

ISBN-10 (pbk): 1-59059-763-X

eISBN-13: 978-1-4302-0362-9

Printed and bound in the United States of America 9 8 7 6 5 4

Lead Editor: Jim Sumser
Technical Reviewers: Brian Davis and Jeff Gennick
Editorial Board: Steve Anglin, Ewan Buckingham, Gary Cornell, Jason Gilmore, Jonathan Gennick,
    Jonathan Hassell, James Huddleston, Chris Mills, Matthew Moodie, Dominic Shakeshaft, Jim Sumser,
    Keir Thomas, Matt Wade
Project Manager: Tracy Brown Collins
Copy Edit Manager: Nicole Flores
Copy Editors: Susannah Davidson, Ami Knox, Bill McManus
Assistant Production Director: Kari Brooks-Copony
Production Editor: Kelly Winquist
Compositor: Lynn L'Heureux
Proofreader: April Eddy
Indexer: Broccoli Information Management
Artist: April Milne
Cover Designer: Kurt Krames
Manufacturing Director: Tom Debolski

Distributed to the book trade worldwide by Springer-Verlag New York, Inc., 233 Spring Street, 6th Floor, New York, NY 10013. Phone 1-800-SPRINGER, fax 201-348-4505, e-mail orders-ny@springer-sbm.com, or visit http://www.springeronline.com.

For information on translations, please contact Apress directly at 2855 Telegraph Avenue, Suite 600, Berkeley, CA 94705. Phone 510-549-5930, fax 510-549-5939, e-mail info@apress.com, or visit http://www.apress.com.

The source code for this book is available to readers at http://www.apress.com in the Source Code/Download section.

*I'd like to dedicate this book to Ashley. My wife truly understands that
"the difference between men and boys is the price of their toys."
Thank you for your support and encouragement.
Up next—our own special, little project . . .*

Contents at a Glance

v

Contents

About the Author

JAMES FLOYD KELLY (Jim) is a freelance technical writer and currently lives in Atlanta, Georgia. With degrees in English and Industrial Engineering, his friends and family often wondered what he was thinking about when he made that decision. Well, he somehow managed to turn his skills into a career where he gets to play with robots, new software, and other technologies. Jim was one of the original Mindstorms Developer Program (MDP) participants selected by Lego to test the new Mindstorms NXT robotics kit, and he contributes with other NXT fans to The NXT Step Blog (http://thenxtstep.blogspot.com). He is also a member of the Mindstorms Community Partners (MCP), a group of NXT testers that continues to work with Lego on the NXT product line.

About the Technical Reviewers

■**DR. BRIAN DAVIS** has been building Lego robots of various types for about five years, programming mostly in NQC on the RCX. He has designed robots to play tic-tac-toe, compete in robotic sumo, and successfully challenge more "conventional" robots in events such as line following and maze solving. He has also worked on community projects like the Great Ball Contraption, a cooperative kinetic sculpture that moves small Lego balls around, and has helped coordinate Lego fan events such as BrickFest and House of Bricks. In 2005 he was contacted by Lego to become a member of the Mindstorms User Panel expansion, a small group of Lego enthusiasts who were consulted on the development of the NXT Mindstorms product. Since then he has immersed himself in the NXT product, building robots, working on studless design, and digging out the details of the NXT-G language and the NXT hardware. He regularly contributes to several online resources, including The NXT Step Blog, LUGNET, and others.

Brian received a PhD in physics from the University of Michigan, and currently lives in northern Indiana. When he is not playing with Lego (actually, even when he is), he is a husband and stay-at-home Dad of three and also teaches college-level physics, biophysics, and astronomy. He can be reached at brdavis@iusb.edu.

■**JEFF GENNICK** is an 11-year-old "Yooper," living in Michigan's Upper Peninsula, about seven blocks from Lake Superior. Jeff has more Legos than his father likes to think about, having seemingly invested all of his father's retirement fund into the little blocks. Legos are everywhere in the house, and Jeff and friends are frequently building and tearing down their various creations. When not playing with Lego bricks, Jeff switches into gamer mode where you'll find him at work conquering games such as Lego Star Wars II, Freelancer, and Veggie Tales: LarryBoy and the Bad Apple. Jeff gets outdoors too, and during good weather you may see him mountain-biking with his father on the local trails.

Acknowledgments

Writing a book is a *lot* of work! And I'm not talking about my work. There are so many people who have contributed some excellent work to the book you're holding, and I'm glad to have this opportunity to thank them for their hard work.

First, thanks go to Jim Sumser, Lead Editor with Apress. Jim read my original proposal for the book and must have seen something promising because I've had nothing but complete support during the entire writing and editing process. When he e-mailed to let me know that Apress wanted to do the book, I think my heart actually skipped a beat when I realized he was serious and that I would actually have to write this thing!

I figured out quickly that I was going to need some serious organizational help with getting this book written. I have to thank Tracy Brown Collins at Apress, my Project Manager, for her work and apologize for any stress I may have caused her. For a book with this many drawings, figures, photos, and screenshots, I am amazed at her ability to keep it all organized and keep me moving forward towards a finished project. Tracy, you helped this writer stay on track, and you did it with kindness and support. Thank you so much!

Evun an Englush major can make spelling and grammur mustakes (just kidding). For helping me clean up the text and fix quite a few errors, I have Susannah Davidson, Bill McManus, and Ami Knox to thank. Going over their fixes and suggested changes was a good review for me—thank you all for the great work!

You might have noticed that this book has a lot of figures. Well, someone had to help me clean them up and redraw my horrid hand sketches. I was fortunate to have a team that really deserves the credit, and this includes April Milne. Thank you all for taking what looked perfect in my head but terrible on paper and turning it into something to be proud of! And a special thank you goes to Kurt Krames for the great cover mixture of Mayan pyramid and NXT robot. Who could imagine these two images sharing a book cover?

And finally, with any technology book, a huge amount of thanks has to go to the technical editor. I was fortunate to have Brian Davis help me with testing the robots and double-checking my programs. He caught quite a few errors and offered up some suggestions for better ways to explain some complicated subjects. The book is much improved thanks to his efforts. Thank you, Brian, for your attention to details and for your feedback.

Another thank you goes to Jeff Gennick who provided questions and feedback during the writing of my chapters. Jeff (and his dad, Jonathan Gennick, another Apress staff member) purchased an NXT kit early on and helped me with early testing of the initial robot designs. Thanks go to both of them for their help.

I'm certain there are others who were working hard behind the scenes, and I'd like to thank everyone who had a hand in getting this book completed.

Introduction

Welcome to *LEGO Mindstorms NXT: The Mayan Adventure*. I don't like to make assumptions, but since you're holding this book, I'm guessing that you are either an owner of the new Lego Mindstorms NXT robotics kit or are interested in the robotics kit and what can be done with it. (Or maybe you just thought the cover looked interesting and were wondering what robots have to do with the ancient Mayan civilization.)

This book is fairly unique, and I'll tell you why. For the earlier version of Mindstorms (called Mindstorms Robotics Invention System, or RIS for short), numerous books were written, most of which focus on building rather extravagant robots, hacking the Mindstorms processor (called the Brick), and doing other wild things with the product. And the books are great! Many of them show you, step by step, how to build and program very unique creations. But after reading them, I felt that a few things were missing.

The first thing I noticed was a minimal amount of "where to start" type information. The first time you open up a Mindstorms robotics kit, you might feel a little overwhelmed at the sheer number of pieces (almost *all* of them small) in the box. You get an instruction manual and some sample robots to build, but there is very little information for those new designers who are asking "How do I start designing a robot?"

The second item I found lacking was incentive. There are lots of robots that can be built, but many Mindstorms owners get stuck trying to come up with a problem to solve. "What should I build?" is a frequently asked question. There are robotics competitions, with fixed tasks to complete and well-defined conditions for winning, but what if you're not into competitions or lack access to them? Where can a person find challenges to take on and accomplish?

The last gap involves training. Many of the books on the market for the RIS are great at telling you how to build and program your robots, but many times the explanations aren't really explanations—they're instructions: "Put this piece here" and "Drop that there." What is missing are the reasons for doing something (or, at least, the authors' reasons).

With *The Mayan Adventure*, I've tried to fill in these gaps as follows:

- To answer the question "How do I start designing a robot?" I've provided something called a Design Journal page. This is a worksheet that I use (and encourage you to use) to demonstrate the development of the book's robots, using a step-by-step method. It's not the only method out there, but it's my hope that you will find it useful as a way to keep your thoughts organized and to help you move forward in a constructive way.

- As for lack of incentive, I've divided the book into five sections, each of which involves a challenge. Each section has part of a fictional storyline that sets up a *reason* for building a robot. The story is fictional, but the challenges give you plenty of encouragement to experiment and develop your own robots.

- And when it comes to training, I provide solutions to the five challenges by walking you through the development of my robots, their construction, and their programming. I give you some "Do this" and "Do that," but always with an explanation.

I don't use a lot of fancy, technical terms. There are some in there (it's unavoidable when dealing with programming), but I think you'll find that the book is written in an easy-to-follow way and, hopefully, you'll also find the process fun.

If you're completely unfamiliar with NXT, you really should install the NXT-G software (the CD that comes with the kit) and go through the included tutorials. These tutorials will teach you the basics of how to use the software as well as give you some basic construction skills. To get the most out of this book, you do need to at least be comfortable with using the NXT components, opening the NXT-G software, creating and saving programs, and uploading programs to your robot. If you're comfortable with this short list, then you're almost ready to start . . .

How This Book Is Organized

As I mentioned earlier, I've divided the book into five sections. Each section is further divided into four chapters. The fictional storyline starts in Chapter 1, continues in Chapters 5, 9, 13, and 17, and concludes in Chapter 21. The storyline is where you find the details of a particular challenge (for that section); these details are important because they help you to determine the robot's objectives.

Chapters 2, 6, 10, 14, and 18 are what I call the "theory" chapters. Don't let that word scare you, though. When I say theory chapters, I simply mean that these chapters give you plenty to think about—what does the robot need to do, what can it *not* do, what parts should be used, and what parts should *not* be used. I use the Design Journal page in these theory chapters, and I've provided five blank copies in the back of the book for you to follow along with me (or use them to develop your own robots).

Chapters 3, 7, 11, 15, and 19 are the building instructions for the robots. In each chapter, you'll find a set of photos that walks you through building my version of the robot. You can follow my steps and build the exact same robots I include in the book, or you can come up with your own creations. (If you find you're missing a part or something just doesn't snap together properly, the best part about Lego robots is that there's always a workaround—another way to connect something or a combination of parts that can be used as a substitute. Don't stress about it—use your creativity and find an alternative solution!)

Chapters 4, 8, 12, 16, and 20 provide the programming instructions. I use *plenty* of screenshots to show you how to configure each block that is used in the NXT-G programming language. If you have used my building instructions, you can also use the programming instructions. These chapters also include instructions for you on how to set up a test environment for testing your robots and see if they can complete the challenges.

Finally, I've included some appendices for you; references, instructions for documenting your own robots, and other stuff. Check them out.

Who Is This Book For?

It doesn't matter if you are 10 years old or 50, building robots is fun. This book is for everyone who wants to build some new Mindstorms NXT robots and have fun. I don't expect you to be a programming guru—I'm certainly not. I also don't expect you to have advanced degrees in robotics, engineering, or computer science. Let's all remember that Lego Mindstorms NXT is, ultimately, a Lego product. It's a TOY! It's supposed to be fun, not stressful.

If you're a kid, this book can be a great way to get your mom or dad interested in your hobby. And if you're a parent, this book can be a great way to have some fun with your kids. I think you'll see that it's fun to create challenges for yourself (or someone else) and then try to build some great robots to overcome those challenges.

What You Need to Use This Book

The only things you need besides this book are a Lego Mindstorms NXT robotics kit and a computer to run the software and upload programs to your robots. There are currently two versions of the Mindstorms NXT kit—the retail version that you can buy online or in stores, and the education version that Lego sells to teachers, schools, and individuals. There are differences in the types of parts that come in the two kit versions, so please be aware that all the robots in this book have been built with the retail version. If you own the education version, that's okay. It just means that if you find I'm using a part that you don't have, you'll have to improvise. Don't let that bother you—just look at it as another challenge to overcome and something new to learn.

Extras for This Book

Extra Design Journal pages can be downloaded from the Source Code page on the Apress Web site, at http://www.apress.com.

CHAPTER 1

Tomb, Trap, and Trigger

Location: Southwest Guatemala

85 miles SW of Guatemala City

Coordinates: 14° 02' N / 90° 42' W

Weather Conditions: 94 degrees Fahrenheit, Humidity 40%

Day 2: King Ixtua Tomb Excavation, 4:42 PM

Evan leaned against a large stone at the base of the pyramid and sprayed more insect repellent on his left arm. The smell was horrible, but unlike the sunscreen, at least it worked. Evan wasn't sure which was more burned, his nose or his ears. He couldn't wait to get inside the pyramid and the shade it offered. The pyramid and the base camp were completely covered by the jungle and not visible from above, but the sunlight still managed to find its way through the leaves and branches and heat the air.

"A slight problem here," said Uncle Phillip as he walked away from the large stone entry door to the Mayan tomb. He continued walking across the camp, with his two assistants, Max and Grace, running to keep up.

Evan turned and ran to catch up with his uncle. "What's wrong?" he asked, almost running into two Guatemalan guides carrying a box of excavation equipment.

"Follow me, Evan, and I'll show you," Uncle Phillip replied as they continued walking towards the communications tent.

Dr. Phillip Hicks was the lead excavator for a newly discovered Mayan tomb, deep in the Guatemalan jungle. Evan's uncle was a professor of archaeology and taught at Florida State University, but he jumped at any chance he could find to leave the classroom and do some hands-on research. Two weeks ago Evan's parents had received a call from Uncle Phillip, asking if Evan would like to tag along; his parents had agreed to let him travel with his uncle for a few weeks to finish off his summer vacation. It would also be a nice break from Evan's younger twin brothers, Les and Wes.

As they entered the communications tent, Uncle Phillip threw his FSU cap on a nearby chair. Sitting next to the chair was a large opened chest with numerous books and strange equipment. Uncle Phillip was an expert in Mayan history, and earlier in the day he had shown Evan a picture of a Mayan glyph from one of the books. Uncle Phillip told Evan that the strangely drawn symbol represented King Ixtua. That same symbol was carved in stone above the tomb's entry door, confirming that the Mayan pyramid was the tomb of the ancient Mayan king.

Uncle Phillip began flipping maps on a large table, looking for something. "Where's the enlargement of the Tupaxu manuscript? That drawing makes sense now," he said.

One of the assistants, Max, was looking on a small side table. Evan stood quietly, not wanting to interfere. The other assistant, Grace, began to dig through the chest of books.

"Have you ever heard the story of King Ixtua, Evan?" asked Uncle Phillip. He continued to shuffle maps and papers on the table.

Evan shook his head. "No, sir. My history grades aren't so hot. Sorry."

"That's okay," replied Uncle Phillip. "I didn't really become interested in history until college. But I think you'll like this story."

Evan's last history grade had not been impressive; science and math were more to his liking. But when his uncle had told him that this pyramid was unopened and had been hidden for more than 700 years, Evan couldn't resist. He had packed his clothes, MP3 player, laptop, and the new robotics kit his parents had given him for his birthday last month, and met his uncle at the airport. If the pyramid turned out to be one big boring rock, he'd have his music and could at least spend some time designing some robots to show his friends when he got home.

"This King Ixtua liked monkeys, you see," said Uncle Phillip as he continued to search through a smaller pile of maps and papers. "He had numerous spider monkeys that he trained to do tricks. The story tells us that King Ixtua had a pyramid built as his final resting place. To keep out tomb robbers and other unwelcome guests, he had the builders design the pyramid so only someone friendly to his monkeys could gain access to the tomb. A nice legend, huh?"

"Weird," Evan said, and then laughed. His uncle smiled at him and laughed, too.

"Here it is!" yelled Max, as he pulled a large sheet off the small table and walked over to Uncle Phillip. Evan watched as his uncle carefully placed the sheet in front of his team.

"Two years ago, Evan, one of my old professors found a Mayan manuscript in a sealed jar on a dig and gave it to me. I translated the writing and found it was written by Tupaxu, the king's pyramid builder. It gave a general description of the location of the pyramid, among other things," said Uncle Phillip. "Look at this," said Uncle Phillip, pointing his finger at a strange drawing on the sheet.

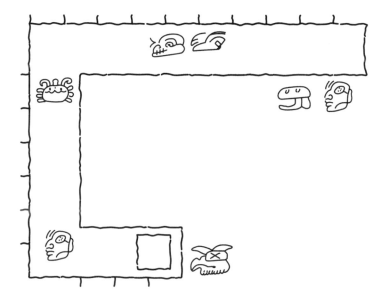

Figure 1-1. *Tunnel drawing*

Evan looked at the small drawing. It was surrounded by the strange Mayan writing he had seen on the various ruins in the camp.

Evan shook his head. "What is it?" he asked.

Grace pointed at the strange writing. "It's a drawing of a small tunnel. Your uncle was right about the monkeys, it seems," she said. "That drawing shows us how to unlock the stone entry doorway to the tomb."

Evan still didn't understand, and he frowned. "What are these symbols?" he asked, pointing at the small shapes.

"Measurements," answered his uncle. "These measurements translate to a tunnel entrance roughly eighteen inches high by eighteen inches wide. Too small for a person, but just the right size for a small spider monkey."

"But if you've found the door, why can't you just drill through it or knock it down?" asked Evan.

Uncle Phillip shook his head. "First, we don't destroy or damage any ruins. And second, the door has a trap that is disabled by a pressure switch. If the switch isn't pressed, the trap, whatever it is, will go off if we open or tamper with the door. Tupaxu was a very smart designer."

"So you just need to find this pressure switch and press it, right?" asked Evan.

"The first part is easy, Evan," said Uncle Phillip. "We found the pressure switch, but it's in a very bad location. Come on, I'll show you."

Tunnel Challenge

Evan pointed his flashlight down the tunnel. The bright beam ended about ten feet ahead where the tunnel turned to the left and continued.

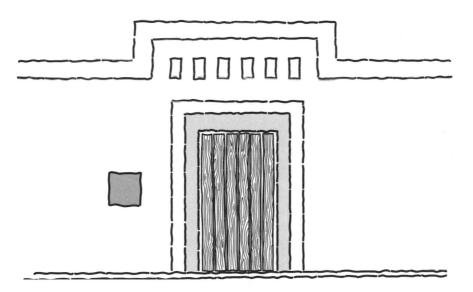

Figure 1-2. *Tunnel at tomb entry*

"According to the manuscript, the tunnel is about ten feet deep. It then goes left about six feet and then turns left again for another three feet. At the end of the tunnel is a small pressure plate," said Uncle Phillip. "If the pressure plate isn't triggered, we can't get in."

Grace was busy taking measurements of the tunnel with a tape measure. She nodded and wrote in her notebook. "It definitely matches the dimensions of the drawing. It looks like you were right; a trained monkey would follow the path and step onto the pressure plate, triggering the release for the doorway," she said. "The legend of King Ixtua is true."

Uncle Philip shook his head. "Unfortunately, the story of the monkeys is also true. I don't think we have any trained monkeys in our tents. And Evan may be too big to send down the tunnel," he replied.

"What!" yelled Evan. "Are you serious?"

Uncle Phillip laughed. "Just kidding, Evan," he said. "We'll find another way."

Evan watched his uncle scratch his head and turn to walk back to camp. It appeared that the exploration of the tomb was at a standstill. Evan felt sorry for his uncle and the assistants, knowing they had spent so much time planning this expedition. It was hard to believe the solution to the problem was something as simple as a small monkey stepping on a pressure plate.

Uncle Phillip, Grace, and Max talked quietly as they walked back to camp. Evan looked down the small tunnel and shook his head. *If only we had a small trained monkey*, he thought.

And then the idea came to him.

"*Wait!*" Evan yelled and then spun to face the others. "I've got it!"

Evan's Solution

Back in the communications tent, Evan set a small, plastic yellow toolbox on the table. Next to it was his dad's old laptop that was currently booting up. Evan opened the toolbox and reached in, pulling out a small rectangular object.

"This is the Mindstorms NXT Intelligent Brick," he said. "This is the brains of any robot I build with this kit." Evan handed it to his uncle and continued pulling out various objects. He watched as his uncle turned the Brick over in his hands and examined it closely.

"And these are sensors and other parts that are used to build a robot." He set a few of the objects on the table in front of the team and then logged into the computer.

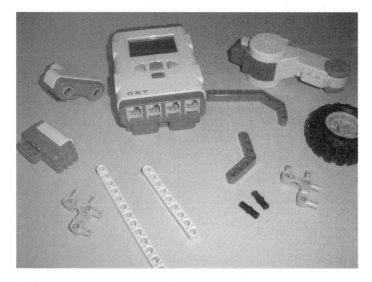

Figure 1-3. *Mindstorms NXT Intelligent Brick and other components*

Max and Grace each picked up some of the components and examined them, and Uncle Phillip handed the Brick back to Evan. Evan set the Brick on the table and pointed at the computer screen.

"This software allows me to program the robot to do various tasks. I can tweak the software until I get the robot to do exactly what I want it to do. Pretty cool, isn't it?" he asked.

Uncle Phillip smiled and nodded. "Are you telling me that you can build a small robot with this stuff that can go down that tunnel and trigger the pressure plate?"

Evan smiled. "Yep. And I don't think it will take me that long, either," he replied. He pulled out a small brown notebook from the laptop case and opened it up. He had been playing with the Mindstorms NXT kit for about a month and had plenty of notes and comments written in it.

Max handed his component to Evan and pointed at it. "What does that do?" he asked.

"That's a servo motor. It does a lot of different things, but I use it mainly to give a robot wheels to move. Grace is holding the sound sensor," Evan said, pointing at a small block that Grace was examining.

Uncle Phillip pulled a chair over to the table and sat down with Evan. He looked over all the parts Evan was placing on the table and nodded.

"This might work," Uncle Phillip said. "How much time do you think you'll need?"

"Well, I'll need to do some planning first, mainly to figure out the best parts to use. The actual building and programming will take some time, too. I'm guessing three or four hours," Evan replied.

Max and Grace looked at Professor Hicks, waiting for his decision.

Evan's uncle looked at his watch. "It's almost dinner time, and the sun will be down in a few hours. There's really no point in trying to open the tomb tonight. If you can get the robot working, we'll let you send it down the tunnel tomorrow," he said. "Is there anything else you need, Evan?"

Evan thought for a moment, looking at the robotics kit in front of him and all the components.

"I just need some time to work through my design notebook. I'll start building and programming after dinner," he said. "This'll be fun."

Uncle Phillip smiled at Evan. "All right, this sounds like a good plan," he said, and stood up. "Dinner is in 40 minutes."

Evan watched as Uncle Phillip, Grace, and Max left the tent, and then he took a deep breath. "Time to get started," he said.

Story continues in Chapter 5 . . .

CHAPTER 2

■■■

ExploroBot—Planning and Design

In this chapter you're going to learn (drum-roll, please—cue the announcer) . . .
A PLANNING AND DESIGN PROCESS!

Please don't let the words scare you. Yes, "planning and design process" sounds boring, but I promise that you'll have fun with this chapter. I know you're ready to start putting pieces together to build a bot, but if you take some time and go through these P&D chapters, you'll be building and programming your own robots in less time, with fewer mistakes.

So, let's get started. That tomb door is still locked, and you're going to need the ExploroBot to open it.

The ExploroBot

Do you have a picture of the ExploroBot in your mind already? If so, I'll bet that it doesn't look exactly like the one pictured here (see Figure 2-1). (If it does, you are an amazing mind reader. Call me—we can make a fortune on the stock market.)

■**Note** There are five blank design journal pages in the back of this book that you can cut out. You're going to use them to design the robots in this book *and* robots of your own. If you need more pages, you can find a file titled DesignJournal.pdf in the Source Code/Download area of the Apress Web site (http://www.apress.com) that you can use to print more pages.

At the top of the design journal page you'll see the words Robot Name. Go ahead and write **ExploroBot** in the box, and pat yourself on the back. The PLANNING AND DESIGN PROCESS has begun. (You could write something else, such as **RobotThatOpensTombDoors**, but you might run out of space.)

Figure 2-1. *The ExploroBot*

Are you wondering how that little robot is going to open the tomb door? Good question. And you're going to answer that question by following along using a page out of Evan's design journal.

The Robot Description

Okay, now that you've named your robot, it's time to describe it. No, I'm not talking about "Short, grey and white, with wheels." What I mean is, what is this robot supposed to do? At this point, I hope you've read Chapter 1. If not, I'll wait . . . Go back and read it. Okay, have you finished it? Good. Now, what is this robot supposed to do? Don't say it, write it.

Look on your design journal page, and you'll see Robot Description and a large blank box. Don't be shy here. This is where you're going to try your hardest to describe accurately what this robot will do for you. Look back to Figure 1-2 in Chapter 1 if you need a reminder about the path the robot needs to follow. Let me show you what I wrote down, and you can compare it to your description, okay? Here goes (see Figure 2-2).

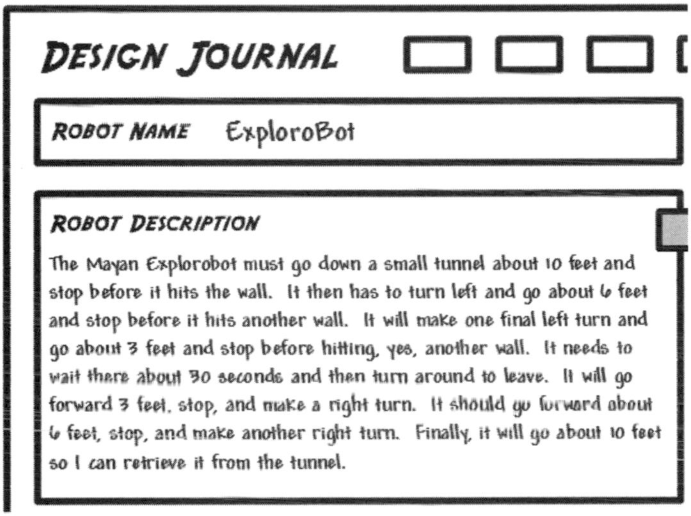

Figure 2-2. *Robot description*

If your description isn't exactly like mine, that's okay. What *is* important is that you got the major points: Robot moves forward about ten feet, stops, turns. Robot moves six feet, stops, turns. And on and on. Trust me—without an accurate description of the robot, it will be more difficult to build (Chapter 3) and program (Chapter 4). Don't worry if your description missed something; you'll get better at this, I promise. You're going to have more opportunities to write robot descriptions later in the book. By the time you're finished, you'll be an expert.

So, what's next, you ask? Okay, I'll tell you—you're going to take the description you wrote and break it down into small, single-item tasks.

The Task List

On your design journal page, locate the Task List section. This section is where you're going to list each individual task that the robot must perform. The *good news* is that if you wrote down a detailed description (see the previous section), then this section is almost already done.

What do I mean by "individual task?" An individual task is something like "Walk forward five feet" or "Turn doorknob." Something like "Press the button and turn the wheel" is not an individual task. Your goal is to list the actions your robot will perform, one at a time. Take a look at my task list (see Figure 2-3).

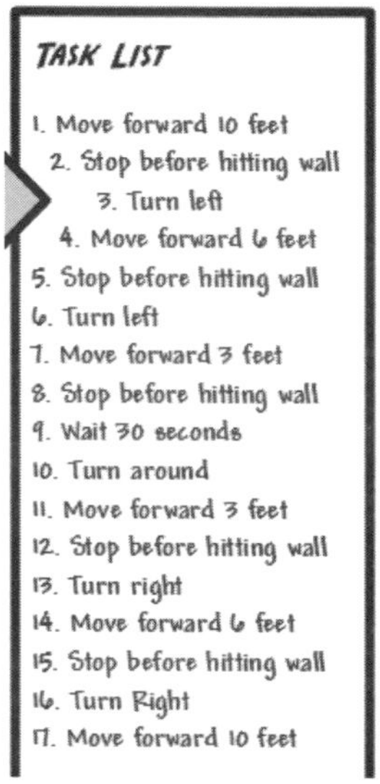

TASK LIST

1. Move forward 10 feet
2. Stop before hitting wall
   3. Turn left
4. Move forward 6 feet
5. Stop before hitting wall
6. Turn left
7. Move forward 3 feet
8. Stop before hitting wall
9. Wait 30 seconds
10. Turn around
11. Move forward 3 feet
12. Stop before hitting wall
13. Turn right
14. Move forward 6 feet
15. Stop before hitting wall
16. Turn Right
17. Move forward 10 feet

Figure 2-3. *The ExploroBot task list*

Compare your task list to mine. Were you able to break down the robot description into individual tasks? These individual tasks will help you in many ways, including assembling the correct form for your bot, picking the appropriate sensors to be used, and later when programming the bot.

I'll give you a small preview of how we'll use the task list later. Look at steps 2, 5, 8, 12, and 15—"Stop before hitting wall." Are you already thinking about how to do this? You've got options, of course. There's the Touch sensor that can be programmed to stop the robot when it's triggered. And what about the Ultrasonic sensor? The sensor sends out a signal that's detected when it bounces back off an object in front of it, such as our wall. So you can see that this task list will help you to start thinking about the NXT components you'll use. For now, let's leave the Task List and move on to the next section of the Design Journal.

Limitations and Constraints

You're going to encounter one obstacle quickly when you begin to design your robots using the Lego Mindstorms NXT kit. What is it? It's the number of parts in your kit.

It would be nice if you had access to an unlimited number of sensors, motors, connectors, beams, and other components. But for this book, and the robot designs included in it, I'm not making any assumptions about your collection of parts except that you have the Lego Mindstorms NXT kit or the Lego Mindstorms Education NXT version of the kit.

When you begin to design your robots, you need to be aware of limitations (or constraints) such as this one. Limitations and/or constraints can come from many different places. Besides the number of parts in your robotics kit, you need to keep in mind things such as the following:

- Robot size and weight (tall, short, heavy, light, wide, thin, square, circular)

- Weather and lighting conditions (outdoors, indoors, artificial light, no light)

- Floor or surface conditions (soft, hard, wet, slippery, and so on)

- Movement requirements (up, down, left, right, forward, backward, diagonal)

There may be some constraints that you won't encounter until you begin building and testing your robots. Don't worry if this happens. Your main goal at this point should be to write down any limitations that come immediately to mind. Just look back at your Robot Description and Task List and the environment or objects where the robot will interact. Do any constraints come to mind? Write them down on your Design Journal page in the Limitations/Constraints area.

Take a look at Figure 2-4. I've written down a few sentences that describe what I think are some major constraints for the ExploroBot. Remember, there may be other constraints that won't show up until we begin testing our design. The important part is to try and identify any obvious constraints before you begin to design and build your bot.

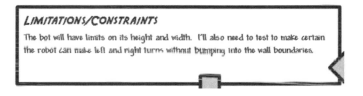

LIMITATIONS/CONSTRAINTS

The bot will have limits on its height and width. I'll also need to test to make certain the robot can make left and right turns without bumping into the wall boundaries.

Figure 2-4. *The ExploroBot has a few constraints to consider.*

The constraints for the ExploroBot aren't too difficult to work around. Let's take a look at the challenge and see how these constraints will affect the robot design.

First, the robot will enter a tunnel that has a fixed height and width. So the robot you build cannot be too wide or too tall or it simply won't fit into the tunnel. We know the measurement of the tunnel is 18 inches tall and 18 inches wide. We'll keep that in mind when we begin to design.

The second constraint is a little trickier. Take a look at Figure 2-5. This is an overhead view of the tunnel and its dimensions. Pay attention to the two corners where the robot will turn.

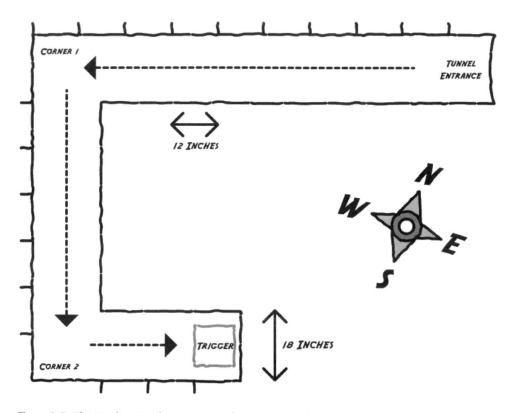

Figure 2-5. *The ExploroBot has to turn a few corners to land on the trigger.*

The robot must stop before it hits the wall at Corner 1. When it stops, it will turn left and proceed to Corner 2. When it's turning, we'll have to be careful to give the robot sufficient space to turn and not bump into the wall. There are numerous methods for building and programming a robot to make a right-angle turn, and I encourage you to experiment with other methods.

So, how will we do this right-angle (or 90 degree) turn and give the robot plenty of room to avoid bumping the walls? Glad you asked.

If you look at Figure 2-6, you'll notice I've zoomed in on the first corner and included some measurements, including the length and width of the ExploroBot. Ideally, we would like the robot to stop a certain distance from the wall and turn left, and the best place for the robot to stop would be directly in the middle of the corner. I don't want this to get too complicated, so just keep in mind that when the robot turns, it cannot be too close to the wall or, when it turns, it will bump the wall with its front right wheel. So be aware that during the building and programming of the ExploroBot, we'll be "tinkering" and "tweaking" to get the bot to perform well in a corner.

Note During the building and programming of the bot, you'll perform many tests. During this phase, you'll test many of the bot's functions—forward speed, stopping speed, detecting the wall, stopping at a proper distance, and more. I'll cover this in more detail in Chapter 3 and Chapter 4.

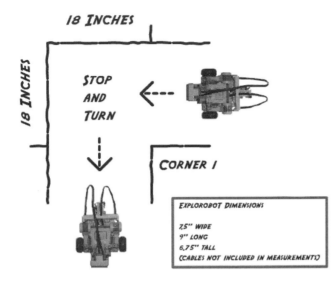

Figure 2-6. *The ExploroBot should turn while centered in the corner.*

The final constraint isn't so much a constraint as it is a condition that might affect the bot. The surface of the tunnel is stone. It's a flat rough surface, not made of sand. I'm including this constraint only to demonstrate that you must always be aware of the external conditions the robot will face. Because the surface is flat and rough, we should be able to use the large rubber wheels to move the robot, because they'll have a good grip on the surface of the tunnel. But this might not always be possible. A wet surface can sometimes cause plastic or thin wheels to simply spin without getting traction, keeping the robot from moving. And what if the robot doesn't have a surface to roll or walk across? I'll answer that question in Chapter 6.

Just try and always keep an open mind when thinking about the obstacles your robot will face. Examine the robot's environment, its tasks, and its overall goal as you start to brainstorm about how you'll solve the problem. And that's what you're going to do next. You're going to brainstorm about this bot's design, components, and overall appearance in this next Design Journal section—Mindstorm.

Mindstorm

Convenient name for this section, huh? The Lego Mindstorms NXT robotics kit uses that unique word, Mindstorms. For us, to mindstorm (or brainstorm) is our chance to use our creativity and start developing ideas for how this bot will be designed and built. This is an easy section to complete. What I want you to do is simply write down your questions, observations, and ideas that have been popping into your head since you became aware of the challenge. There are no incorrect items to place in this section except for sketches—those come last. So, to get you started, take a look at Figure 2-7. You'll see some of my initial thoughts on this challenge, this bot, and the direction I want to take for my initial design.

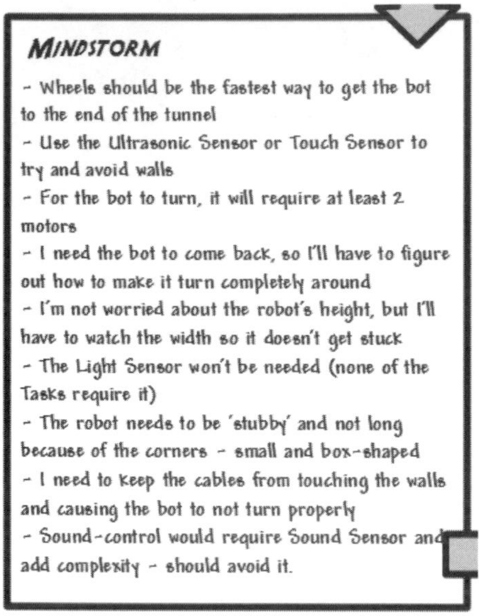

MINDSTORM

- Wheels should be the fastest way to get the bot
to the end of the tunnel
- Use the Ultrasonic Sensor or Touch Sensor to
try and avoid walls
- For the bot to turn, it will require at least 2
motors
- I need the bot to come back, so I'll have to figure
out how to make it turn completely around
- I'm not worried about the robot's height, but I'll
have to watch the width so it doesn't get stuck
- The Light Sensor won't be needed (none of the
Tasks require it)
- The robot needs to be 'stubby' and not long
because of the corners - small and box-shaped
- I need to keep the cables from touching the walls
and causing the bot to not turn properly
- Sound-control would require Sound Sensor and
add complexity - should avoid it.

Figure 2-7. *The Mindstorm section contains my initial thoughts.*

I'm not going to cover all my `Mindstorm` items here, but I would like to mention a couple and explain how and why I wrote them.

One of my observations was "For the bot to turn, it will require at least 2 motors." This might seem like common sense, but then again, maybe not. In order for a bot to turn, it has to have a force that makes it turn. Two wheels, connected to a single motor, only give forward and backward motion. For the bot to turn left and right, it requires another motor. By spinning one motor (and its wheel) in one direction and spinning the other motor in the reverse direction, we can cause the bot to turn. This can also be accomplished simply by locking the second motor in place and keeping it from spinning. One wheel will spin, the other wheel will not spin, and the bot will turn.

Another observation was "Sound-control would require Sound sensor and add complexity—should avoid it." One of my initial ideas was to control the bot by using different sounds and tones. One tone would stop the bot, another tone would make it turn right, and yet another would make it turn left. Then it occurred to me that this would be just too much trouble. My goal is to make the bot as independent as possible and allow it to find its way down the tunnel and back. So the Sound sensor was eliminated.

Your main objective here is simply to have some fun and write down some of your initial thoughts on what you'd like to do with your bot design. You might have to take a completely different direction after some testing. You might find you exhaust your supply of a particular component. What you write down isn't going to lock you in to a particular design. You can change the design anytime—even start over completely. Print out another Design Journal page and try a different design. It's supposed to be fun, so make it fun. Go crazy with your ideas—the crazier, the better!

Now you're done with the `Robot Description` and the `Task List` is full. You've identified some `Limitations/Constraints` and your `Mindstorm` items section is overflowing with your thoughts and observations. It's now time to finish up with the Design Journal's final section—Sketches.

Sketches

When I draw stick figure people, they tend to have very short legs and very long arms. I still color outside the lines with crayons. I guess what I'm trying to say is that if you're a professional artist, you don't have to worry about any competition from me.

I can, however, draw shapes that are fairly close to squares, circles, rectangles, and triangles. And that's good enough for what I'm going to ask you to do in this section. I want to give you some suggestions before starting on the building of your bot, and I'm going to take my own advice and show you my actual sketches for the ExploroBot.

I'm going to reference some of the ideas I wrote down in the Mindstorm section and show you how I came up with the size and shape of the ExploroBot. First, I'll start with the shape. Take a look at Figure 2-8 and notice that I started with a basic shape to help determine the placement of sensors, motors, and other parts.

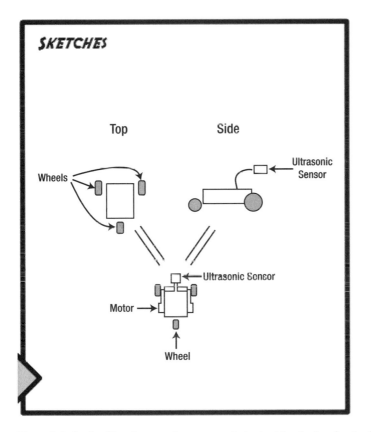

Figure 2-8. *In the Sketches section, try and start with placing basic shapes.*

First, I need to decide between the Touch sensor or the Ultrasonic sensor for detecting an approaching wall or obstacle. If I use the Touch sensor, it will need to be placed far in front of the bot, possibly on a long neck or pole, to allow it time to stop the bot and give it room to turn. But if I use the Ultrasonic sensor I can place it closer to the bot's body because it can detect a wall or an obstacle from a distance and it doesn't require an impact with the wall or obstacle. Because my goal is to keep the ExploroBot as short in length as possible, I'm going to use the Ultrasonic sensor.

My ExploroBot will require two motors (for turning), the Ultrasonic sensor, and the Intelligent Brick. And unless I want the Brick to scrape the ground while it moves, I'll need to give it one or two extra wheels. I'll try to save some weight and keep the size down by using three wheels.

What I'm envisioning is using the Intelligent Brick as the main body. Two motors, one on each side of the Brick, will spin the two wheels used for forward and backward motion and for turning. I'll configure a small third wheel that will pivot to make the bot's turning a little smoother and give less resistance.

What do your sketches look like? Have you taken a different approach to the design of the ExploroBot? Remember, there is no *right* or *wrong* solution. If your ExploroBot reaches the end of the tunnel, lands on the pressure plate, and then returns to the tunnel entrance, you've succeeded in opening the tomb door.

In Chapter 3 I'm going to walk you through the assembly of my version of the ExploroBot. Feel free to change it up! Move the Ultrasonic sensor to the back or simply change it to the Touch sensor. Try giving it four wheels instead of three. Chapter 4 will show you how to program the ExploroBot; at the end of the chapter I'll also give you some ideas on how to set up the challenge and test your bot.

Now, let's build the ExploroBot!

CHAPTER 3

■■■

ExploroBot—Build It

Before you begin building the ExploroBot, take a look at Figure 3-1. Remember, this is just one possible version of the ExploroBot. Some of you might choose to design and build your own version without going through this chapter, but for those who would like to build the one pictured, I have a few suggestions.

Figure 3-1. *Evan's version of the ExploroBot*

Never Be Afraid to Experiment

I've chosen to include actual pictures of the construction of the ExploroBot. I've tried to provide enough detail in each figure for you to discern what parts are used and where those parts are placed. If you find that what you're holding in your hands doesn't quite look like the picture, do the following:

1. Take a deep breath.

2. Remember this is supposed to be fun.

3. Go back to the previous step and confirm you've made it that far.

4. Look at the current step, and examine the figure's details for clues to where components should be placed. Things like counting holes to determine where two or more parts connect is useful. So is skipping ahead a few figures to try and see the parts from another angle.

5. When in doubt, take your best guess and move forward.

If you do hit a roadblock and just can't figure out how to move forward, try taking a look at the next few steps. Sometimes another figure will show the ExploroBot from a different angle and you'll see the solution. Enjoy the building process and realize that if your final bot doesn't look *exactly* like the one in this chapter, that's okay. Remember: getting the bot to work and solving the challenge is your main goal.

■**Note** If you modify or try to create your own version of the ExploroBot (or any other bot in this book), please take a picture and e-mail it to me. I would enjoy seeing your final bot in action. I've included my e-mail address in the Introduction.

And now, on to the construction of the ExploroBot!

Step by Step

I'm going to break the ExploroBot into four sections. The first section will be the Ultrasonic Sensor and the "neck" used to support it. The second section will be the body, including the two motors and two wheels. The third section will be the rear-wheel assembly and the frame used to keep the cables tidy. You'll finally assemble the ExploroBot in the fourth section using the head/neck, body/motors, and frame/rear-wheel subcomponents.

For each section, I'm simply going to jump from figure to figure. I'll make comments where I feel a tricky area might exist or where I feel you need to be made aware of a special assembly instruction.

Pay special attention to those figures showing the individual parts lying unassembled. These will help you to determine what parts to locate for upcoming assembly figures.

Here we go . . .

First Section: Ultrasonic Sensor and Neck

Starting with Figure 3-2 and continuing through Figure 3-9, you'll be assembling the Exploro-Bot's head and neck. Take a look at Figure 3-2 and Figure 3-4. These are the figures that show the majority of the parts you'll be using in this section.

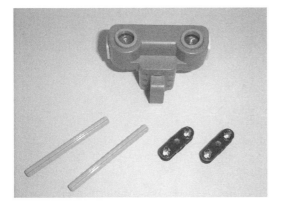

Figure 3-2. *These are the parts you'll need for the ExploroBot's head.*

Figure 3-3. *The fully assembled ExploroBot head—set this aside for now*

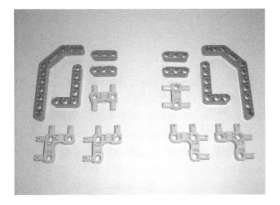

Figure 3-4. *Parts for the left and right sides of the neck that will hold the ExploroBot's head*

Figure 3-5. *Partial assembly of the left and right sides of the neck*

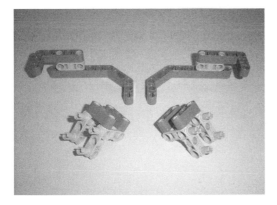

Figure 3-6. *Place the L-shaped beams.*

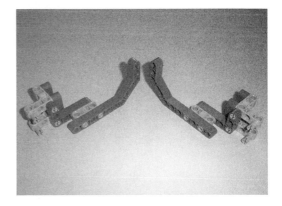

Figure 3-7. *The fully assembled left and right sides of the neck*

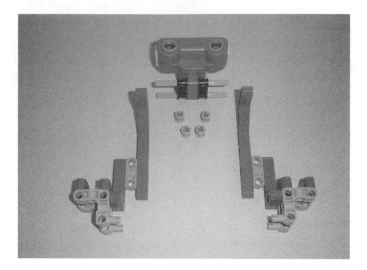

Figure 3-8. *The left and right sides of the neck, ExploroBot's head, and four round connecting pins*

■**Note** What I call a "round connecting pin" is also called by its official Lego name: Part # 3713 Technic Bush. Why do I tell you this? Because I want you to be aware that Lego gives a unique part number to every component it sells. Also, because this is where I tell you that I'm going to avoid using the official part numbers unless absolutely necessary. If you're unable to determine the identity of a component from a figure, take a look at the next figure or two. You'll most likely be able to determine what the component is by seeing it from a different angle or by seeing it where it's placed.

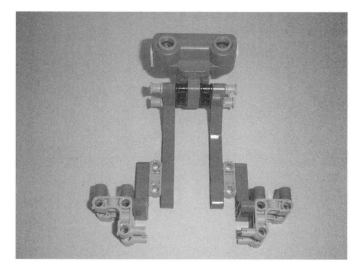

Figure 3-9. *The fully assembled ExploroBot head and neck—set this aside for now.*

It's time for a quick check here. Take a look at your ExploroBot head and neck. Does it look like the one shown in Figure 3-9? If not, try and identify where the difference is and go back to the figures showing the assembly. If the difference is extremely obvious, spend a few minutes looking at the parts and you'll find the mistake. When working with such small parts, it's not uncommon to connect a part in reverse or upside down—I do it all the time.

When you're satisfied with the ExploroBot head and neck assembly, set it aside for now. We'll come back to it after you've completed the main body and rear-wheel sections.

Second Section: Bot Body and Motors

In this section, you're going to build the ExploroBot's main body and its two motor/wheel combinations. Take a quick look at Figure 3-10 and Figure 3-12. These two figures show the majority of the parts you'll be using in this section.

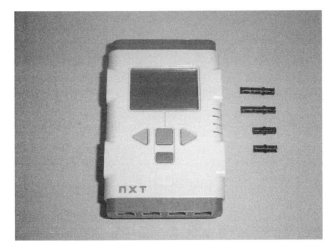

Figure 3-10. *The body will be made of the Intelligent Brick and a few connectors*

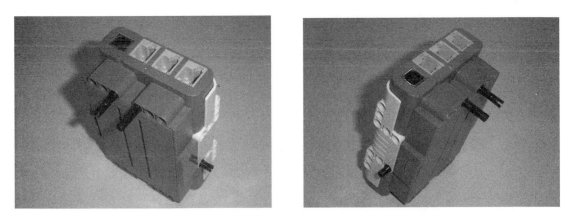

Figure 3-11. *Left and right side views of the Intelligent Brick and placement of the connectors*

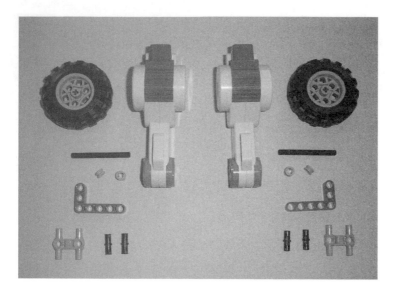

Figure 3-12. *Components for the left and right side motor/wheel combinations*

■**Note** In Figure 3-12, you can determine the length of the black rod by comparing it to the length of the L-shaped beam. Please also note that in the figure there are two round connector pins *and* two half-thickness round connector pins. These two half-thickness pins are shown standing up so you can see the thin groove. These are used as spacers to keep the rubber wheels from touching the orange motor face. Figure 3-13 shows the proper assembly in more detail.

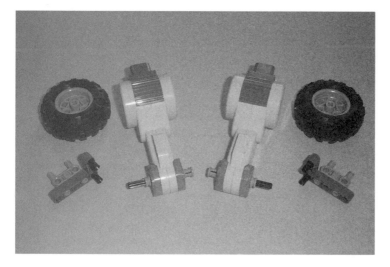

Figure 3-13. *Partial assembly of the left and right motor/wheel combinations*

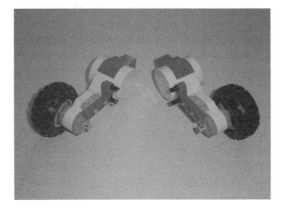

Figure 3-14. *The fully assembled motor/ wheel combinations*

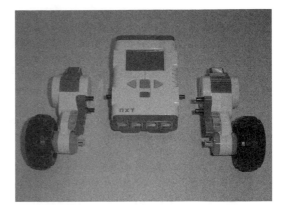

Figure 3-15. *The Intelligent Brick and the motor/wheel combinations before assembly*

Figure 3-16. *Components for the left and right side motor/wheel combinations*

Okay, it's time again to check your work. Compare your ExploroBot body with the one shown in Figure 3-16. You can use Figure 3-16 to compare things such as the location of the black connectors in the L-shaped beams to make sure you've got the motor/wheel combinations located properly.

Again, the key here is to look for any major differences between your ExploroBot's body and the one shown in Figure 3-16. If you find any differences, just go back and examine the figures carefully where the mistake appears to have been made. If necessary, take the assembly apart and start over. You've got plenty of time and you're having fun, right?

Are you happy with the ExploroBot's body? Congratulations! You're half done with the ExploroBot. We're going to move on to the third section, which is a little longer and a little more complex due to the number of parts being used. Just take your time on this section and enjoy the building process. Remember my advice—if you get stuck, just take a deep breath and remind yourself that this is fun. You can't make a mistake because you can always start over—no harm done!

Now let's finish the ExploroBot's rear-wheel section and then get this bot assembled . . .

Third Section: Rear-Wheel Assembly and Frame

There's a *lot* to build in this section. First you're going to build a small frame that will help you to control the cables you'll install in the fourth section. Then you're going to build a small rear-wheel and a base to hold the rear-wheel. This base has a lot of parts, but you'll find that it helps to strengthen the bot and reinforce the rear-wheel.

Take a quick look at Figure 3-17, Figure 3-20, and Figure 3-25. These figures show the majority of the parts you'll be using in this section, but in some later figures you'll notice I've added some new parts. My best advice is to pull out the parts you see in the three figures I've mentioned. You'll know when I've added some new parts because you'll have used all the previous ones you set aside! And again . . . when in doubt, just pause and examine the figures more closely. I've made sure to include enough detail for you to figure out what parts are being added to the mix.

Now, let's start with Figure 3-17 and the cable frame.

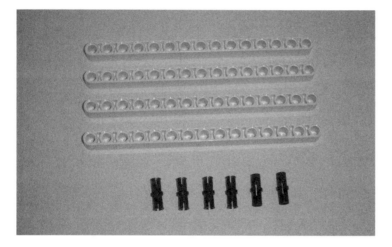

Figure 3-17. *Parts needed for the ExploroBot's rear frame, used to keep cables untangled*

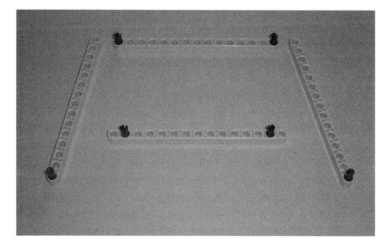

Figure 3-18. *Partial assembly of the cable frame*

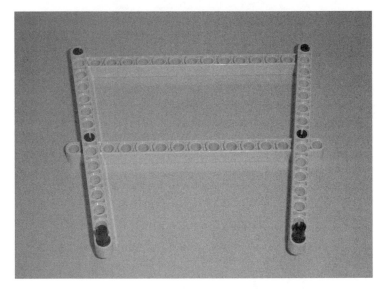

Figure 3-19. *The final cable frame assembly—set this aside for now*

Next, Figure 3-20 shows the start of the rear-wheel.

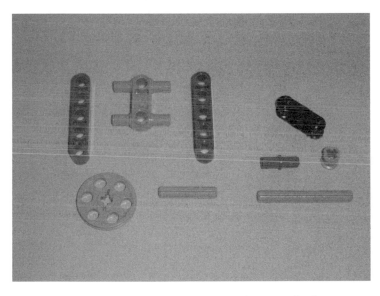

Figure 3-20. *These are the parts for creating the rear-wheel.*

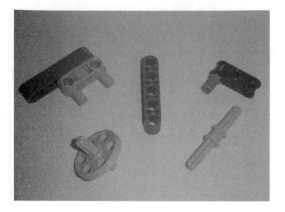

Figure 3-21. *It's not quite a rear-wheel yet, but keep going . . .*

Figure 3-22. *The rear-wheel is starting to come together . . .*

Note In Figure 3-22 you'll notice that I've added two new parts that weren't seen in Figure 3-20. This will happen again in later figures, so be on the lookout for it. As I mentioned, if you set out the parts that you need for each section, when I add parts like this to a figure it will be very obvious to you—"Hey, that's not in my parts pile!"

Figure 3-23. *The rear-wheel is almost done . . .*

Figure 3-24. *The final rear-wheel assembly—set this aside for now*

Finally, Figure 3-25 shows the parts needed to start the rear-wheel base.

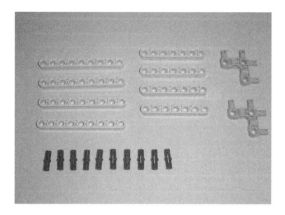

Figure 3-25. *Locate these parts to start the base that will hold the rear-wheel.*

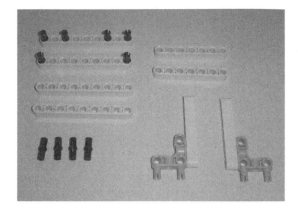

Figure 3-26. *Begin by connecting the parts as shown . . .*

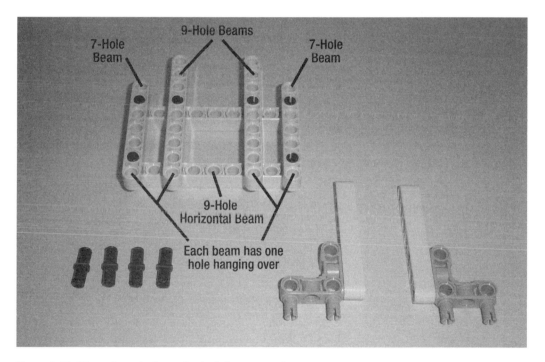

Figure 3-27. *Place the 7-hole and 9-hole beams as shown . . .*

■Note In Figure 3-27, the two 9-hole beams and the two 7-hole beams are placed so that each beam has one hole "overhanging" the horizontal 9-hole beam (at the bottom). This is also a good place to mention that I'll occasionally use "callouts" in the figures. These "callouts" are simply text in the figure itself, sometimes with lines or arrows. Figure 3-27 uses callouts to indicate the 7-hole and 9-hole beams, and how they "overhang" the horizontal 9-hole beam.

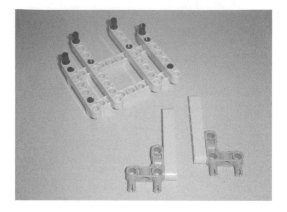

Figure 3-28. *Place the four connectors in the top of the 7-hole and 9-hole beams.*

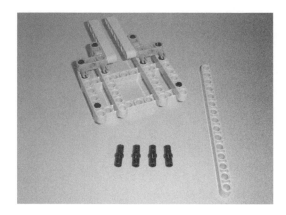

Figure 3-29. *Connect the parts as shown. The four connectors and 15-hole beam are new.*

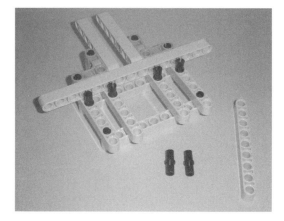

Figure 3-30. *Connect the new parts as shown. The two connectors and 9-hole beam are new.*

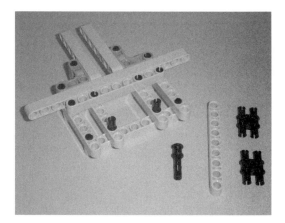

Figure 3-31. *Connect the new parts as shown. Locate the 9-hole beam and the two quad-connectors shown.*

■**Note** Between Figure 3-31 and Figure 3-32, be sure to spin the rear-wheel base around. You'll see in Figure 3-32 that the base is now facing the opposite direction. Look at Figure 3-32 carefully—you'll see that the 9-hole beam has two holes overhanging at the back and that the two quad-connectors are connected facing rearward.

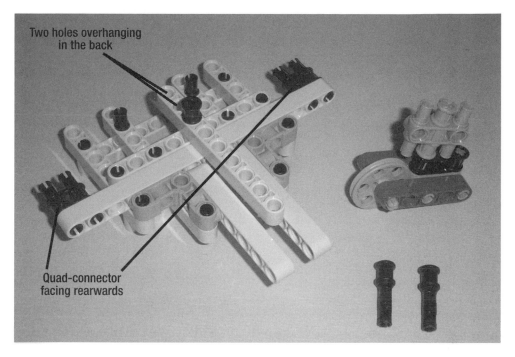

Two holes overhanging
in the back

Quad-connector
facing rearwards

Figure 3-32. *Connect the new parts as shown. Locate these two connectors and the rear-wheel.*

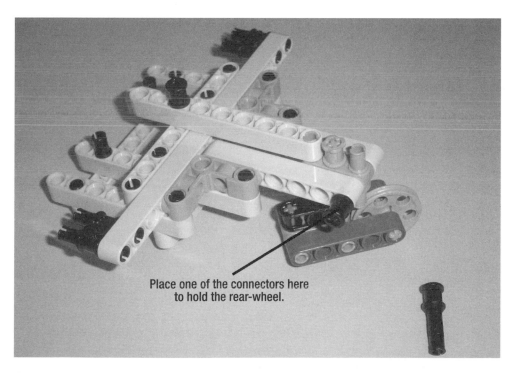

Place one of the connectors here
to hold the rear-wheel.

Figure 3-33a. *You'll use the two connectors to connect the rear-wheel to the base. One connector is placed on the left side and the other on the right side.*

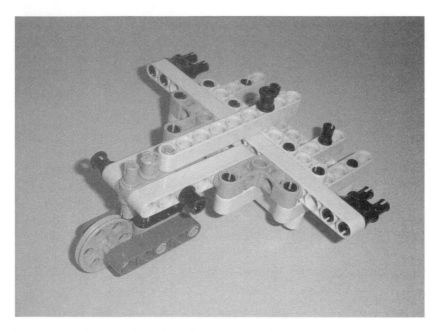

Figure 3-33b. *Another view of the final rear-wheel base*

Congratulations! You've finished the rear-wheel base. Do a quick check and compare the base you assembled to the one shown in Figures 3-33a and 3-33b. If you're satisfied with it, now it's time to pull all the sub-assemblies together.

You should have the following ready to go:

- Head and neck assembly

- Main body with motor/wheel combinations

- Rear-wheel base

- Cable frame

Place them all within reach. It's time to finish building the ExploroBot.

Fourth Section: Put It All Together

Take the main body assembly and the rear-wheel/base and turn them upside down. You'll see this in Figure 3-34.

■Note Connecting the rear-wheel/base and the main body can be a little tricky. Before attempting it, take a good look at Figure 3-34 and Figure 3-35. I've used callouts again in Figure 3-34 to show you where the two sub-assemblies will connect. Between the two figures, you can see that the two quad-connectors will connect to the back of the motors. The two connectors on the back of the Intelligent Brick (see Figure 3-11) will go up into the 9-hole beam as indicated in Figure 3-34.

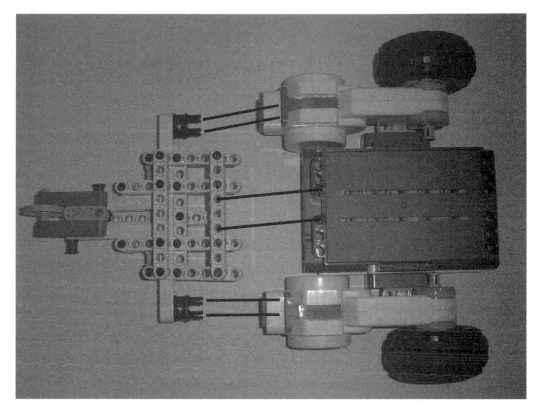

Figure 3-34. *Turn the main body and the rear-wheel/base upside down to connect them.*

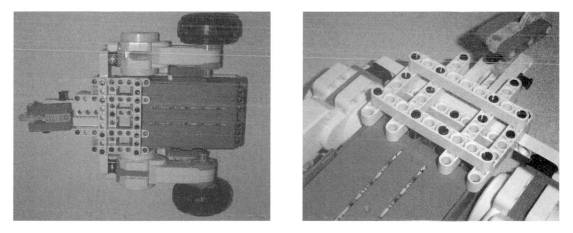

Figure 3-35. *Two different views showing how the main body and the rear-wheel/base connect.*

Figure 3-36 shows the assembled main body and rear-wheel/base as well as the head/neck assembly and cable frame.

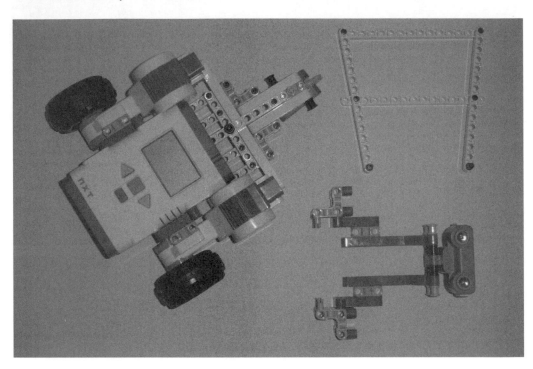

Figure 3-36. *Head/neck, cable frame, and the main body and rear-wheel/base assembly*

Next, connect the cable frame to the main body as shown in Figure 3-37a.

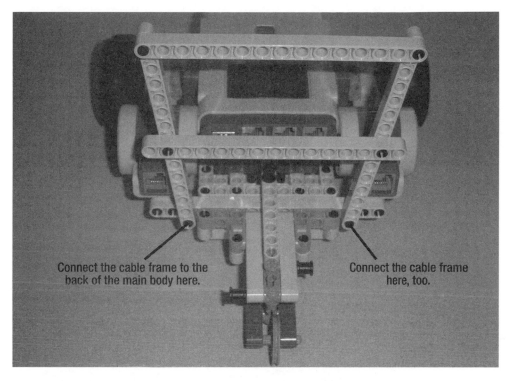

Connect the cable frame to the
back of the main body here.

Connect the cable frame
here, too.

Figure 3-37a. *The cable frame connects to the back of the main body.*

Figure 3-37b. *Another view of the connected cable frame*

Finally, on the front of the main body, you're going to connect the head/neck assembly as shown in Figure 3-38.

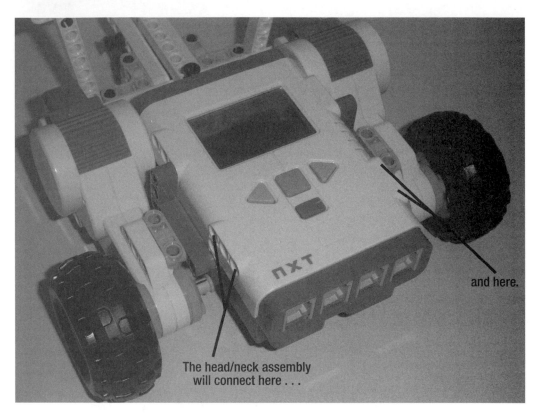

The head/neck assembly will connect here . . .

and here.

Figure 3-38. *The head/neck assembly will connect to the main body here.*

You'll see the head/neck assembly connected to the main body in Figure 3-39. Take a close look and you'll see exactly where the left and right neck components connect to the Intelligent Brick.

Figure 3-39. *The head/neck assembly connected to the main body*

Guess what? You're done with building the ExploroBot. To complete the actual bot, you need to do the following:

1. Connect a cable from the Ultrasonic Sensor to Port 4 (see Figure 3-40).

2. Looking at the back of the ExploroBot (see Figure 3-41), connect a cable from the left motor to Port C.

3. Connect a cable from the right motor to Port B (see Figure 3-41).

Figure 3-40. *The Ultrasonic Sensor connects to Port 4.*

Left motor (viewed from rear)
connects to Port C

Right motor (viewed from rear)
connects to Port B

Figure 3-41. *The motors are connected to Port B and Port C.*

And that's it. You've built the ExploroBot.

Figure 3-42. *The completed ExploroBot*

But you're not done. Sorry.

Chapter 4 is going to cover the programming of your ExploroBot. Without the programming to tell the bot how to behave, you've got a nice paperweight. And a locked tomb door.

So, on to the next chapter.

CHAPTER 4

■ ■ ■

ExploroBot—Program It

Your ExploroBot looks nice, but it really doesn't do much yet, does it? That's about to change. In this chapter you're going to create the program that sends the bot down the tunnel (and back) to trigger the locked tomb door. So, let's get started.

Some Experience Required

This chapter isn't about teaching you the basics of the software. Included with the Lego Mindstorms NXT software is a collection of software tutorials. At this point, I'm making the assumption that you've built the bots included with the Mindstorms NXT kit and you've gone through the tutorials for programming the bots. During these tutorials, you received some basic skills in selecting programming blocks, dropping them into the workspace, and configuring the blocks.

In this chapter, I'm going to show you how to use your completed Design Journal sheet for the ExploroBot to help you construct the program, block by block. So go ahead and open up the Lego Mindstorms NXT software (see Figure 4-1).

Figure 4-1. *The Lego Mindstorms NXT software*

You're going to create a new program, so type **ExploroBot** into the blank text field labeled **Start New Program**, then click the **Go** button (see Figure 4-2).

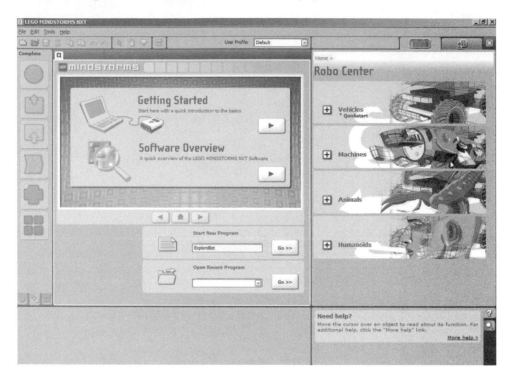

Figure 4-2. *Enter a name for the new program and click* **Go**.

■**Note** To have more workspace visible on your screen, close down the RoboCenter area on the far right by clicking the small red X in the upper-right corner of the software.

Now, before we start dropping blocks all over the place, we need to think about what this program is supposed to do. Remember the Task List from the Design Journal? This is where that Task List is going to come in handy (see Figure 4-3).

We're going to use each of the numbered items from the Task List to determine what types of programming blocks will be placed on the workspace. Like the construction of the actual ExploroBot, there are also numerous ways to program the bot. As you experiment with the Lego Mindstorms NXT software, you'll probably discover new (and better) methods for programming. You might find a way to shorten the program so it takes less memory space in the Intelligent Brick. Or you might choose to switch out the Ultrasonic Sensor with the Touch Sensor, which requires slightly different programming blocks. My point is this: there's no *perfect* method for programming the ExploroBot. With that in mind, let's do a little planning before dropping some blocks.

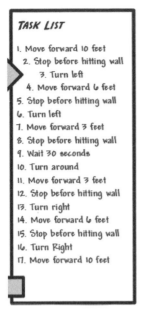

Figure 4-3. *The Task List will help us to program the ExploroBot.*

Take a look at the Task List's first item: "Move forward 10 feet." What do you think—maybe throw in a Light Sensor block? Just kidding. The bot first has to move forward down the tunnel, so that means a MOVE block (see Figure 4-4).

Figure 4-4. *The basic MOVE block*

■**Note** You can drag and drop a MOVE block from many different locations. One is located on the COMMON palette, and the other MOVE block can be found on the COMPLETE palette. In this chapter, I'm not going to point out every place for you to grab a block. In most instances, just look around on the COMMON and COMPLETE palettes and you'll find the necessary blocks. This will help to familiarize you with all the other programming blocks available. If you find one you're not familiar with, drop it on the workspace and play around with it for a few minutes . . . there's no rush.

We'll configure the MOVE block a little later. For now, let's move to the next Task List item: "Stop before hitting wall." Obviously, this would use a Touch Sensor or Ultrasonic Sensor. The ExploroBot in Chapter 3 uses the Ultrasonic Sensor, so we know we'll be configuring it later.

One interesting thing to note is that the bot will make four left turns during its travel down the tunnel. How did I come up with this number? Take a look at Figure 4-5 and you'll see all four turns.

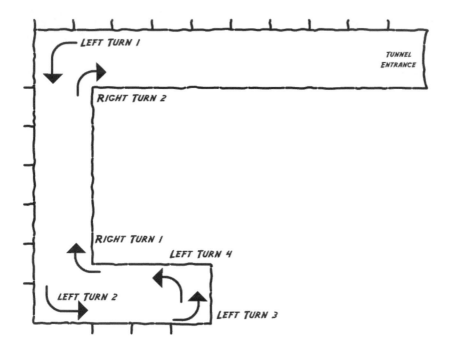

Figure 4-5. *The ExploroBot will make four left turns and two right turns during its travels.*

After the robot has reached the end of the tunnel and turned completely around, it will make two right turns on its way out of the tunnel (see Figure 4-5).

Now, why is this important? Because when programming, sometimes it pays to try and reduce the amount of work you need to do. And the Lego Mindstorms NXT software comes with a useful block we're going to use here that will save us some time. That block is the LOOP block (see Figure 4-6).

Figure 4-6. *The basic LOOP block*

The final block I want to discuss is the WAIT block (see Figure 4-7). When the ExploroBot reaches the trigger, I want it to stay there for a short period of time, just to make sure the pressure plate is triggered.

Figure 4-7. *The basic WAIT block*

With these four blocks, you have all the tools you need to program the ExploroBot to perform its duties.

Into the Tunnel

To save some time, I want you to look at the Task List again. I'm going to group some of the tasks together like this:

(Group 1) Forward – Detect Wall – Stop – Turn Left (first corner)

(Group 2) Forward – Detect Wall – Stop – Turn Left (second corner)

(Group 3) Forward – Detect Wall – Stop – Turn Left (end of tunnel)

Turn Left (this final turn is so the bot is pointed in the direction to leave)

Notice the first three groups are *identical*. When programming the ExploroBot, you could choose to place a MOVE block, another block for the Ultrasonic Sensor to detect the wall, another block to stop the motors, and another block to turn the bot left. And this will only get you past the first corner! You've still got group 2 and group 3 to go!

This could take a while. But not really. You're going to use the LOOP block in such a way that you can have the ExploroBot do all three groups with minimum programming. First, place a LOOP block on the sequence beam (see Figure 4-8). It's not much to look at, but hang on.

Figure 4-8. *You'll start with the LOOP block to save some time.*

The LOOP block repeatedly executes blocks within it (inside its orange borders) an unlimited amount of times *or* a specified number of times. The LOOP block can also repeatedly execute a sequence of blocks inside it until a condition is met (such as a sensor block being triggered). You can even put a LOOP block inside a LOOP block!

■**Note** Putting a LOOP block inside another LOOP block is called "nesting." We're going to use this concept with the ExploroBot. Keep reading.

Because you have three groups of similar tasks, you're going to set this first LOOP block to run three times. After you've dropped the LOOP block onto the workspace, take a look at the configuration panel (see Figure 4-9).

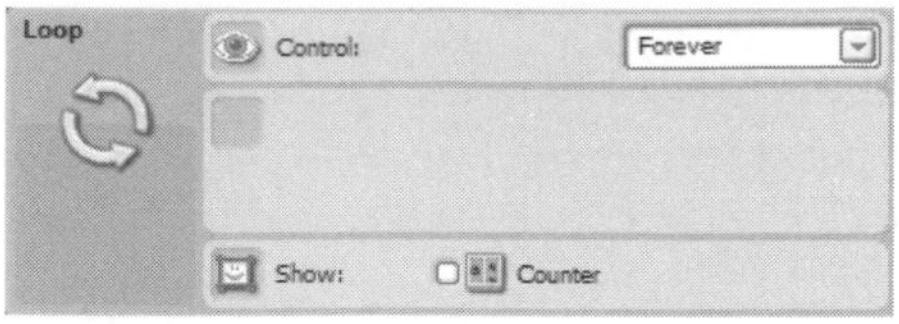

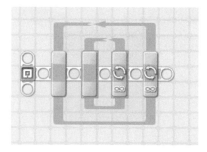

Figure 4-9. *The configuration panel for the LOOP block*

From the **Control:** drop-down menu, select **Count**. In the **Count:** text box, enter the numeral **3**. Now, any blocks or actions that you place inside this loop will be performed three times before this LOOP block is finished and the program continues. Now, what goes in the loop? Would you believe another LOOP block?

You want the ExploroBot to begin rolling down the tunnel and continue until the Ultrasonic Sensor detects the first corner, right? Well, to program this you need the MOVE block to continue turning motors B and C until the Ultrasonic Sensor detects the wall. To do this, you place a MOVE block inside a LOOP block that's configured to use the Ultrasonic Sensor to break the loop. Just drop another LOOP block inside the first LOOP block (see Figure 4-10); it will expand to allow the new LOOP block.

Figure 4-10. *Nest another LOOP block inside the first LOOP block.*

Now you need to configure the inner LOOP block to use the Ultrasonic Sensor (see Figure 4-11). Using the configuration panel for the inner LOOP block, change the **Control** section to **Sensor**. In the **Sensor** section of the drop-down menu, select **Ultrasonic Sensor**. Also, set the **Distance:** setting to 5 (inches). You could also select **Centimeters** from the **Units** drop-down menu in the **Show** section, but you're going to leave it at the default, **Inches**.

Figure 4-11. *Use the configuration panel to configure the inner LOOP block.*

■**Note** At the end of this chapter, I'll cover testing of the ExploroBot. The setting of five inches might not be correct for your ExploroBot. You'll have to test different sensitivities of the Ultrasonic Sensor to determine the proper distance for the Ultrasonic Sensor to break the LOOP and stop the bot's forward movement.

Next you'll drop in the MOVE block (see Figure 4-12) and use its configuration panel to configure it. You want the motors to turn continually and only stop when the Ultrasonic Sensor breaks the LOOP block. You're also using motors B and C and motion set to forward.

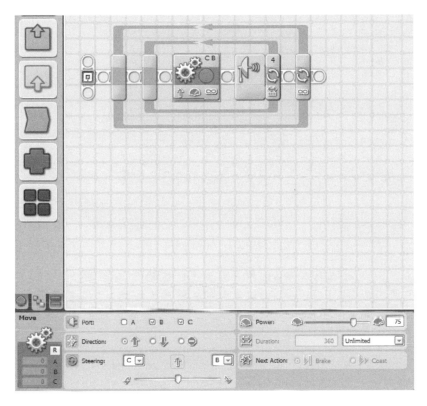

Figure 4-12. *Place a MOVE block inside the inner LOOP block.*

Once the LOOP block is broken (by the Ultrasonic Sensor), the bot needs to stop the forward motion and turn left. This also is done three times (see the earlier three groups). Now you need to drop in a block to stop the motors, and another block to turn the bot.

First, let's drop in a MOVE block to stop the motors (see Figure 4-13). It's easy to configure. Just select the **Stop** action (as shown) instead of forward movement.

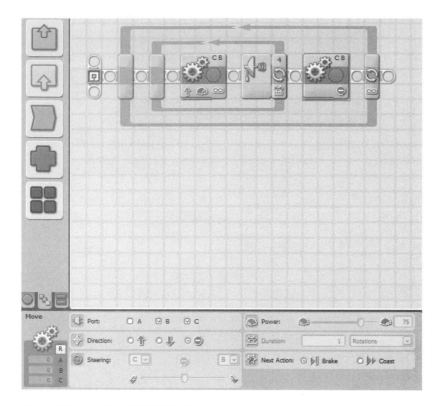

Figure 4-13. *Another MOVE block stops the motors from turning.*

The final action for the outer LOOP block is to turn the bot to the left. Drop in another MOVE block and configure it as shown in the configuration panel (see Figure 4-14).

■**Note** Only one motor (B) is configured to turn in this MOVE block. When motor B turns and motor C is motionless, the bot will turn left. At the end of this chapter, I'll show you how to determine the proper number of degrees needed to make a good left turn—for now, let's set it to 360. We'll also cut the power down to 25 for this block to make the turn slow and steady.

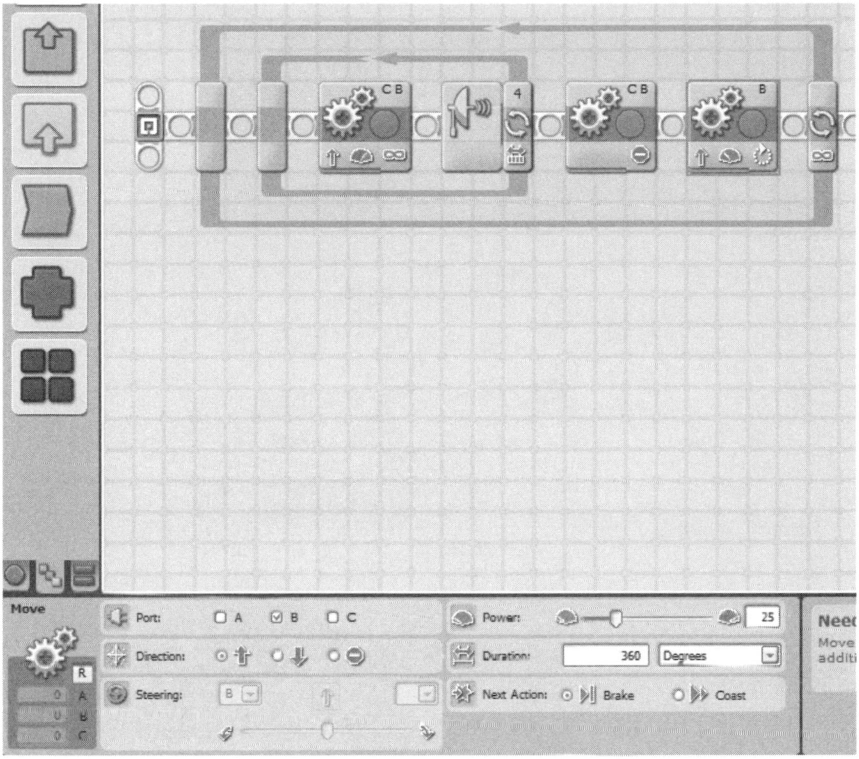

Figure 4-14. *This MOVE block turns the bot to the left.*

Let's pause here and take a look at what we've done. I'm also going to ask you to add some comments to your program. Comments are a built-in feature of the software and will come in handy if you ever want to make changes later or give the program to a friend. With comments, someone else looking at your program should be able to follow along and better understand what your program does and why.

At this point, you've got an outer LOOP block that will run three times. Everything inside it will occur three times and three times only. This means the bot will move forward until the Ultrasonic Sensor detects an obstruction in its path (the tunnel wall), stops moving, and turns left—three times. If you go back to Figure 4-5, you'll find that when the outer LOOP block completes, the bot should be sitting on the trigger and facing north.

I suggest that you use the Comment tool (see Figure 4-15) and type in a description of the blocks that you've just created. In Figure 4-15, I've included my comments for you to see.

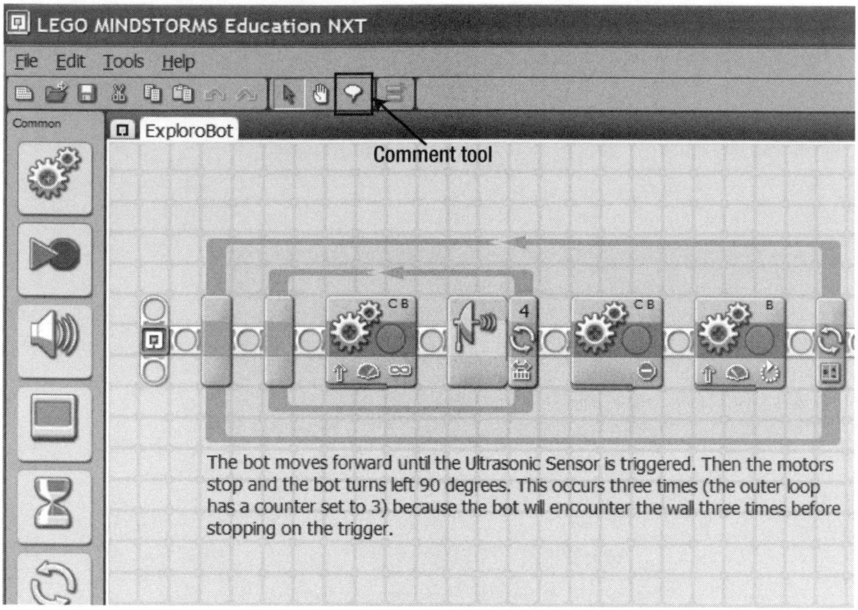

Figure 4-15. *Place comments for your blocks using the Comment tool.*

Now that the robot is on the trigger, let's go back to the Task List. Step 9 is for the bot to pause for 30 seconds. This is simple—just drop a WAIT block at the end of the program and set it for 30 seconds (see Figure 4-16).

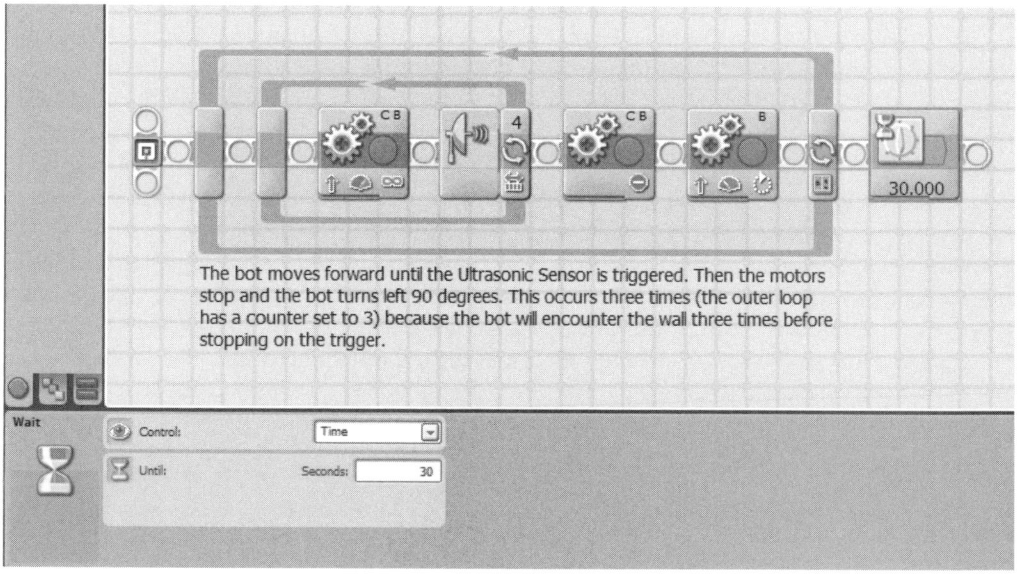

Figure 4-16. *A WAIT block is added for the bot to pause on the trigger.*

Because the bot is facing north, you need it to make one more left turn (see Figure 4-5) so it can go back the way it came and leave the tunnel. Easy enough. Just drop a MOVE block in and configure it like the other MOVE block that turns the bot (see Figure 4-17). Like the earlier MOVE block, let's set this one with a power setting of 25 and duration of 360 degrees until we determine the actual turn required.

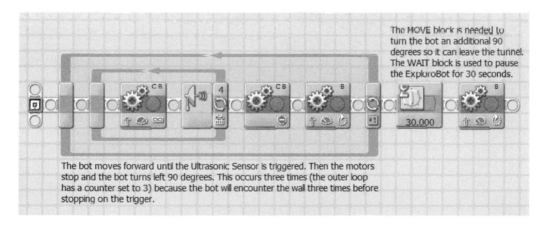

Figure 4-17. *A MOVE block is added to make the final left turn.*

Figure 4-18 shows a comment I've added at this point in the program. Again, I highly recommend comments. You never know when you might come back to this program—having comments will quickly help you to refresh your memory of how things work and are configured.

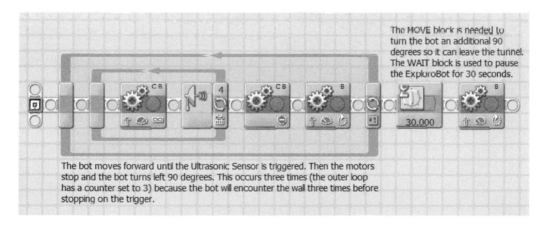

Figure 4-18. *I've updated the comments in the program.*

At this point, it's time to program the exit of the ExploroBot.

Out of the Tunnel

Right now, the ExploroBot is facing west, ready to begin its exit from the tunnel. Just like the entrance, the bot will make some moves that are duplicates:

(Group 1) Forward – Detect Wall – Stop – Turn Right (second corner)

(Group 2) Forward – Detect Wall – Stop – Turn Right (first corner)

Turn Right (this final turn allows the robot to leave the tunnel)

So, once again, there's an opportunity to use two LOOP blocks, one nested inside the other. There are just a couple differences with these two LOOP blocks:

- The bot will be making right turns instead of left turns.

- The bot will make two right turns, so the outer LOOP block should only need its **Count** set to 2 instead of 3.

Knowing this information, let's place the two LOOP blocks and configure the outer LOOP for three repetitions and the inner LOOP for the Ultrasonic Sensor (see Figure 4-19). But didn't I say that it only needed to make two right turns? After that second right turn, you want the bot to keep rolling. It won't encounter another wall, but it should encounter your hands, waiting for it to come out of the tunnel. For that reason, you can configure this LOOP with a count of 3, even though it won't make an actual third turn.

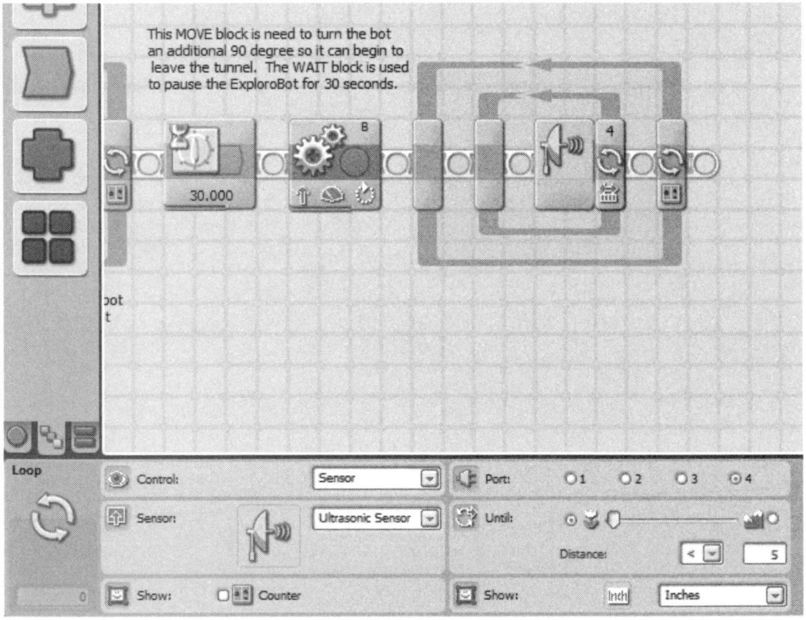

Figure 4-19. *Two LOOP blocks placed and configured*

Next, place three MOVE blocks: one for moving the bot, one for stopping the motors, and one for turning the bot. The first MOVE block is configured with **Unlimited** duration for motors

B and C. The second MOVE block is configured to stop motors B and C, and the third MOVE block is configured to turn *only* motor C at a power level of 25 and a duration of 360 degrees (see Figure 4-20).

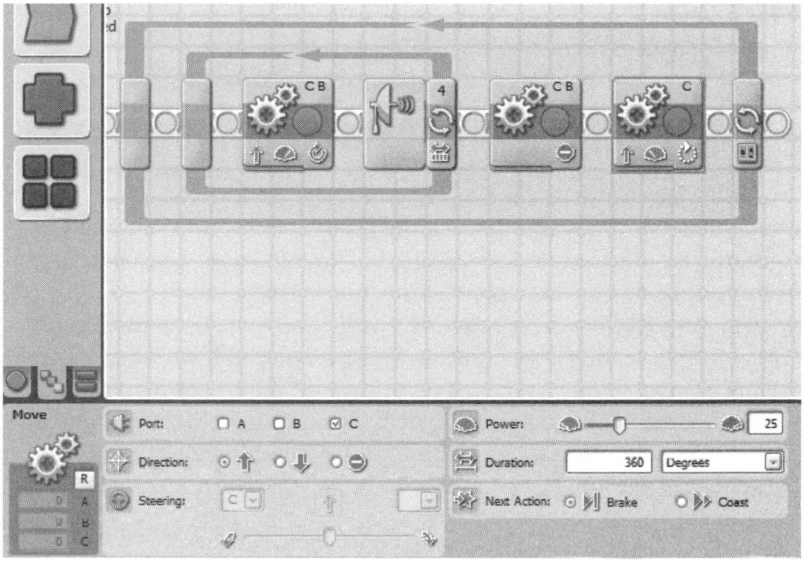

Figure 4-20. *Place three MOVE blocks here.*

Comments are placed describing these new LOOP and MOVE blocks (see Figure 4-21).

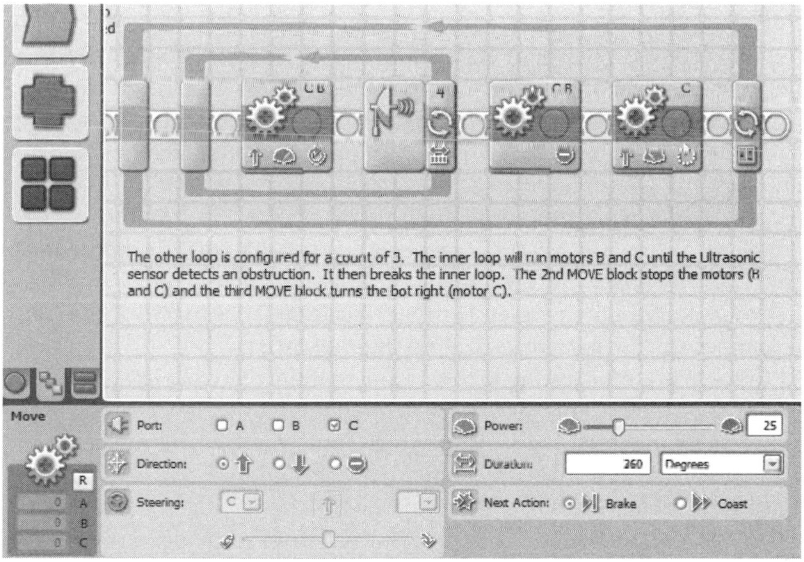

Figure 4-21. *Comments are added to describe these new blocks.*

That's it. Well, not quite. But we're close. Remember all those MOVE blocks that turn the bot? We set them to 360 degrees. That was just a guess. When I downloaded this program to my ExploroBot and ran it, those 360 degrees of rotation on the motors actually turn the bot only about 20 degrees to the left. To make those right and left turns, we're going to need the motors to turn quite a bit more. Luckily, the Intelligent Brick comes with a nice little tool to help you determine the correct number of degrees needed to turn the bot. Read on . . .

What the Degree, Kenneth? (With Apologies to REM)

First, I need you to turn on the Intelligent Brick.

Using the Brick's right or left button, scroll through the list of options until you find **View**. Press the orange select button on the Brick and, using the right or left buttons, scroll through this list until you find **Motor degrees**. Once again, press the orange select button.

Now, you're going need to select the port to monitor. The first turn will be done by motor B, so use the left or right button to scroll and find **Port B**. Select it and you'll notice a small box on the LCD screen with the number 0 (zero) in it. Just for grins, turn the wheel on motor B and watch what happens on the screen. That number tells you how many degrees the motor turns. If you turn the motor forward, you'll get a positive number (1 and climbing). If you turn the motor backward, you'll get a negative number (-1 and dropping). Press the orange select button to reset the degree counter.

Now, place the ExploroBot on a flat surface, and press the orange select button again to reset the counter. Next, you're manually going to turn the ExploroBot 90 degrees to the left. For best results, try and keep the wheel for motor C from rotating. Just twist and turn the Exploro-Bot left so that the wheel on motor B turns. When you're done, take a look at the LCD screen. Your results might vary, but for my ExploroBot I got a reading of 535. Now do the same thing for **Port C**. A true right turn, done the same way, should give you the same result (or very close).

The number you get for motor B and motor C is the number you'll enter for the **Duration** setting for the MOVE blocks used to turn the ExploroBot. (See Figures 4-14, 4-17, and 4-20 for coverage of the three MOVE blocks used for turning.) Go back and enter the number for all three MOVE blocks (two for motor B and one for motor C). Save your changes and upload the updated program to your ExploroBot.

Keep in mind that your ExploroBot will be different from every other ExploroBot—some motors are little more stiff, some less stiff. My rubber wheels might behave a little differently on a wood floor versus a cement floor. Battery levels will be different. There are so many factors that can affect how your ExploroBot operates. Don't get frustrated . . . just tweak and tweak and then tweak some more (see my tweaks later in the chapter).

At this point, you'll have to do some testing to determine that the right and left turns are as close to 90 degree turns as possible. Don't take risks—if the bot is off by a few degrees, you'll take the risk that your bot might not go straight and get stuck somewhere where you can't reach it. You want the bot to turn as close to 90 degrees as possible and then move forward on a straight path. Tweak the individual **Duration** settings until you're happy that the bot is turning left and right correctly (see Figure 4-22).

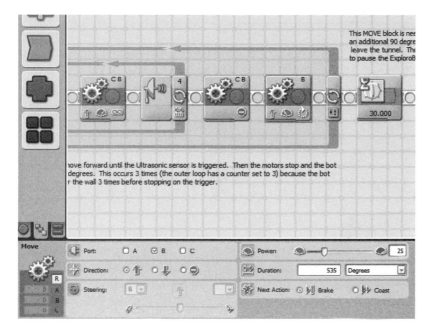

Figure 4-22. *I've entered **535** for the **Duration** settings on my three MOVE blocks for turning.*

Opening the Tomb Door

Now it's time to simulate (test) the tunnel challenge. If your ExploroBot navigates a test tunnel and returns successfully, great job. You can rest assured that the real tunnel would be no challenge to your well-designed bot.

Here are my suggestions for setting up your test tunnel.

Note You don't have to construct a real test tunnel to get results. Remember, your bot simply needs to move in fairly straight lines, react properly to obstacles (by turning left or right), stop on the "trigger" and wait, and come back to the starting point.

For my test "tunnel," I used the wooden floors of my home. I found a large open area and measured out a distance of ten feet. At the end of the ten feet I stood up a hardback book to simulate the wall of the first corner.

Next I measured six feet to the left and placed another hardback book to simulate the wall of the second corner.

For the end of the tunnel, I measured three feet left from the second corner and placed three hardback books to simulate the dead end (see Figure 4-23).

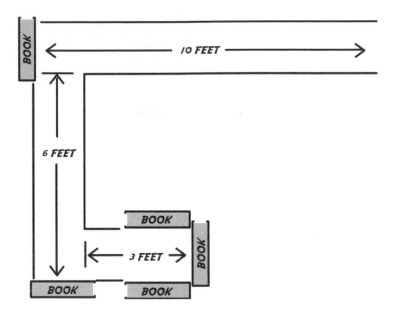

Figure 4-23. *Bird's-eye view of my test "tunnel"*

And my results? It took four runs before I was successful in having my ExploroBot return to me. Here's a summary of the runs:

- *First run*: My ExploroBot got too close to the wall before stopping. The simple fix for this was to change the Ultrasonic Sensor setting from five inches to seven inches. The Ultrasonic Sensor detected the wall earlier and was able to stop the bot so it had room to turn properly.

- *Second run*: When the ExploroBot successfully stopped at the wall and turned left, it turned just a little less than I needed. My original setting was 535 and I changed it to 550.

- *Third run*: I had the same problem as the second run, but this time it turned a little too much. I had to change the setting again from 550 to 548. This time it worked.

- *Fourth run*: On the exit trip, I had motor C set to 535. I changed it to 548 and it worked great. The ExploroBot "exited" the tunnel and was back in my hands.

I could hear some odd noises behind the tomb door as the pressure plate was triggered and the tomb door lock was released . . .

CHAPTER 5

■ ■ ■

String, Pebbles, and Gravity

Location: Southwest Guatemala

Weather Conditions: 87 degrees Fahrenheit, Humidity 88%, Rain 20%

Day 3: Inside King Ixtua's Tomb, 8:13 AM

Evan looked into the tunnel. The ExploroBot was about four feet away but still moving towards the tunnel exit. A few minutes earlier the ExploroBot had reached the trigger; some unusual sounds were heard behind the tomb door and then a loud BANG! While Evan listened for his bot to turn around and return, his uncle and a few other team members began pushing on the large stone door.

"It's opening!" yelled Uncle Phillip. "Keep pushing."

As the ExploroBot reached the end of the tunnel, Evan picked it up, looked it over for any damage, and then turned it off. He then turned to watch as Uncle Phillip, Max, and Grace finished pushing against the large stone door. Beyond the door, all Evan could see was darkness.

Uncle Phillip picked up a large flashlight, turned it on, and shone the beam into the tomb. Evan stepped closer for a look. As Uncle Phillip moved the light around the small inner room, the group could see a stone floor, but that was about it; few details could be seen.

"It doesn't appear that any damage was done when we opened the door," said Uncle Phillip.

"Good, I was worried my robot might not actually be able to trigger the pressure plate," replied Evan.

Uncle Phillip turned to Evan and smiled. "Evan, if I were your history teacher, I'd give you straight-A's for the rest of the school year. That was amazing," he said.

Max and Grace nodded and smiled.

"Thanks," Evan replied. "Glad I could help. So . . . what's next?"

Uncle Phillip took off his cap and scratched his head. "Well, I think we need to go and review the manuscript again."

Evan raised his eyebrows. "More traps?" he asked with a smile.

Evan watched as Uncle Phillip instructed one of the Guatemalan guides to guard the door and let no one inside. Uncle Phillip then waved his hand. "Come on. Let's go take a look at that manuscript."

More Monkey Business

Back in the tent, Uncle Phillip had pulled out the enlargements of the Tupaxu manuscript. Each enlargement was actually a photograph of a page of the manuscript. From what Evan could determine, the original pages were slightly larger than notebook paper sheets, but the enlargements were poster-sized.

Max took one of the enlargements, clipped it to a clothesline running across the tent, and then turned to Uncle Phillip.

Uncle Phillip was seated next to Evan and Grace. "Okay, this is the page that corresponds to the tomb's reception room. Grace, you're a better translator than I. What do you think?"

Grace stood up and walked over to the hanging picture. She then pointed at some of the Mayan writing. "One of the written legends about King Ixtua mentioned the word 'akh.' The translation is 'vine.' This drawing here contains the Mayan glyphs for vine and monkey. Take a closer look at this sketch right here," she said, pointing to a small picture.

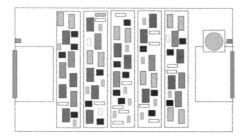

Figure 5-1. *Sketch of the reception room*

"Keep in mind," Grace continued, "that Tupaxu was well known for designing other tombs with elaborate triggering mechanisms. Some of these triggers were to open doors or passageways . . . and some were to trigger traps. What I think you're looking at here is a combination of the two."

Uncle Phillip, Evan, and Max examined the small picture.

"That looks like a jar or cup," Evan said, pointing to the image. "And that's got to be another door, right?"

Uncle Phillip nodded. "Yes. The manuscript does mention a series of obstacles before reaching King Ixtua's burial chamber. If this is one of those obstacles, my guess is that there is a trigger in this room to open that door," he said.

Grace pointed at a small block of Mayan symbols below the picture. "This roughly translates to 'Chuen Ra Rock Drop.'"

"What's a 'Chuen Ra'?" asked Evan.

"Chuen means monkey," said Max. "The monkey's name must be Ra."

Grace nodded. "Yes, and this little bit of writing here is very important." She pointed to some more Mayan glyphs. "This translates to 'shaky ground.' I think this part of the reception room floor is a trap," she said.

Uncle Phillip pointed to a tiny round circle in the picture. Above the circle was a line drawing of a monkey and below it was the jar Evan had pointed out. Several of the tiny circles were drawn inside the jar as well. "Could that be a pebble?" he asked.

"We'll need to examine the actual space, but I have a guess about this room," said Grace. "I think the floor is a trap and cannot be crossed until this jar is filled with pebbles. The jar is probably sitting on a small trigger that will open the next door when the weight of the pebbles in the jar becomes heavy enough. It'll probably also allow us to cross the floor without triggering a trap."

"I think you're right," said Uncle Phillip. "And it does fit with the legend about using monkeys to enter the tomb. I don't think this vine would be strong enough for a person to cross, do you? Okay, it's time to go take a look."

Vine Challenge

At Uncle Phillip's request, a few of the expedition's guides installed two large tripod lamps just inside the tomb entryway. Thick power cables ran out of the tomb and were plugged into a small generator that was running. Bright light from the tripod lamps flooded the reception room.

Max and Grace had followed Uncle Phillip into the reception room. Evan had been asked to wait until it was determined the room was safe. After a few minutes of quiet discussion, Evan heard his uncle yell out "Come on in, Evan!"

Evan walked slowly into the tomb. To his right were the two tripod lamps. Uncle Phillip, Max, and Grace were standing on a stone platform, approximately eight feet wide and six feet deep. Beyond the stone platform, the floor was a pattern of small rust-brown bricks that extended for another fifteen feet, and on the other side of the room were another small platform and a door.

"Stay on the platform, Evan," said Uncle Phillip.

"Yes, sir," Evan replied.

Grace pointed at the floor. "The bricks are probably covering pressure plates. If we step on them, the far door will probably be blocked for good," she said.

"Or worse," replied Max. "The Rupa tomb was designed by Tupaxu and it had poisonous spears that dropped from holes in the ceiling."

The group all looked up at the tomb's ceiling and took a few steps back.

Evan looked across the room. "There's the jar, right where the picture indicated. And what's that above it?" he asked.

To the left of the door was a raised platform with a small carved wooden jar sitting on top. Three feet above the jar was a small wood peg that was embedded in the wall.

Grace turned and looked to her left. "It's a peg. Identical to this one," she replied and pointed. On the left wall near the tomb entrance was a similar wood peg, embedded in the wall at the same height as the other peg.

"Those pegs are where the vine was tied," said Max. "Of course, 700 years has passed and the vine has decayed." Max scratched his head. "You know, if we could manage to get a rope tied to both pegs, someone could climb over to the other side."

Figure 5-2. *Near the stone door are a wooden jar and a stone peg.*

Uncle Phillip shook his head. "It won't work. Look at those pegs. They're small, and I doubt they'd hold the weight of any one of us. Tupaxu designed them correctly. Only a monkey could get across."

"Or a small robot," replied Evan.

Uncle Phillip, Max, and Grace all turned and looked at him.

Evan's Solution

"I think the hardest part is going to be getting some string around that far peg," said Evan.

Uncle Phillip had gathered his team in the equipment tent. Everyone was busy digging in boxes, looking for a ball of string or twine. "That's if we can even find some," Max replied.

"Keep looking. I know we brought some strong twine," said Uncle Phillip. "Okay, Evan. Tell us again what you have in mind."

Evan had pitched his idea quickly in the tomb about using a robot, but hadn't given any details. He took a deep breath and spoke slowly. "From what I could see, the monkey would cross to the other side of the room on the vine, holding one or two small pebbles with his feet, and drop the pebbles into the jar. So what I need to do is create something that holds a small pebble, crosses over on a string or some twine, drops the pebble, and comes back for another pebble."

"Found it!" yelled Grace. She held up a small ball of tan-colored twine.

Uncle Phillip pulled a small chair over to where Evan was seated and sat down. "It would have to be fairly lightweight, Evan. I don't think those pegs will hold much weight. And you'll have to figure out a way to drop a pebble accurately into the jar."

Evan nodded. "I'm pretty certain I can do this," he said. "What I need someone else to do is find a way to get that string tied to the far peg."

Max walked over to Evan and sat down. "How long do you think you'll need to create the bot?" he asked.

"I'm not sure," replied Evan. "At least four or five hours. Sorry."

Max smiled. "Don't apologize. It might take us that long to get the string looped around the peg."

"I have an idea," said Uncle Phillip. "We might be able to take some of the lightweight fiberglass rods that we use to reinforce our tents and tape them together to make a long pole. They won't bend or break."

Grace nodded. "If we tie the twine to a small ring, we could slide the ring off the pole and onto the peg," she said. "I think we can do this."

Uncle Phillip nodded. "Okay, then. Evan is going to get started on the robot. Grace and Max are going to get the string attached to both pegs. And since it's almost lunch time, I'm going to go and get all of you some sandwiches so you don't have to stop working."

While Max and Grace began to talk about locating the fiberglass poles, Evan opened up the yellow toolbox and pulled out the small brown notebook. He flipped it open to a blank journal page and began to write.

Story continues in Chapter 9 . . .

CHAPTER 6

■ ■ ■

StringBot—Planning and Design

What's needed to solve this latest challenge is a bot that can move along a string, carry a small object, drop that object at a specific location, and return for another object to do it all over again. In this chapter, we're going to figure out how to make that happen.

Design and Planning

I'm sure I didn't fool you by reversing the words in the section title. Since you are no longer scared by the phrase "planning and design," I'm just a little worried you might become a little bored with it and try to skip it. So I'm going to shake it up a bit in this chapter . . . challenge you a little bit to come up with something truly unique. The jar isn't going to magically fill with pebbles, so you've got some work to do.

The StringBot

In Chapter 2, I gave you an advanced look at the ExploroBot before we began working on the Design Journal page. While I've got my version of the StringBot ready to go, try to keep from skipping ahead to Chapter 7 to look at it. I want you to start seeing your own StringBot in your head without my design influencing you.

We're going to use the Design Journal page again in this chapter. If you followed along in Chapter 2 carefully, this chapter will follow the same steps. Get a blank Design Journal page and a pen and let's start designing.

■Note There are four blank Design Journal pages left in the back of this book (if you used one for Chapter 2). If you need more pages, feel free to make photocopies of the Design Journal page or visit the Apress Web site to download the page in PDF format.

At the top of the Design Journal page, in the Robot Name box, go ahead and write **StringBot**. Feel free to create your own name for the bot; names such as TwineBot, MonkeyBot, or Gort are available. (You get Big Bonus Points if you recognize the "Gort" reference.) Once you've got your bot's name selected, it's time to work on the Robot Description.

The Robot Description

Remember, the Robot Description doesn't need to be pages and pages of written text. Your goal is to keep it simple and uncluttered. As I said in Chapter 2, this isn't where you describe the bot as "lightweight, a mixture of parts, some motors, and maybe a sensor or two." This section is where you try to accurately describe the overall process the robot will follow.

Ask yourself the question, "What is this robot supposed to do?" and start writing inside the Robot Description box. Write "visually." What do I mean by this? Picture a box (a shoebox, for example) in your hands—the box doesn't have any sensors or motors or any other items yet, it's just a box. Imagine this box doing what you believe needs to be done to solve this challenge (refer to Chapter 5 if you need a reminder). Now compare what you wrote down to my Robot Description in Figure 6-1.

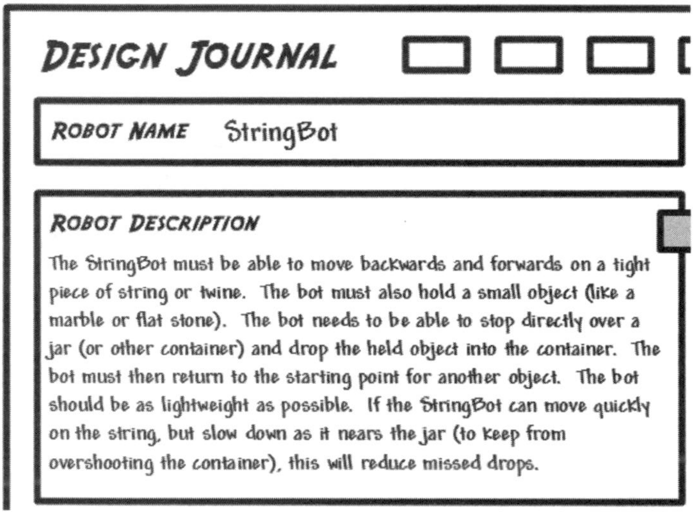

DESIGN JOURNAL ☐ ☐ ☐ ☐

ROBOT NAME   StringBot

ROBOT DESCRIPTION

The StringBot must be able to move backwards and forwards on a tight piece of string or twine. The bot must also hold a small object (like a marble or flat stone). The bot needs to be able to stop directly over a jar (or other container) and drop the held object into the container. The bot must then return to the starting point for another object. The bot should be as lightweight as possible. If the StringBot can move quickly on the string, but slow down as it nears the jar (to keep from overshooting the container), this will reduce missed drops.

Figure 6-1. *The StringBot's Robot Description should be short and simple.*

Did you cover the major requirements? Again, don't worry if your Robot Description doesn't match mine exactly. Although it wasn't mentioned in the challenge (Chapter 5), I had a thought that if the bot were moving too quickly on the string, it might overshoot the jar. So I added "If the StringBot can move quickly on the string, but slow down as it nears the jar (to keep from overshooting the container), this will reduce missed drops." You might not have added that to your Robot Description—maybe you have an idea to prevent that from happening. Great! Put it into your Robot Description.

The major items you need in your Robot Description are the bot's need to traverse the room on a string, backwards and forwards, and to be able to hold a small object and drop it into a container. Make sure that the bot returns for another object (it will take many visits to fill the jar) and that you have a good Robot Description, and you are ready to move on to the next step—the Task List.

The Task List

If you'll remember back to Chapter 2, the Task List takes your Robot Description and breaks it down into the bot's individual functions—move forward, stop, drop rock, etc. Look on your Design Journal page. As I stated before, if you have a good Robot Description written down, the Task List almost writes itself. Go back and review your Robot Description and start listing the individual tasks the StringBot will perform. I've made my list for the StringBot, and you can view it in Figure 6-2.

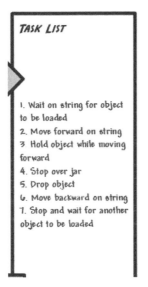

TASK LIST

1. Wait on string for object to be loaded
2. Move forward on string
3 Hold object while moving forward
4. Stop over jar
5. Drop object
6. Move backward on string
7. Stop and wait for another object to be loaded

Figure 6-2. *The StringBot's Task List is almost identical to the Robot Description.*

The Task List is one of the most important sections of the Design Journal; each of the tasks you list will affect the construction of your bot. Since each item is an action item, each action must be paired up with a physical assembly that will either perform the action or assist with the performance of that action. Have you ever heard the phrase "form follows function?" Basically what it means is that the shape of an item (its form) is usually determined by what it will do (its function). Your bot is no different. In order for your StringBot to perform its duties, you must keep its main job in mind while you are designing it.

Now, back to your Task List. Read over it again and look at your Robot Description. Did you catch everything? Did anything new come to mind?

In my Task List, you might have noticed that the first item, "Wait on string for object to be loaded," isn't mentioned in my Robot Description. That's okay! This task was an afterthought. While the idea is fairly common sense (what good is sending the bot down the string if it's not holding an object, right?), I decided to add it to my Task List anyway. I could have gone back and added this at the end of my Robot Description, but as long as I have it *somewhere* on my Design Journal page, I should be okay.

I want you to keep in mind that your Design Journal page is for you to keep track of *all* of your thoughts on this project. It doesn't have to be neat and clean—as a matter of fact, the best Design Journal page will have scribbles and notes and things crossed out—a real mess! Later, if you want to record your work for history, feel free to rewrite your Design Journal page all nice and clean.

The final point I want to make on the Task List is an item that is *not* listed. Look back at the last sentence of my Robot Description—"If the StringBot can move quickly on the string, but slow down as it nears the jar (to keep from overshooting the container), this will reduce missed drops." Do you see it on my Task List? Why isn't it there?

Well, it turns out that this really isn't a task. It's an observation that I want to remember later on when I start designing. It would fit perfectly in the Mindstorm box, but I didn't want to take the chance that I'd forget my thought later, so I put it down in the spot I was currently working—Robot Description. I mention this only as another example to you of how important it is to write down everything that comes to mind! That great thought you have now might slip away in 30 minutes when you're sketching or skateboarding or eating lunch. Remember: when the thought pops into your head, write it down! (I'll revisit that last sentence in my Robot Description later in the "Mindstorm" section.)

This Task List was shorter than the one for the ExploroBot (mainly because this bot goes back and forth with one task in mind—the ExploroBot moved forward different distances, which were each given their own task), but each item is just as important.

Limitations and Constraints

I want to remind you here that you should write down in the Limitations/Constraints box *only* limitations that come quickly to mind. Don't spend too long thinking over this section because, truthfully, until you start building, you really can't imagine all the limitations that you are going to run into. Just visualize the StringBot (or the shoebox) moving down that string and write down where you think you might run into trouble. Spend five to ten minutes (max) thinking about a bot that moves along a string to drop a pebble in a jar. What could go wrong? Well, take a look at Figure 6-3 to see what I came up with for the Limitations/Constraints box.

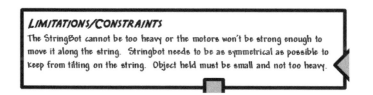

Figure 6-3. *The StringBot does have some limitations to overcome.*

One *huge* constraint that we really need to focus on for the StringBot is how it will move.

When it comes to the StringBot's size and weight, we need to keep it at a minimum. Think about a simple piece of string or twine tied between two poles (or pegs). If you put something extremely heavy on that string, the string will dip down. If it dips down too much, it might slide to the center of the string and stop moving completely. And even if the string doesn't dip down, another problem can occur. If a bot's motor spins too fast *or* if the motor is simply too powerful, the bot might just spin in place and not move at all! The NXT parts are made of plastic; like a rubber tire on a wet road, if you try to move plastic parts on a string too quickly, it can be difficult for the plastic parts to "grab" on and move. Figure 6-4 demonstrates these two problems.

Figure 6-4. *Problems with a heavy bot on a string (left image) or a motor that spins so fast that the bot doesn't move on the string (right image)*

The next item on my `Limitations/Constraints` list is "StringBot needs to be as symmetrical as possible to keep from tilting on the string." If you didn't think of this one here, don't sweat it. It would have become *very* obvious once you started building. When it comes to your StringBot, what is on the left side of the string needs to be fairly symmetrical to what's on the right side. If one side has more components or motors, it will tend to pull the bot in that direction and can cause the bot to slip off the string (see Figure 6-5).

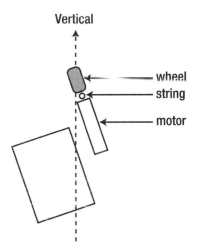

Figure 6-5. *A nonsymmetrical bot can lean.*

The final constraint, "Object held must be small and not too heavy," is also a fairly important consideration. You can design the most lightweight bot on the planet, but if all you've got available for it to carry is a steel padlock or other heavy item, the bot isn't going to go anywhere.

The design of the bot should include some sort of "carrier" that has been built for a small item. Sure, it will take a lot of trips to fill a jar with smaller, lighter items, but the bot will also travel faster. A larger, heavier bot designed to carry a heavier item will take longer to make the round trip. Ultimately, it's your call. A heavier load will use up battery power faster because the motors will draw more electricity. But it could be argued that with a lighter object, it will take many more trips to the jar, which in turn will use up the batteries. (If you're really curious, try it both ways—design a HeavyStringBot and a LightStringBot and see which one solves the challenge faster.)

We might encounter more constraints as the project moves forward. Or maybe you've come up with a constraint or two not mentioned here. Perfect. Keep them in mind when designing your own version of the StringBot.

Mindstorm

I like this section. It's my favorite part of the process before I actually start grabbing and putting pieces together. When you are mindstorming, there are no right or wrong ideas. Just find a comfortable chair and start thinking about your bot. You've probably already got a ton of ideas floating around in your head; this is the time to put the best of them down on paper. And if you think you're not that creative, let me make another suggestion.

Sometimes I have difficulty "getting creative." I might be tired or just not in the mood to do some heavy thinking. If this happens to you, especially now that you're trying to get your StringBot design started, it can be frustrating. What I do when I find that my creative energies are not at full strength is to play a game called "Won't Work."

With "Won't Work," instead of focusing on solutions to the challenge, you're going to think about solutions that (ta-da) won't work. The idea is that if you're not feeling creative (typically considered a positive emotion), you can be anti-creative. (Okay, I made up that word, but it does work. Trust me.) By thinking about things that won't work, I typically begin to start finding things that *will* work . . . and then I'm thinking creatively. Here are a couple of examples of my "Won't Work" session:

1. I'll never get the bot to cross the string by walking across like a human—it requires too much balance.

2. I can't lower the bot into the jar (its weight might set off the trigger). If the weight isn't enough, I won't get the bot back for further attempts.

Your vision of the StringBot is probably going to be very different from mine. Whether you use the "Won't Work" trick or immediately start putting your thoughts down on the Design Journal page, you're beginning to finalize the design of your StringBot and how it will work.

Take a look at Figure 6-6 and you'll see the ideas I've written down for the Mindstorm section of the Design Journal page.

The first Mindstorm entry came to me fairly quickly—"I need to find a way to add friction to the string so plastic rims or wheels won't spin in place." I know from playing around with my Mindstorms NXT kit that most of the pieces are made of very smooth plastic. My thoughts for the StringBot don't include hands and arms like a monkey. I plan on building a StringBot that moves along a string like a cable car (see Figure 6-7). I'm concerned that if I use one or two pulley wheels, the small wheels will slip on the string. When I begin to build, I'm going to try to incorporate one of the rubber wheels, because I think the rubber probably won't slip on the string.

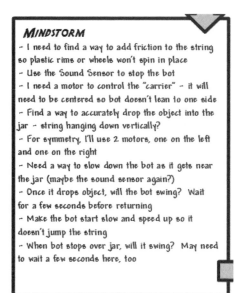

MINDSTORM

- I need to find a way to add friction to the string so plastic rims or wheels won't spin in place
- Use the Sound Sensor to stop the bot
- I need a motor to control the "carrier" – it will need to be centered so bot doesn't lean to one side
- Find a way to accurately drop the object into the jar – string hanging down vertically?
- For symmetry, I'll use 2 motors, one on the left and one on the right
- Need a way to slow down the bot as it gets near the jar (maybe the sound sensor again?)
- Once it drops object, will the bot swing? Wait for a few seconds before returning
- Make the bot start slow and speed up so it doesn't jump the string
- When bot stops over jar, will it swing? May need to wait a few seconds here, too

Figure 6-6. *The Mindstorm section will help you to complete your StringBot design.*

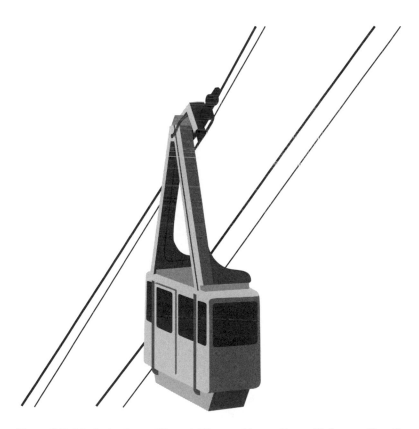

Figure 6-7. *My StringBot will work like a cable car. But will the small pulley wheels slip?*

I won't go through every item on my `Mindstorm` list, but there are a couple more items I feel are important for me to explain. The first is, "Find a way to accurately drop the object into the jar – string hanging down vertically?"

Most jars that I own have small openings at the top. I don't want my StringBot wasting time moving down the string and missing the drop. Maybe for your challenge setup you'll use a large jar or box, but where's the fun in that? So it occurred to me that I better come up with a way for my bot to accurately drop its held object right into the jar. I'll obviously test my bot many times by observing where the object falls when the carrier releases it. What I think I'll do is tie a piece of loose string around my bot. Gravity will keep the string hanging straight down; when the string moves over the jar and is roughly in the center of the jar, I'll know to stop the StringBot and release the object.

Two other items in my `Mindstorm` box mention making the bot pause after certain actions. I believe (because I haven't tested it) that the bot will swing a little when it comes to a stop *and* after it drops the object. I want the bot to stabilize before it drops the object, and then again before it begins its return trip. If the bot is swinging, the dropped object might miss the jar. Also, a swinging bot might jump the string, and then it won't be able to return.

Your main objective here is to simply have some fun and write down some of your initial thoughts on what you'd like to do with your bot design. You may have to take a completely different direction after some testing. You may find that you exhaust your supply of a particular component. What you write down is not going to lock you in to a particular design. You can change the design anytime—even start completely over. Print out another Design Journal page and try a different design. It's supposed to be fun, so make it fun. Go crazy with your ideas—the crazier, the better!

The final `Mindstorm` item I want to quickly discuss is, "Make the bot start slow and speed up so it doesn't jump the string." I added this item because, in my earlier NXT experiments, I've seen that when the motors start spinning quickly, sometimes the power of the motors can make a bot twist or "jump" and can slightly alter its direction. I offer this only as a suggestion—sometimes it's best to slowly increase the power of your motors while testing your bot to determine the best speed. Keep that in mind when you begin testing your StringBot.

Well, we're almost done with the Design Journal page. It's time to take everything you've collected—`Robot Description`, `Task List`, `Limitations/Constraints`, and `Mindstorm` information—and start with some rough sketches to help you when you begin construction.

Sketches

Even though we're not in the same room, I'll know if you're snickering. I told you before that I'm not an artist, so keep that in mind when you begin to look at my sketches of the StringBot.

Luckily, I know a little bit about what I'm looking for in terms of the shape and size of the StringBot. One of my constraints mentioned keeping the StringBot symmetrical. I know that if the bot isn't symmetric, it will lean to one side . . . and if it comes off the string, that will be bad, right?

In my `Mindstorm` box, I indicated that I want to use two motors, one on the left and one on the right. If I do this, I'll have to place that third motor near the middle of the bot to keep it from leaning. Since I'm going to use the idea of a cable car, I want the pulley wheels to be on top. And since I know my StringBot won't work without the Intelligent Brick, I've got to decide whether to have the Brick mounted horizontally, with the buttons parallel to the ground, or mounted vertically, so I can view the LCD screen as the bot moves away from me.

Okay, so it's time to draw. I tend to draw using basic shapes like rectangles, squares, and circles, so my sketches will consist of components drawn using their most basic shapes (the motor, for example, is two circles connected by a small rectangle). Figure 6-8 shows my initial sketches for the StringBot—no laughing!

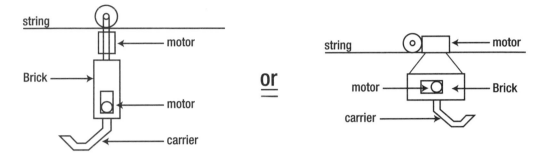

Figure 6-8. *I use basic shapes to define the StringBot in the Sketches area.*

I've got quite a few concepts to test out when I start building. I might find that the vertical mounting of the Brick doesn't balance as well on the string as mounting the Brick horizontally. Or I might find that the weight of the third motor (for the carrier) isn't properly balanced and causes the bot to lean. Ultimately, if the StringBot moves to the end of the string, drops the object, and returns, I don't care what it looks like. (Okay, maybe I do—everyone loves a nice-looking bot.)

Chapter 7 is going to show you how to assemble my version of the StringBot. Compare it to my sketches and maybe you'll see the final version hidden in those rough drawings. Feel free to build my version. Or, if you're really proud of your design, go ahead and build YOUR StringBot. Remember—if your bot can fill a jar with dropped objects, you shouldn't have any trouble completing this challenge. Time to build the StringBot!

■ ■ ■

CHAPTER 7

StringBot—Build It

Figure 7-1 shows my version of the StringBot. It's a strange-looking device, but it does work. If you ever want to have some fun, try showing your bot design to others who are unfamiliar with it. Ask them "What do you think it does?" and be ready for some surprising answers! I showed this to a couple of people and the most surprising response was this: "How does it roll along the floor with only one wheel? The smaller wheels don't look like they'll help hold it up." Just goes to show that you cannot judge a book (or a bot, in this case) by its cover.

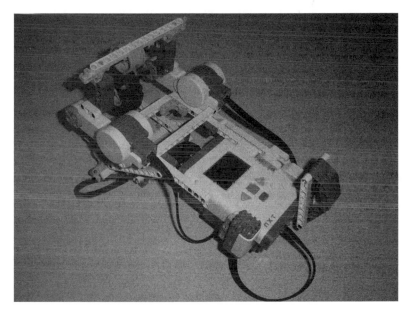

Figure 7-1. *Evan's version of the StringBot*

Where to Start?

Some people have no trouble just clicking pieces together. Others have more difficulty and find themselves sitting and staring at all those wonderful plastic pieces with no idea where to start. I find myself in both situations often. Some days I'm ready to go, with ideas flowing so fast I have difficulty deciding which one to build first. Other days, I pick up a few pieces, snap them together, shake my head, and take them apart. It can be frustrating.

Hopefully by now you're starting to see the importance of the Design Journal page. It can help you to at least start building something—ANYTHING—with a basic shape and concept. Just sit down with your Design Journal page and look over the sketches. Read over the Mindstorm section and see if anything sticks out as a good place to start. I always start with the Intelligent Brick. Since it's a required part for all bots, it just seems to me to always be the best place to begin.

Before we move into the actual building instructions for the StringBot, I want to mention a few things that happened during my initial construction:

1. I mounted the motors on the sides of the Brick, with the Brick parallel to the floor. It worked, but I couldn't see the LCD screen when the bot moved away from me. I chose to mount the Brick hanging vertically.

2. I tried to run my StringBot on the string without the rubber wheel. As predicted, at high speeds the pulley wheels would just spin and the bot wouldn't move. I had to set the motors to a very low speed for it to move. It took too long to reach the jar and come back.

3. I used the small pulley wheels initially to ride the string. But no matter what happened, the StringBot kept jumping the string. So I used the wider rubber wheel rims (minus the rubber) with a couple of beams used as "string guides" to keep the bot going straight. And it works great.

One thing I would suggest is to keep a builder's notebook (along with your Design Journal pages). In this notebook, you should write down observations while you are playing—I mean building—robots. Write down things like you see in the above list. The next time you decide to build a robot that possibly rides a string, a quick review of your notebook will remind you that the small pulley wheels aren't the best method. You can also use it to draw sketches of bots, special assemblies, and other things that you might use in the future.

This is the last time I will mention it (because most people don't like to be told things twice), but as you're following along with the building instructions, if you get stuck or can't figure out the next step, just take a short break. Look ahead at the next few figures in the chapter and see if you can use the different angles to determine the proper placement of a confusing piece. Trust me, I've built these bots over and over again to test the instructions. I've done my best to give you clear views from the right angles for where parts should be placed. Count holes on beams to determine where I've placed those small connectors (for example, 5 holes from the top on the 15-hole beam) or skip ahead and look at the final bot image. If your StringBot looks similar to this one with a couple of minor differences—that's okay! You might have found a better solution anyway!

You'll figure it out, so don't let the StringBot stress you out. You're still having fun, right?

■**Note** I would enjoy seeing your modifications to the StringBot—or maybe you've created something completely different. Take a picture and e-mail it to me. My e-mail address is in the Introduction.

Okay, let's go build the StringBot.

Step by Step

I've broken the StringBot building instructions into three sections. The first section consists of the Intelligent Brick, framework, and motors. The second section will add in the wheels-on-string system and the string guides. The third section will be the carrier arm and motor assembly that will be used to drop objects. These three sections will be connected and wired up and you'll have your StringBot.

I'll continue to add comments to the sections where I think a little help is needed. And when you see an image with text and arrows, pay special attention because there might be a tricky placement that you need to focus on.

Just like the ExploroBot instructions, I'll add new parts to an image shortly before those parts are going to be used.

First Section: Brick, Framework, and Motors

Figures 7-2 through 7-19 show you all the components used to build the initial StringBot frame with motors. Let's start off with the pieces you see in Figure 7-2.

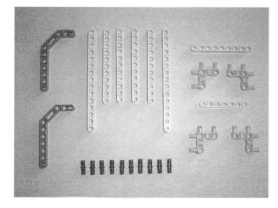

Figure 7-2. *Starting pieces for the StringBot*

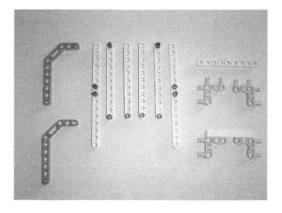

Figure 7-3. *Place the ten small black connectors in the beams as shown.*

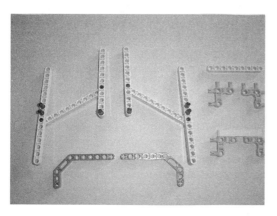

Figure 7-4. *Connect the beams like this—count the holes to help determine placement.*

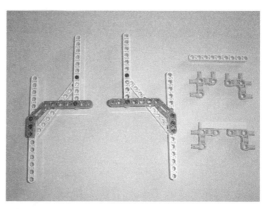

Figure 7-5. *Place the angled dark gray beams to add strength to the frames.*

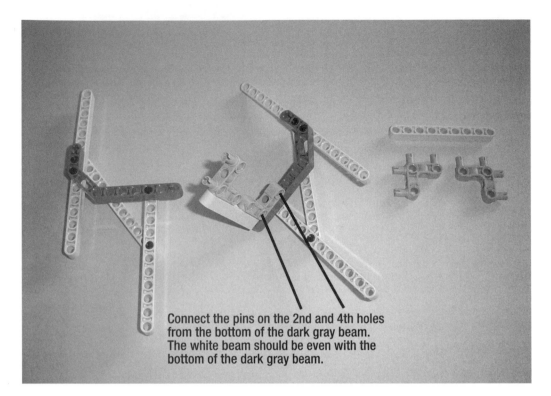

Connect the pins on the 2nd and 4th holes
from the bottom of the dark gray beam.
The white beam should be even with the
bottom of the dark gray beam.

Figure 7-6. *Connect the small 7-hole beam to the right-side frame as shown.*

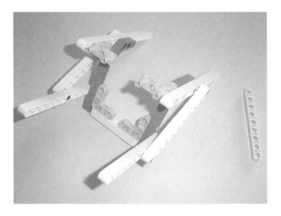

Figure 7-7. *Connect the left-side frame to the right-side frame.*

Figure 7-8. *Grab the Brick and six small black connectors (often called friction pins or friction pegs).*

■**Note** What I call the "small black connectors" have an official Lego part number. I don't like using numbers to reference parts unless absolutely necessary—but if you must have this information, the part number is 2780.

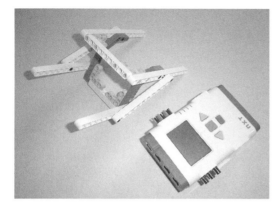

Figure 7-9. *Orient the Brick as shown and get ready to attach it to the framework.*

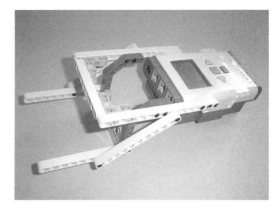

Figure 7-10. *Connect the framework to the Brick.*

At this point, take a short break and compare your StringBot frame to Figure 7-10. Do they match? If not, try and correct the problem by going back through the figures to find the difference. You'll be connecting the motors in very specific locations, so it's important to have your framework match as closely as possible the one shown in Figure 7-10. Okay, let's continue . . .

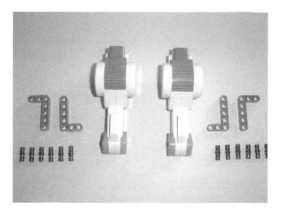

Figure 7-11. *The motors and the components used to connect them to the framework.*

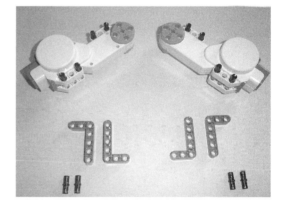

Figure 7-12. *Place the small black connectors in the motors as shown.*

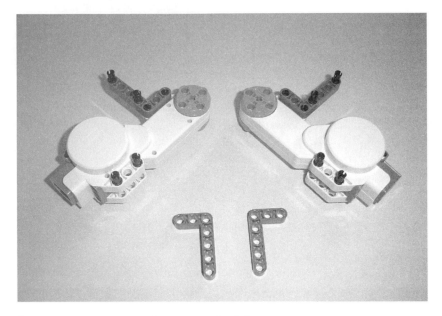

Figure 7-13. *Connect an L-beam to each of the motors.*

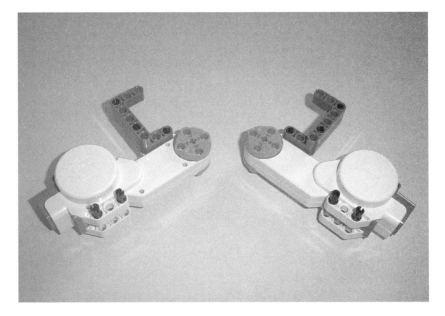

Figure 7-14. *Connect the next L-beam to each of the motors.*

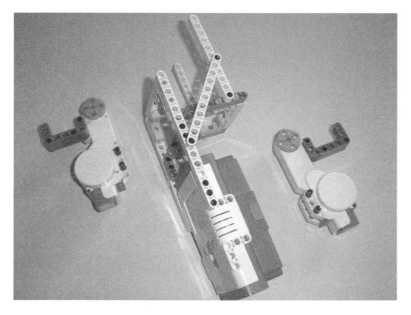

Figure 7-15. *Grab the Brick/framework and orient it with the motors as shown.*

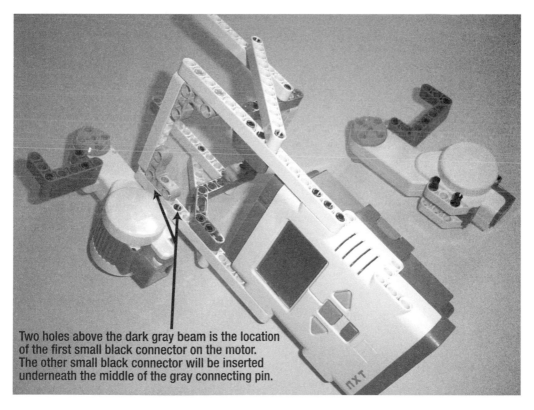

Two holes above the dark gray beam is the location
of the first small black connector on the motor.
The other small black connector will be inserted
underneath the middle of the gray connecting pin.

Figure 7-16. *Connect the left motor as shown.*

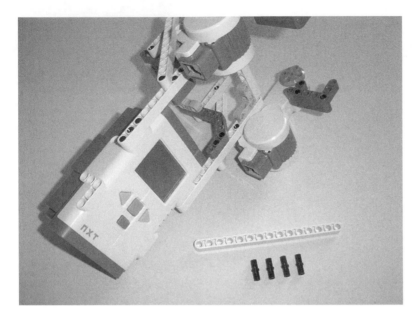

Figure 7-17. *Connect the right motor as shown.*

The final step for this section is to reinforce the two motors with a 15-hole beam. Figure 7-18 shows the pieces used, and Figure 7-19 shows how to connect them to the motors. (And while you're at it, go ahead and grab the other components shown in these figure because you'll need them for the second section.)

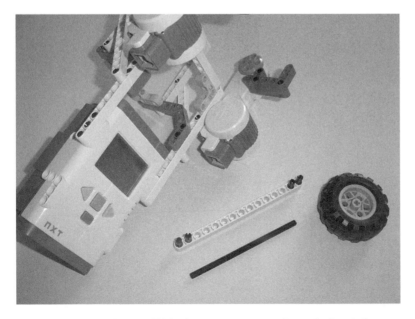

Figure 7-18. *Insert the small black connectors into the 15-hole reinforcement beam.*

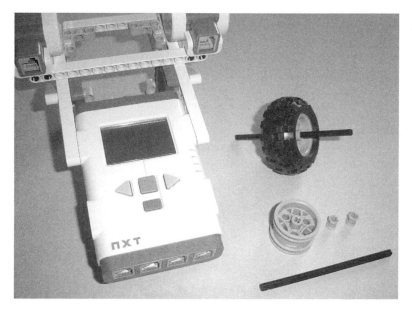

Figure 7-19. *Place the 15-hole reinforcement beam as shown.*

Now let's get the wheels-on-string system created . . .

Second Section: Wheels-on-String System and String Guides

When I say "wheels-on-string system," I'm talking about the pieces needed for the StringBot to roll along the string. For this version of the StringBot, there will be two small rims used as guides (take off the rubber tires) and one rubber wheel (with rim inside) used to apply friction to the string. There will also be two 15-hole beams used as "string guides"—these will help keep the bot from jumping the string and not returning to you. We're going to start from Figure 7-19 where you'll see some of the parts used. Figure 7-20 shows the first wheel rim assembly.

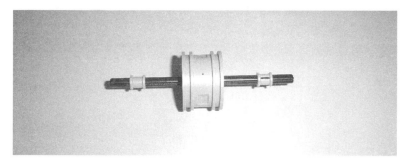

Figure 7-20. *Assemble your first wheel rim guide as shown.*

In Figure 7-21 the Brick/framework assembly has been flipped over. You can also use this image to count holes for correct placement of the first wheel rim guide (third hole back on each side).

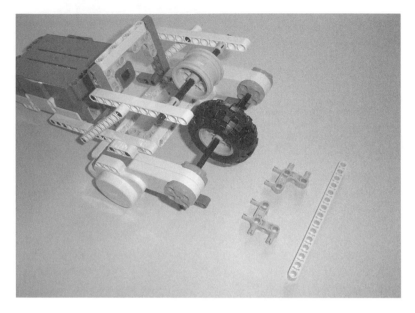

Figure 7-21. *Place the rubber wheel and your first wheel rim guide as shown.*

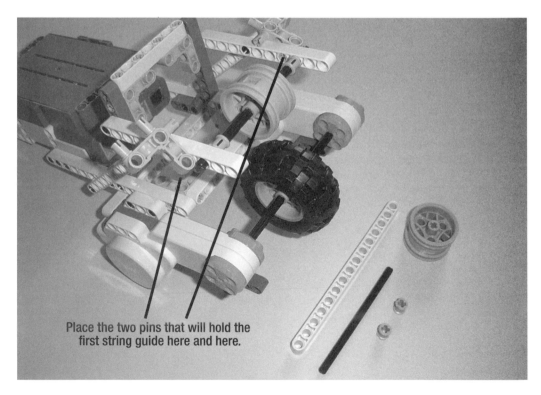

Place the two pins that will hold the
first string guide here and here.

Figure 7-22. *Place the pins that will hold the first string guide.*

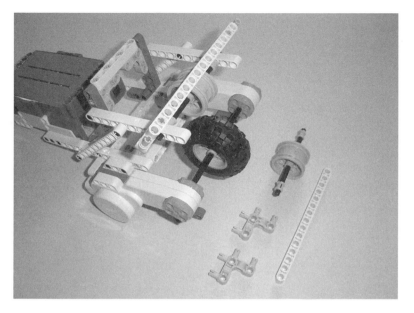

Figure 7-23. *Place the 15-hole string guide beam and assemble the second wheel rim guide.*

In Figure 7-24 you'll see that the Brick/framework has been flipped over. This is where you'll place the pins for the final string guide. You'll also place the final wheel rim guide.

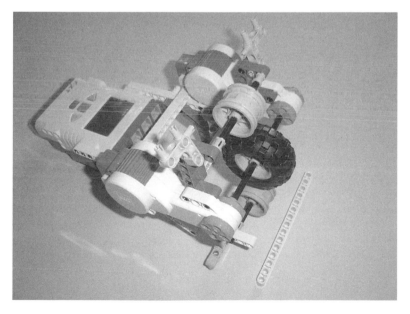

Figure 7-24. *Insert the final wheel rim guide and connect the pins for the final string guide.*

Figure 7-25. *Place the final 15-hole string guide.*

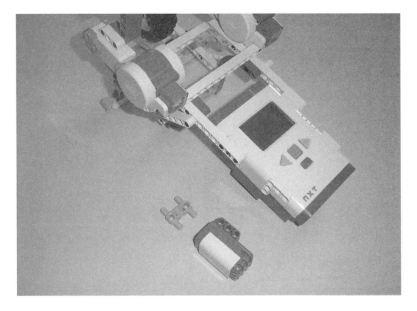

Figure 7-26. *The sound sensor and pin are needed next.*

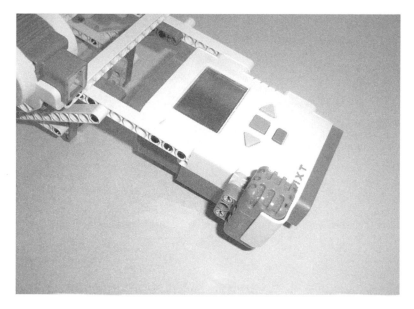

Figure 7-27. *Connect the sound sensor to the Brick.*

Okay, the StringBot is almost finished. Are you beginning to see how it will work? You'll feed a string through one of the middle holes on the front string guide. The string will then go under the first rim, then the rubber wheel, and then the second rim. Thread the string through the final string guide, and your StringBot will be able to move along the string.

That covers movement on the string, but you still need to be able to drop small objects in the jar. That's accomplished with the carrier arm.

Third Section: Carrier Arm and Motor Assembly

You're almost done. We're going to build a small carrier arm for the StringBot that will be used to carry a pebble or small coin to be dropped in the jar. The third motor will be used to control the carrier, and we'll place it on the bottom of the current StringBot assembly.

Figure 7-28 shows the majority of the pieces you'll need for this section. Go ahead and grab them and let's start building.

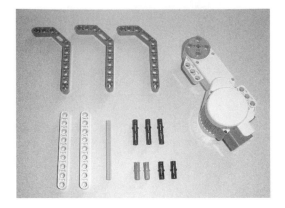

Figure 7-28. *Locate these pieces to build the carrier arm and motor assembly.*

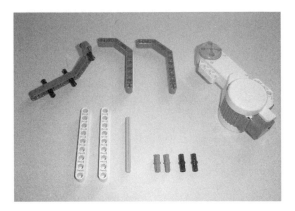

Figure 7-29. *Place the small black connectors in the first dark gray beam.*

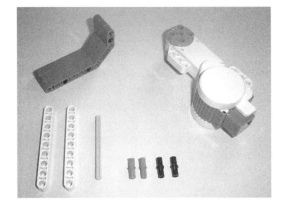

Figure 7-30. *Connect the other two dark gray beams to the first one.*

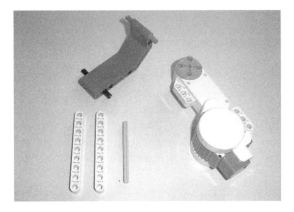

Figure 7-31. *Insert the small black connectors and blue connectors as shown.*

Go ahead and locate a 15-hole beam and black pin as shown in Figure 7-32. You'll use these shortly to connect the carrier arm and motor assembly to the main body of the StringBot.

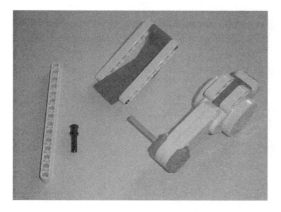

Figure 7-32. *Insert the gray axle into the motor and connect the side beams to the carrier.*

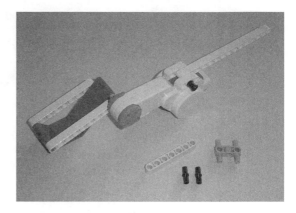

Figure 7-33. *Connect the 15-hole beam to the motor as shown.*

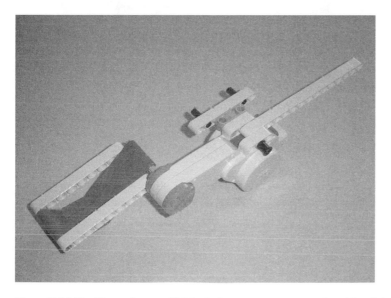

Figure 7-34. *You'll use the small 7-hole beam to connect to the side of the Brick.*

Now, using the main StringBot assembly (with the Brick), you're going to connect the carrier motor assembly as shown in Figure 7-35.

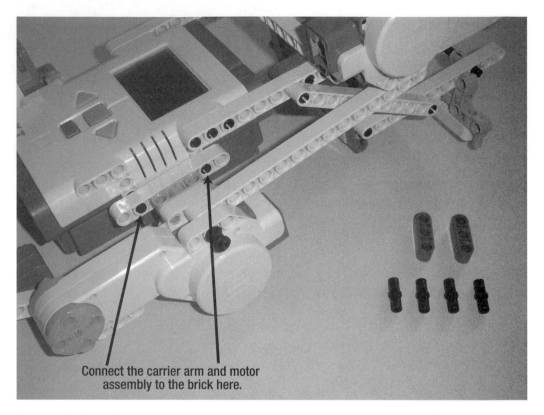

Connect the carrier arm and motor
assembly to the brick here.

Figure 7-35. *Two different views showing how the main body and the rear wheel/base connect*

In Figure 7-36, notice where I've placed the four small black connectors. These will be used with two small 3-hole beams to strengthen the connection and keep the carrier arm assembly from "wobbling."

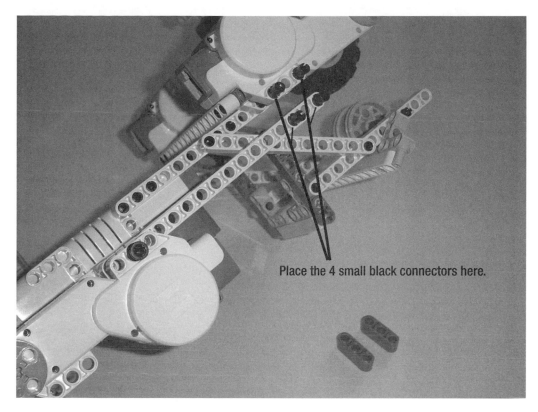

Place the 4 small black connectors here.

Figure 7-36. *Place the four small black connectors as shown.*

Next, connect the cable frame to the main body as shown in Figure 7-37.

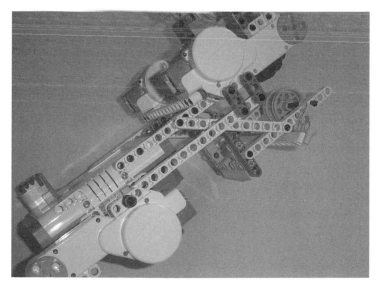

Figure 7-37. *Place the 3-hole beams as shown.*

And that's it! You are now the proud owner of your very own StringBot. We still have the programming to complete, but at this point if you have some string, you can place your StringBot on the string and test to see how it will roll along the string.

What I would suggest is tying one end of the string to a doorknob (on a closed door, of course). You'll feed the string through the StringBot and then tie off the other end of the string to something heavy or possibly another doorknob. Cut yourself a long piece of string so you'll have plenty of options. And my last bit of advice: tie the string so that it is as tight as you can make it with the StringBot sitting on the string. If there's too much slack in the string, the StringBot will slide towards the middle of the string. It also might not have enough power to move along the string.

Figure 7-38 shows how I've fed the string through the front string guide, under the first wheel rim, under the rubber tire, under the second wheel rim, and then finally through the rear string guide.

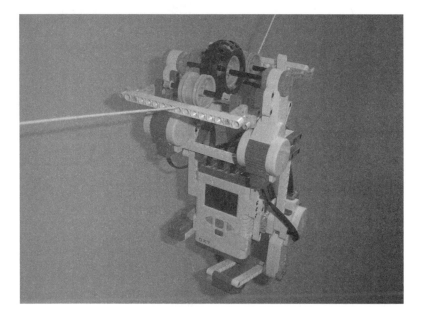

Figure 7-38. *String up your StringBot.*

Once you've got the StringBot programmed, this little fellow will move forward on the string, stop when you tell it to stop, and then move slowly towards the jar until you tell it to stop for the final time. At this point, the carrier arm will drop whatever object it is holding, pause for a few seconds, close the arm, and then return to you. Simple!

Chapter 8 will show you how to program the StringBot to do all this . . . and more. I'm going to give you some ideas on increasing the functionality of the StringBot with some additional programming. Once you've got your StringBot working, you'll fill that jar with some coins or small rocks to trigger the pressure plate—the trapped floor won't be dangerous anymore and the expedition crew will be able to cross the room and continue investigating the tomb.

CHAPTER 8

■■■

StringBot—Program It

The StringBot is a unique little bot. When you ask someone to describe a robot, my guess is that he or she will probably have a mental picture of a wheeled robot or a bot with legs. Our StringBot has neither—it's going to move along a string. But whether your bot has wheels, legs, or some other method for moving, it has to be programmed properly to accomplish its desired tasks. The StringBot needs to move along a string, successfully drop a small object into a jar, then return to you. This chapter will show you how to make that happen.

Get Familiar with the Blocks

In Chapter 4, you used the MOVE, WAIT, and LOOP programming blocks to get the ExploroBot to complete its task. For the StringBot, you're going to use these same blocks. With the ExploroBot, you used the Ultrasonic Sensor, but with the StringBot, you're going to use the Sound Sensor.

Just like you started doing in Chapter 4, I'm going to ask you to refer back to your completed Design Journal page for the StringBot to help determine the proper blocks to use. Go ahead and get the StringBot Design Journal page out and open up the Lego Mindstorms NXT software (see Figure 8-1).

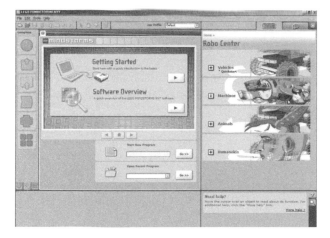

Figure 8-1. *The Lego Mindstorms NXT software*

Because you're creating a new program, go ahead and type **StringBot** into the blank text field labeled **Start New Program** and then click the **Go** button (see Figure 8-2).

Start New Program

StringBot   Go >>

Figure 8-2. *Enter* **StringBot** *for the new program name and click* **Go.**

■**Note** To have more workspace visible on your screen, close down the RoboCenter area on the far right by clicking the small red X in the upper-right corner of the software. You can also maximize the window to cover the whole screen.

Take a look now at the Task List on your Design Journal page (Figure 8-3). Our Task List wasn't as long as the one for the ExploroBot, but we still need to go back through it to help us with the bot's program.

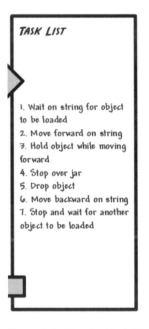

Figure 8-3. *Use the Task List to help with programming the StringBot.*

Let's go down the Task List and place potential programming blocks next to each step. This might help you to understand what the final program's structure will look like. At this point, you're just guessing about the blocks you might use, but at least this will get you thinking about what might be needed.

1. Wait on string for object to be loaded: WAIT, LOOP

2. Move forward on string: MOVE, LOOP-UNTIL-SOUND-SENSOR

3. Hold object while moving forward: MOVE

4. Stop over jar: STOP, WAIT

5. Drop object: MOVE

6. Move backward on string: MOVE

7. Stop and wait for another object to be loaded: MOVE, LOOP-UNTIL-SOUND-SENSOR

I also reviewed the Mindstorm section of the Design Journal page, and there are a couple items in there that I'd like to implement using programming:

1. Need a way to slow down the bot as it gets near the jar

2. If bot might swing, build in some wait time before beginning a new task

We'll keep these in mind as we begin to assemble our StringBot program. We're going to use the same blocks covered in Chapter 4: MOVE, LOOP, and WAIT, plus a new block—STOP.

There's not much to say about the STOP block (see Figure 8-4). In a nutshell, when you place the STOP block in your program, the bot will cease all function when it reaches that block—no further programming blocks will be executed by the Intelligent Brick.

Figure 8-4. *The basic STOP block*

However, you need to be aware of some things when it comes to the STOP block. First, the STOP block doesn't need to be configured. There are no special settings for it. Second, if any motors are running when the STOP block is reached in the program, they'll coast, not brake. The final item I want to mention about the STOP block requires a short diversion in our discussion. I want to introduce to you another programming block: the SWITCH block.

The SWITCH block will allow you to program your bot to perform actions based on input conditions. For example, the most basic SWITCH block will test for two conditions. If one condition is met (TRUE), then one path of the SWITCH block will be taken. If the second condition is met (meaning the first condition is FALSE), then the second path of the block will be taken. We'll use the SWITCH block for a later bot design, but for now I want you to look at Figure 8-5. In this example, the SWITCH has been programmed to execute a MOVE block and then a STOP block to stop the program. These program blocks will execute if the Touch Sensor is pressed (TRUE/condition met). If the Touch Sensor isn't pressed (FALSE/condition not met), then the programming block in the lower port of the SWITCH block will execute—a picture will be displayed on the LCD screen. The program will then continue by leaving the SWITCH block, and a SOUND block will play a sound file forever (or until you turn off the Brick or program).

If the Touch Sensor is pressed and the STOP block is executed, the SOUND block will never play its sound file because the program will, well, stop on the STOP block!

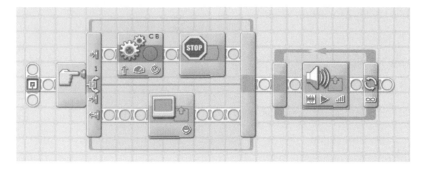

Figure 8-5. *The basic SWITCH block*

█Note The SWITCH block is located on the COMMON palette and on the COMPLETE palette. In most instances, just look around on the COMMON and COMPLETE palettes and you'll find the necessary blocks. If it helps, you can hover the mouse over a block for a few seconds—a small "hint" block will appear telling you the name of the block.

Okay, let's get back to programming the StringBot.

Getting to the Vase

As you begin to put the program together, I want to suggest that you start adding comment text as you move forward. The comments you add will help you remember not only *why* you're using a certain block, but they can also be used to tell you how a block is configured. In the remaining programming figures, I'll include comments so you'll see what I mean.

Now, what was that first Task List item? Fairly simple: wait on the string while an object is loaded in the carrier. You're going to use a LOOP block, but this one is a little different from the one seen in Chapter 4. With this LOOP block, instead of testing for a sensor to be triggered (such as the Sound Sensor or Ultrasonic Sensor), you're going to have the block wait for a button on the Brick to be pressed. (You could use a simple WAIT block configured to wait for a button to be pressed, but you're using the LOOP block because you can later add more blocks inside the LOOP block if you wish, and add more options for your bot later on.) Take a look at Figure 8-6 to see how I did this.

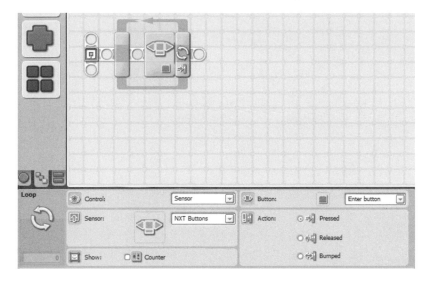

Figure 8-6. *Using a LOOP block to hold the StringBot until an object is placed in the carrier*

In Figure 8-6, I've configured the LOOP block to check and see if the **Enter** button (orange button) on the Brick has been pressed. Once the button has been pressed, the rest of the program will begin to execute. I could just as easily have included the Touch Sensor on my StringBot and had the LOOP block test to see if the Touch Sensor was pressed. But because I wanted to keep my StringBot light in weight, reducing the amount of sensors was important. The Brick has to be included, so I might as well use its buttons in place of the Touch Sensor, right?

So, while the StringBot is sitting on the string, waiting, we'll place an object in the carrier. Once the carrier is loaded, the next step is to start the StringBot moving along the string. If you remember, one of our conditions was that we wanted the StringBot to slow down as it neared the jar. We then want the motors to spin again, but slowly, so that we have more control over the accuracy of putting the bot over the jar. To do this, you're going to use LOOP blocks again. The first LOOP block will run the motors at high speed and the second LOOP block will run the motors at a reduced speed. You'll use your voice (with the Sound Sensor) to control when the bot switches from high speed to low speed. You'll place the first LOOP block as shown in Figure 8-7.

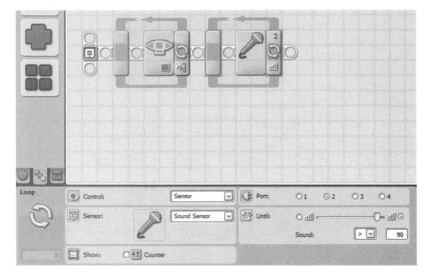

Figure 8-7. *This LOOP block will allow you to stop the high-speed bot with your voice.*

In Figure 8-7, I've configured the LOOP block to use the Sound Sensor. I set the threshold to 90 (I'll probably have to yell) so the LOOP will end when the Sound Sensor is triggered. Now you need to place the MOVE block so the motors will run at high speed (see Figure 8-8).

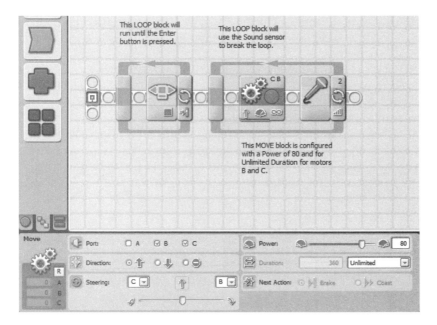

Figure 8-8. *This MOVE block runs the motors at high speed.*

After the Sound Sensor is triggered, you want the motors to stop. Figure 8-9 shows the program so far.

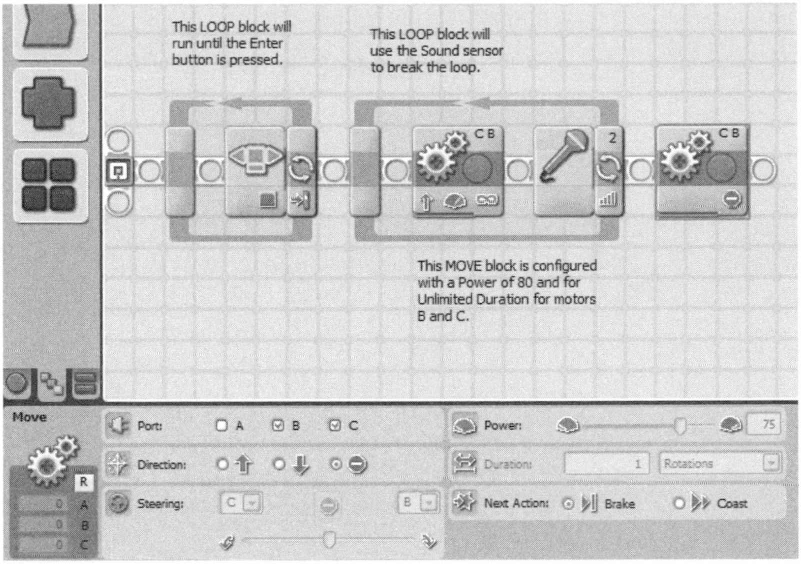

Figure 8-9. *Now the motors need to stop.*

Next, you want the bot to pause for a short period just in case it's swinging on the string. Drop in a WAIT block for this and configure it for three seconds (see Figure 8-10).

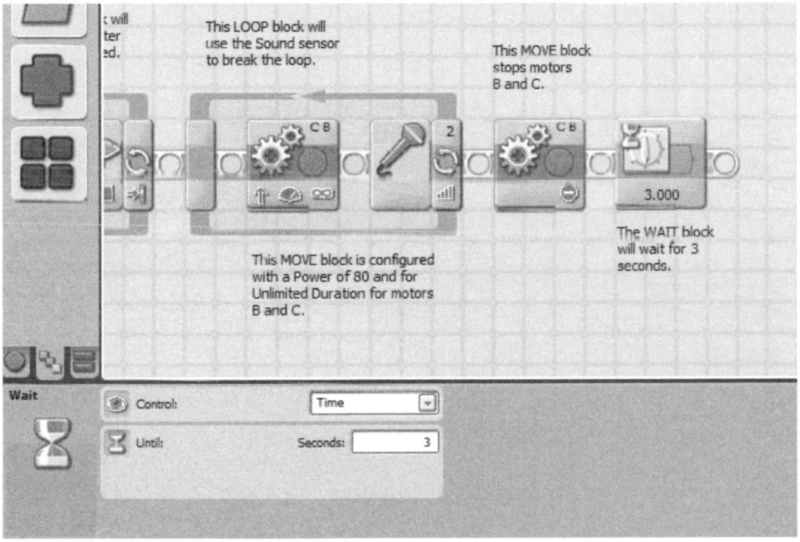

Figure 8-10. *The WAIT block allows the bot to stop swinging.*

Now that the bot is stopped, you need to configure the program to start the bot moving again, but this time at a slower speed. This is done just as before, with a LOOP block configured to break when the Sound Sensor is triggered with the Sound level set to greater than 90 (>90).

Configure the MOVE block inside it at a slower power setting—40. Figure 8-11 shows the final
LOOP block configured.

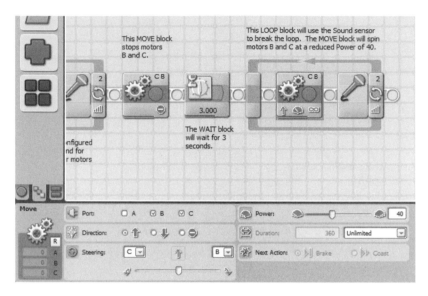

Figure 8-11. *The motors run at a slower speed until the Sound Sensor is triggered.*

When this LOOP block is broken, you need to stop the StringBot's movement and give it
time to stop swinging. What you'll do is throw in a MOVE block that will stop the motors (see
Figure 8-12).

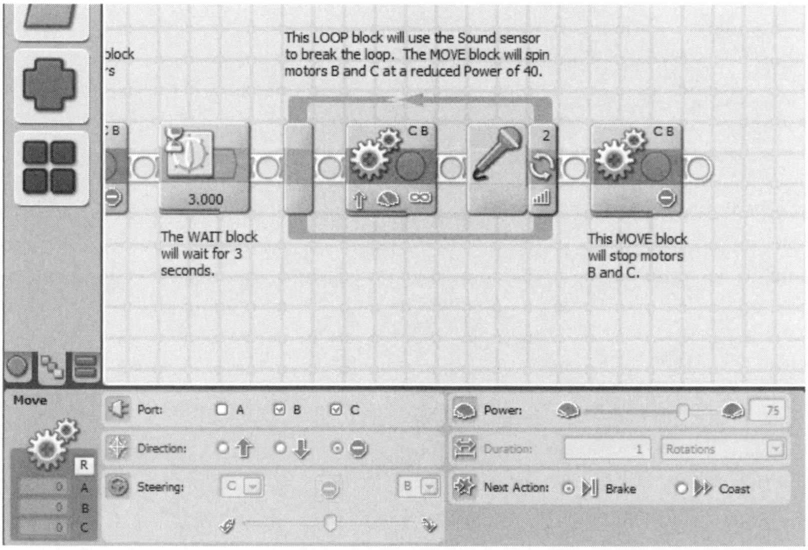

Figure 8-12. *Now stop the motors—the StringBot should be directly over the vase.*

Your StringBot should be directly over the vase at this point, but it might be swinging. Add in a WAIT block (see Figure 8-13) before releasing the object from the carrier—a five-second wait should do it.

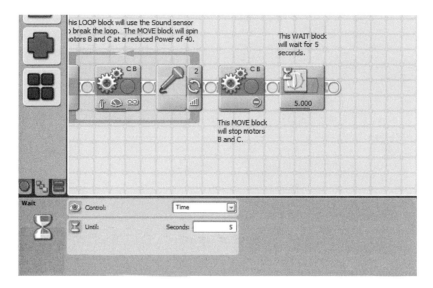

Figure 8-13. *Add in a WAIT block to allow the StringBot to stop swinging above the vase.*

Above the Vase

Now you've got the StringBot directly over the vase. That wasn't too bad, was it? Well, the next part is even easier. All you need to do is have the carrier release the held object and return to its starting point, ready for another object to be loaded.

During my testing, I did find that if I had the carrier move too quickly, I didn't have very accurate control when the object dropped. I began to tweak the speed of the motor and found that a slower release resulted in a more accurate drop. By the way, I was dropping quarters and nickels. I experimented with dropping multiple coins at the same time; sometimes both coins dropped in the vase, sometimes neither did. You'll have to experiment with your own StringBot to determine what you want to drop and how many you wish to attempt to drop at the same time.

The other factor is how far back you wish the carrier to spin—experimentation with my StringBot revealed that a 90-degree rotation was sufficient for the object to fall out of the carrier and into the vase. You might also need to experiment to determine the proper rotational setting.

Take a look at Figure 8-14. I've added the MOVE block that will slowly lower the carrier. For now, I've set the speed of the motor to 25.

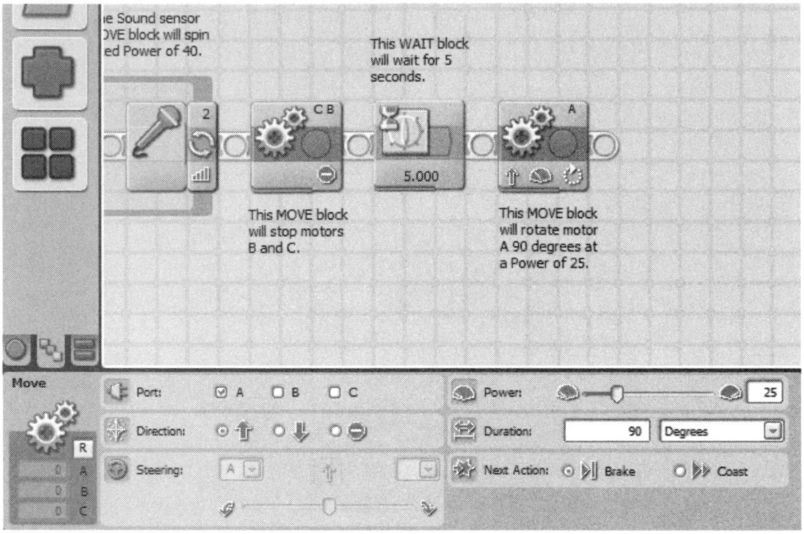

Figure 8-14. *Use a MOVE block to control the carrier's release speed.*

Okay, so now that the carrier has released its object, let's wait a few seconds and then close the carrier. Technically, we don't have to close the carrier, but I just don't like the look of the StringBot with the carrier hanging down.

First, add a WAIT block (see Figure 8-15).

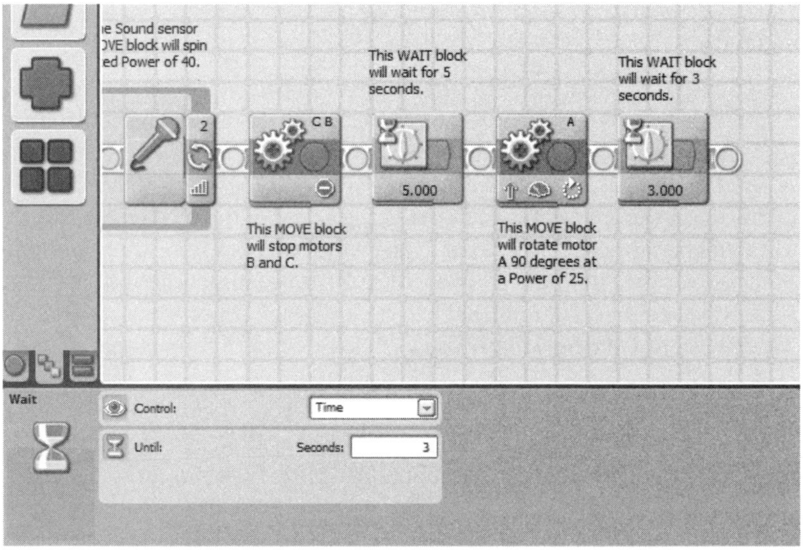

Figure 8-15. *After the object is dropped, we'll wait for a few seconds before starting back.*

Then, add the MOVE block to close the carrier (see Figure 8-16).

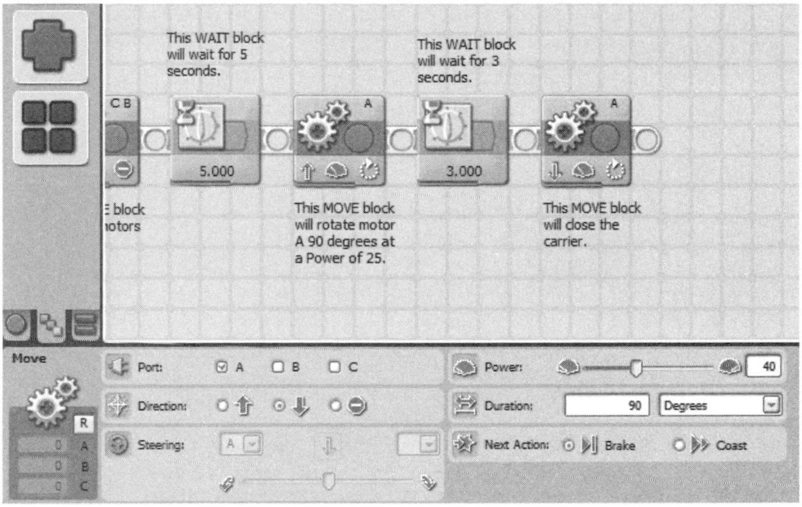

Figure 8-16. *Another MOVE block closes the carrier.*

Before you program the StringBot to return to its starting position, throw in one more WAIT block, just in case the StringBot is swinging on the string (see Figure 8-17).

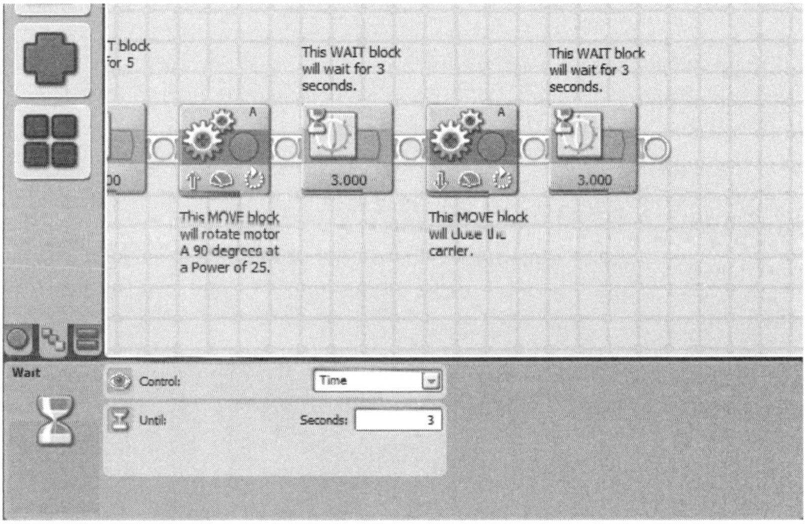

Figure 8-17. *This WAIT block lets the StringBot stop swinging before returning.*

Back for More

Our final task for the StringBot is to return to its starting position and get another object to drop. But before finishing up the programming, I do want to talk about the importance of testing your bot before putting it into actual use.

During my first test of the StringBot, I made a *huge* mistake. Take a look at Figure 8-18 and you'll notice that the final bit of programming I added was a LOOP block with a MOVE block inside. The MOVE block was configured with a **Duration** of Unlimited, and the LOOP block was again configured to respond to the Sound Sensor. And that was my mistake.

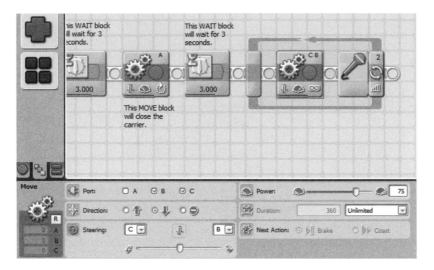

Figure 8-18. *The StringBot program had a big mistake that could have spelled disaster.*

On the fourth or fifth practice return trip, my phone rang. The Sound Sensor picked up the ringing of the phone and the StringBot stopped. That's what it's supposed to do, right? Well, my StringBot had only traveled about six inches. If this were the real situation, my StringBot would be stuck in the middle of the room without any way to retrieve it! I might have been able to rig up something to reach out and grab it, but maybe not.

Fortunately, I was testing the StringBot in my kitchen. I just walked over and grabbed the StringBot and brought it back to its starting position. If I had only performed the test once or twice, I would probably not have caught my mistake. So, let me repeat it again and again—test your bot, and test it often.

Once I caught this mistake, I deleted that final LOOP block. In its place, I used another LOOP block. This one I left set to loop Forever (see Figure 8-19).

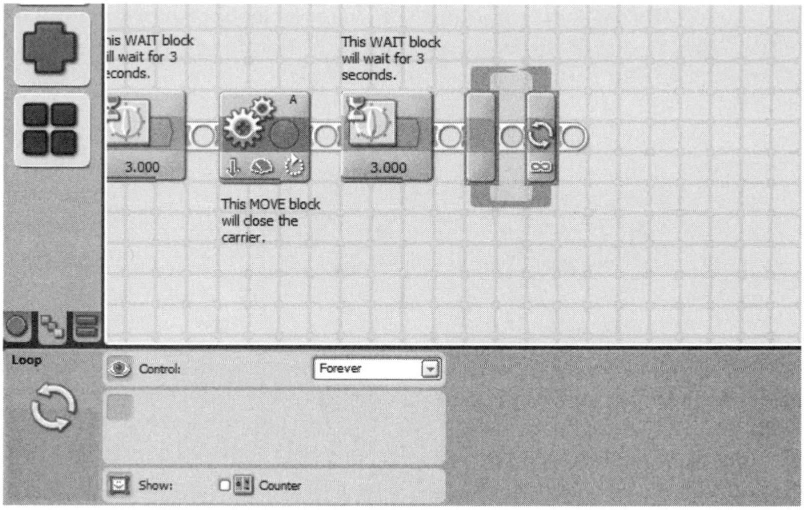

Figure 8-19. *Set the last LOOP block to loop Forever.*

Now place another MOVE block inside this LOOP block and configure it with a **Duration** set to Unlimited and a **Power** of 50 (see Figure 8-20).

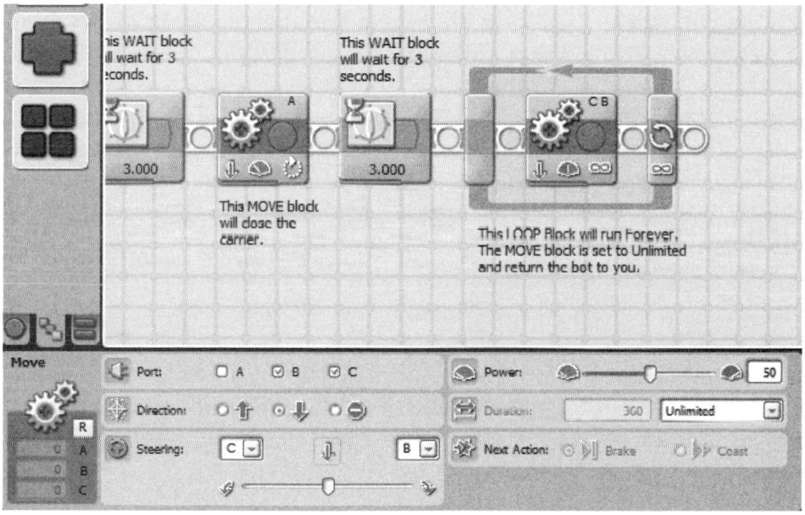

Figure 8-20. *This MOVE block returns the StringBot to you.*

There's no Sound Sensor this time to stop the StringBot, so when it returns to the starting position, you'll have to grab it and stop the program manually by pressing the **Cancel** button on the Brick.

One final programming item I'd like to mention is the addition of the STOP block (see Figure 8-21). Although the STOP block isn't really needed in this program, I find it's a good habit to use the STOP block anyway at the end of a program. It's an old habit, but many programmers will tell you that it's still a good habit. In some programs you'll create, the STOP block is good to have because it will tell the Brick to exit the program and you won't have to press the **Cancel** button on the Brick.

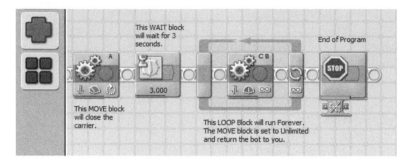

Figure 8-21. *Put a STOP block at the end of your programs.*

Guess what? You're done with programming the StringBot! All that's left is to upload your program to the Brick and test it.

Filling the Vase

Okay, you've got your StringBot built and you've uploaded your program to the Brick. It's now time to set up the challenge so you can put your bot to the test.

When I tested my StringBot, I didn't need to spend a lot of time creating a test environment. To start, I simply tied one end of a piece of string to the doorknob of a closed door. I then cut the string to a length of around 20 feet. Take a look at Figure 8-22 and you'll see that I fed the string through the "rear" string guide (the string guide on the back side of the Brick). The string then goes under the wheel rim, under the rubber tire, under the second wheel rim, then finally through the "front" string guide. I tied the other end of the string to a heavy chair and then moved the chair away from the door to tighten the string. The final setup element was placing a small jar a few feet from the door and directly beneath the string.

One thing I did have some fun with during my testing was changing the angle of the string. In one test the string was parallel to the floor, with the StringBot hanging about four feet above the ground. In another test, I tied the string to the bottom of the chair. The StringBot was forced to climb at a fairly steep angle, but it did work. You'll have to experiment with your own String-Bot to determine the maximum angle it can climb.

The key with testing your bot is to try and have some fun. Play around with your StringBot in different ways—try tying the string higher than the doorknob so the StringBot has to drive at a downward angle. Experiment with a larger carrier. Maybe even try to attach a heavier object to your StringBot that can be released and dropped into the vase. How heavy of an object can your StringBot carry?

Figure 8-22. *The string is fed through the front and rear string guides.*

I ran a series of tests using my StringBot and I want to share them with you. Some were surprising, some were disappointing, and a few of the tests were perfect:

- *First test—string parallel to floor*: My StringBot carried a single quarter. I was able to get the bot to drop the quarter directly in the jar on the first attempt. Because of this, I got a little cocky on the next few tests.

- *Second test—string parallel to floor*: This time, I put a few quarters and nickels in the carrier. About halfway across the string, one of the coins dropped out of the carrier. And when the bot reached the vase and dropped the coins, only one nickel fell accurately into the jar.

- *Third test—string tied to bottom of chair*: I wanted my StringBot to climb the string at a large angle. About halfway up, the StringBot didn't have enough power to finish the climb and it stopped moving.

- *Fourth test—string tied to middle of chair*: I changed the angle of the string this time, reducing the angle. This time, the StringBot successfully carried two quarters and dropped them into the jar.

- *Fifth test—string tied higher than doorknob*: I changed the angle again, this time with the StringBot moving "down" the string. This was a *bad* idea. The StringBot slid at one point and the swinging motion caused most of the coins to fall out of the carrier.

- *Sixth test—string tied higher than doorknob*: I reduced the angle, making it less steep. The StringBot successfully made it to the vase, but when it dropped the coins, a slight swing in the bot caused the coins to miss the jar.

As you can see, the StringBot had some successes as well as failures. In the most basic test (first test), the bot did what it was supposed to do. However, I ran the first test 12 times in a row (16 minutes), and only one run failed. With these results, I imagine that I could fill that jar with about 50 to 60 trips in a little more than an hour.

When the vase was about half full, a loud cracking sound was heard underneath the floor. I think it might be safe to cross the reception room floor . . .

CHAPTER 9

■ ■ ■

Scroll, Key, and Camera

Location: Southwest Guatemala

Weather Conditions: 94 degrees Fahrenheit, Humidity 46%, Rain 0%

Day 3: Tomb Reception Area, 6:08 PM

It had taken Max and Grace more than an hour to get the string properly looped over the reception area room's far peg. They had taped four fiberglass tent rods end to end, making one long rod that looked like an odd fishing pole. They were careful not to let the long pole dip too far down—it could accidentally tip over the jar and then the expedition would be in real trouble.

Before tying the other end of the string to the peg nearest the entry door, Evan had fed the string through the StringBot's string guides and under the rims and rubber wheel. When the string had finally been tied to the other peg, the StringBot was sitting on the string, about five feet above the floor. Over the past hour, the StringBot had dropped about 30 pebbles in the vase with only 4 pebbles missing the target.

Uncle Phillip, Max, and Grace had brought in some chairs and everyone was taking turns preparing the StringBot.

"Want me to take over, Evan?" asked Uncle Phillip.

Evan nodded. "Let me just load the carrier," he replied, placing a small pebble in the carrier. Uncle Phillip had asked Evan to use pebbles, explaining that if it was good enough for King Ixtua, it should be good enough for them to use. Evan had agreed.

"Okay, here goes. Remember, no talking," said Evan. He pressed the orange button on the front of the Brick and the StringBot began to move.

The team watched as the small bot began to move forward on the string. The spinning of the motors was the only sound in the quiet room. The bot moved quickly to the other side of the room, getting closer to the jar.

"Stop!" yelled Evan. He took a deep breath, hoping the bot worked just like in his earlier tests. The Sound Sensor triggered and the StringBot quickly stopped, swinging slightly left and right on the string. It then began to move again towards the jar, but this time at a slower speed.

Evan watched as the bot's carrier approached the opposite wall. He had practiced dozens of times so he could determine when to stop the bot properly so the carrier could drop the pebble into the jar. The bot moved a little closer . . .

"Stop!" Evan yelled again, louder this time so the StringBot's Sound Sensor would be triggered.

Uncle Phillip, Max, and Grace all held their breath as the StringBot stopped directly above the jar.

A few seconds passed, and then the carrier slowly swung down. The small pebble slid from the carrier and dropped straight into the mouth of the jar.

CRACK!

A few loud popping sounds were heard coming from the opposite side of the room, followed by another loud CRACK underneath the stone floor.

"Yes!" yelled Uncle Phillip, jumping to his feet. He smiled at Evan. "I think it worked!"

"Way to go, Evan," said Grace. "Your little robot is amazing."

Evan's face turned red; he wasn't used to this kind of attention. He watched the StringBot's carrier arm close and then the motors began to spin again. The StringBot began its return on the string, ready for another small pebble to be loaded.

When the StringBot reached Evan, Evan pressed the **Cancel** button on the front of the Brick. "What now?" Evan asked, looking at the team.

Max and Grace quickly stepped outside and then returned a few seconds later, holding opposite ends of a large metal chest. "We test the floor," Max said, as he and Grace placed the chest on the floor and then walked back outside the tomb.

"Evan, let's go outside for a minute," Uncle Phillip said.

Evan followed Uncle Phillip out of the tomb. As he stepped outside into the heat and bright sunlight, he saw Max holding a thick wooden rod about ten feet in length. He placed the wood on the floor and pushed it into the tomb until it connected with the metal chest. "Ready?" Max asked.

Uncle Phillip nodded.

Max pushed on the end of the wooden rod and the chest slid off the platform and onto the floor of the reception area. He pushed some more and the chest slid further to the middle of the chamber.

"Well, it looks like the trap in the room has been disabled," said Uncle Phillip with a smile. "Are we ready to see what's next?"

Max, Grace, and Evan all nodded.

"Alright, let me cross to the other side. Everyone can follow, one at a time, when I'm across." Uncle Phillip walked slowly across the floor to the darkened corridor.

The King's Library

Max had moved one of the large tripod lamps across the room. The dark corridor was now well lit, and the team could see that the tunnel extended about 20 feet forward but with a downward slope. Halfway down the corridor, Evan saw a small square opening at the bottom of the left side wall. The corridor was only four feet wide, so the team had followed Uncle Phillip down the hallway, one at a time.

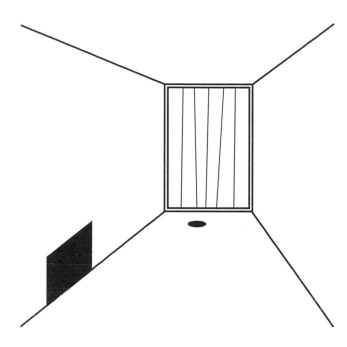

Figure 9-1. *Sketch of the corridor with the square opening and locked doorway*

"Just like the manuscript describes," said Uncle Phillip.

Grace, walking behind Uncle Phillip, pointed further down the hallway. "And there's the hole in the floor for the pa'aachi," she said, pointing at a wooden doorway at the end of the corridor.

"Pa'aachi?" asked Evan, looking around Grace and Uncle Phillip to try and get a glimpse.

"It means key," said Uncle Phillip. "The manuscript indicates that a basket, called a hu'un, was placed in the king's library. Inside the basket is a carved bone that needs to be inserted into that hole before the door will open. And by the look of that hole, it's going to be a very large key."

"Where is the key?" asked Evan, already suspecting the answer.

Uncle Phillip stopped and pointed at the square opening in front of him. "In there."

Evan watched as his uncle dropped to the floor and turned on his flashlight. He pointed the flashlight into the opening and squinted. "It's hard to see, but the room's dimensions look about right."

"Can you see the basket?" asked Max.

Uncle Phillip tried to angle his head so he could see deeper into the opening. "Nope. If it's in there, it won't be visible to someone looking in. Once again, Tupaxu's design appears to require one of the king's trained monkeys."

"Another robot?" asked Evan.

"I don't know, Evan," said Uncle Phillip as he stood up. "This room's a little different and I don't know if your bot will work here."

While they were talking, Grace had moved down the hallway and was examining the door. She took some measurements of the door but didn't push against it. "The door may or may not be locked, but we cannot open it without the pa'aachi. The manuscript says if we open the door without the key being inserted, it will trigger another trap," she said.

Uncle Phillip scratched his head. "Well, it's getting late and I'm hungry. Let's go get some food and talk this over. Evan, I'll show you a picture of the room so you'll understand why I'm worried about using a robot. Everyone back to the tent."

Evan nodded and turned, walking with his uncle out of the tomb.

Key Retrieval Challenge

While Evan finished his macaroni and cheese dinner, his uncle walked over with one of the manuscript enlargements and placed it on the table. Evan set his plate aside and stood up to take a look.

"King Ixtua had one of the largest collections of scrolls and carved tablets in existence at the time of his death. Tupaxu had the scrolls and tablets copied and placed in the tomb. This could be one of the biggest discoveries of Mayan history ever found," said Uncle Phillip.

Max pulled a chair closer to the table. "The manuscript doesn't indicate that the library has any traps. Maybe I could crawl through the opening and get the key," he said. "The opening is large enough for a person to fit through. And I might be able to open the throne room door from the inside. I believe there's a door in there that accesses the throne room directly."

Grace smiled at Max. "Or I could crawl through," she replied. "I am smaller than you."

"Rock, Paper, Scissors?" asked Max, holding up his hands, ready to compete for the chance to see the library first.

Uncle Phillip raised his hands. "No one is going into the library until we determine it is completely safe," he said. "And I'm certain that the door in the library is probably locked as well. There will be plenty of time to examine the library and its contents later, but we need to get that key. Now, Grace, what can you tell us about this room?"

Grace stepped closer to the table and looked down at the large document on the table. She then pointed to the left side of the page. "Against this wall are jars and tables that supposedly hold the scrolls and tablets. There's no information on how many of these artifacts were placed in the library, unfortunately. On the opposite side of the room are some large tables, probably used by visiting priests or the king's family to sit and read."

"The king's family would come in to read?" asked Evan. "Why?"

Uncle Phillip smiled. "The king's family was always welcome to visit his tomb. Priests would keep the tomb clean, bring fresh flowers for all the rooms, and other tasks. King Ixtua was considered a great king and was very good to his people. The library was the king's way to make his family more comfortable when they came to visit him."

"Weird," said Evan. "Sorry to interrupt, Grace."

"No problem," she replied. "Now, here's the important part. To get into the library, visitors would have to place the pa'aachi to open the door in the corridor. The next room will be the king's throne room, and I'm certain there's a door in there that will allow us to access the library. That key is found in the basket right here," she said, pointing to the drawing.

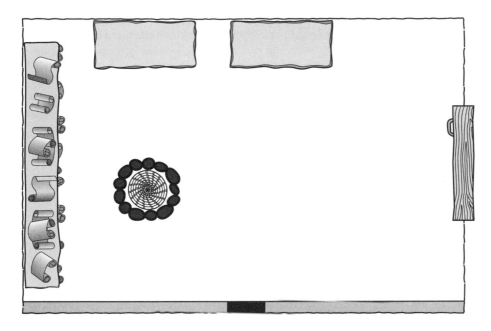

Figure 9-2. *View of King Ixtua's library and the basket holding the pa'aachi*

Evan looked at the drawing. The hand-drawn basket was surrounded by a black ring. "What is this black ring?" asked Evan.

"Probably obsidian," replied Max. "It's a type of glass that comes from lava that has cooled. The Mayan people used it to make weapons, but they also used it for other purposes because of its shiny black color. It's probably set into the stone floor for decoration."

Grace nodded. "King Ixtua probably had a monkey trained to find the black ring and then bring out the basket with the key inside. The real question is whether the rest of the floor is safe to walk across," she said.

Uncle Phillip finally sat down in his chair. "It's too dark inside the room to tell, and we can't just throw a flashlight in there to check. My guess is that the room isn't trapped, but I'm certain that if the basket is there with the key inside, it's probably too heavy for one of Evan's robots to bring back."

Evan nodded. "The motors are pretty powerful, but there's no guarantee it could grab the key or even push the basket back to us."

"And it's dark, too," said Max. "Won't your robot at least need some light?"

"Well, I have a Light Sensor that can create its own light with a small LED, but it's only useful for determining changes in color," replied Evan. "It's not bright enough to light up the room."

"Wait a minute," said Grace. "I have an idea."

Grace's Solution

"You said one of the sensors could detect a change in color," said Grace. "Can it be programmed to detect the change between the rock floor color and the black obsidian ring around the basket?"

Evan scratched his head for a moment, then nodded. "Maybe. It might be possible to have a bot search out the ring, but I still agree with Uncle Phillip that the basket and key are probably too heavy for my little bots to push. We could try it, but if the bot isn't strong enough, we won't be able to get it back," replied Evan.

Grace walked over to one of the boxes holding equipment and began to rummage.

"Do you have something in mind for the weight problem, Grace?" asked Uncle Phillip.

"Yes," she said. "If I can only find the . . . Here it is!" she yelled. She turned and held up a large ball of heavy twine.

"Twine?" asked Max.

Grace nodded. "It's just an idea, but what if we tie the twine to the bot, send it out and around the basket, and then back to us. We untie one end of the twine from the bot and cut the other end off the ball. If we pull on the two ends of twine, we might be able to pull the basket towards us."

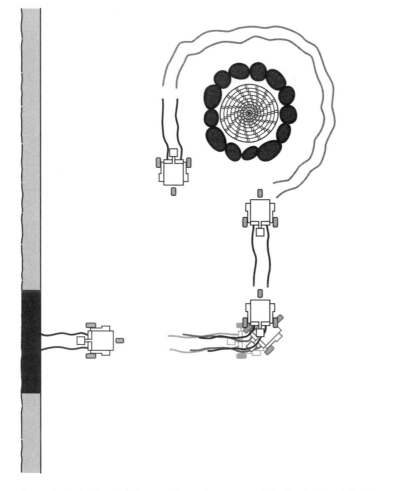

Figure 9-3. *The bot will wrap the twine around the basket and the team can pull it out.*

Uncle Phillip smiled. "Grace, I think you've got the right idea. How about we make it stronger by sending out two separate lines of twine? We could have one line go around the bottom of the basket and maybe one around the middle," he added. "What do you think, Evan?"

Evan had been listening to the discussion, trying to imagine what kind of bot he'd have to build to accomplish this task. An idea began to form and he smiled.

"I think I can build a little bot to do that," Evan replied. "I'll have to do some testing with the Light Sensor, though. But I'm fairly sure I can do this."

"Excellent. It looks like that little robot kit of yours is really saving us time and money. Max, when we get back home, remind me to put in a request for the archaeology department to buy a couple of them, okay?"

"Sure. I think it'll be a great investment," Max replied, then frowned.

"What's wrong, Max?" asked Uncle Phillip.

Max sighed. "Well, I just wish we could see the library as it is now—something to record this little bit of history."

Evan raised his eyebrows and thought about the request. "Well, I could attach a small camera to the bot and have it take a picture before it moves around the basket," he said.

"You could do that?" asked Uncle Phillip.

"Sure. I'll just need a small camera," Evan replied.

Grace smiled. "I have a small disposable camera that has a few shots left on it. Would that work?"

Evan nodded. "Give me some time to do some testing, and I'll have it ready by morning."

Uncle Phillip stood up. "Well, we've got about three hours before the camp has lights out. If you can't finish tonight, take what time you need tomorrow and we'll test Grace's idea," he said. "We need to take care of some paperwork, Evan. So if you need us, just yell."

"Okay. I'll get started right now."

Max, Grace, and Uncle Phillip walked out of the tent, and Evan pulled out his robotics kit and design journal. As he was looking for a pen in his backpack, Uncle Phillip poked his head through the tent flaps.

"Evan, thanks for all your help. We're really glad you came along," Uncle Phillip said. "You're doing great work."

"You're welcome, Uncle Phillip," he said. "Thanks for inviting me on the trip."

Uncle Phillip disappeared, leaving Evan to his work.

Story continues in Chapter 13 . . .

■ ■ ■

CHAPTER 10

SnapShotBot—Planning and Design

There are a *lot* of elements to this challenge's bot. First, we've got to figure out how to properly place the bot in the room. Then, the bot needs to take a picture of the library. After that, the bot needs to circle around the basket (still holding the twine) and return to the team so that they can pull the two ends of the twine to retrieve the basket and the key. Like I said, we have a lot to accomplish with this little bot. So let's get to work.

SnapShotBot Planning and Design

In Chapter 6, I didn't show you an initial picture of my final design for the StringBot. This was intentional, because I wanted you to start developing your own ideas for how the bot should look and function. I'm going to do the same in this chapter—I don't want to show you the final design of my SnapShotBot because I don't want to influence your planning and design ideas. That's the great thing about building bots with the Lego Mindstorms NXT kit: no two bots are likely to ever look the same because you're going to have your own ideas about how you want to solve challenges. So, no skipping ahead to Chapter 11 just yet. This is a challenging little bot to build and I want you to begin to focus on your own version of the SnapShotBot.

Once again, get a blank Design Journal page and pen and let's move forward.

Note There are three blank Design Journal pages left in the back of this book (if you used only one for Chapter 1 and one for Chapter 2). If you need more pages, feel free to make photocopies of the Design Journal page or visit the Apress Web site to download the page in PDF format.

In the Robot Name box, go ahead and write **SnapShotBot** or, again, feel free to create your own name for the bot. Possible alternative names are LibRover, CamBot, or maybe StringBot2. After you've selected a name for your bot, it's time to move on to its description.

The Robot Description

The secret to success with a robot that has this many jobs to do is to try to keep the Robot Description as simple as possible. Visualize the tasks the robot needs to perform and write down your Robot Description once you can see it in your mind.

Ask yourself this question: "If I were walking behind this bot taking notes of its actions, what would I see?" Write the answers inside the Robot Description box. Just as with the earlier bots, simply picture a small box on the ground and visualize this box doing what you believe needs to be done to complete the challenge (the box is a placeholder for your SnapShotBot, because you don't know what it really looks like yet). Feel free to compare your Robot Description to the one I came up with, shown in Figure 10-1.

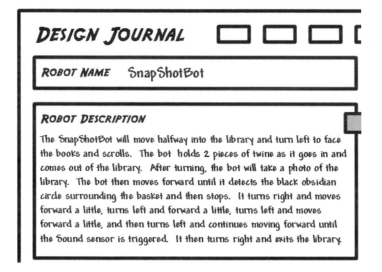

Figure 10-1. *The SnapShotBot Robot Description is the best place to start planning its design.*

I'm guessing that your Robot Description doesn't match mine word for word. And that's okay. The main objectives you should have covered in your Robot Description include holding the twine, taking the picture, discovering the obsidian ring around the basket, navigating around the basket, and somehow returning to the team. Did you get all of it? If not, that's perfectly okay. Why? Because sooner or later during your actual building of your SnapShotBot you would have realized that your bot was missing a task to perform and you would simply go back and write in the missing task into the Robot Description box. Simple!

Here's another test you can do to make certain you've caught everything: pretend *you* are the bot! Look at Figure 10-2 for the layout of the library. Place a basket (or some other item) in the center of a room. Now walk through the tasks you need your bot to perform and compare them to your Robot Description—if you've missed something, just add it:

1. Move to the center of the room (holding two pieces of string) and turn left. (Easy . . .)

2. Take the picture of the library. (Piece of cake . . .)

3. Move towards the basket and stop. (Simple . . .)

4. Walk around the basket. (Check.)

5. Move back to your starting position. (Done.)

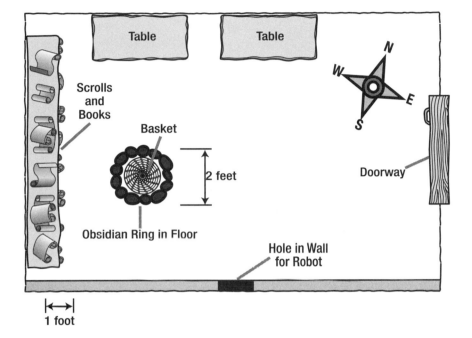

Figure 10-2. *The King's library*

You'll find that pretending to actually be the robot can reduce your design time because you'll have a better understanding of the jobs your little bot must soon perform.

Okay, now it's time for the Task List.

The Task List

Remember the purpose of the Task List? From your Robot Description, the Task List will help you to break down the bot's individual functions so that you can properly build a solution for each of its tasks—move forward, take a picture, stop when sensor is triggered, etc. Review your Robot Description and begin writing down each separate task the SnapShotBot will perform. My Task List for the SnapShotBot is shown in Figure 10-3.

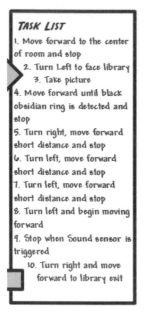

TASK LIST

1. Move forward to the center of room and stop
2. Turn Left to face library
3. Take picture
4. Move forward until black obsidian ring is detected and stop
5. Turn right, move forward short distance and stop
6. Turn left, move forward short distance and stop
7. Turn left, move forward short distance and stop
8. Turn left and begin moving forward
9. Stop when Sound sensor is triggered
10. Turn right and move forward to library exit

Figure 10-3. *The SnapShotBot Task List is built from the Robot Description.*

The Task List is probably *the* most important part for this Design Journal page; there are so many things going on with the SnapShotBot, and a well-documented Task List will help you to keep track of all the actions for this challenge. Because this is such an important Task List, I'm going to cover each item in the list in a little more detail.

Task 1

The first task is "Move forward to the center of room and stop." Seems pretty simple, doesn't it? If you look back to Figure 10-2, you'll notice that the room is square-shaped and that the distance from the bot's starting position to the rear wall is 12 feet. Well, the halfway point will be 6 feet, but how do we tell the SnapShotBot to stop at 6 feet?

When you program the motors, you can only specify the number of rotations, the number of degrees of rotation, or the time in seconds to spin. There are various ways you can get you your bot to stop at 6 feet—I'm including three of them here, but there are many more methods:

- *Time in seconds*: Using a stopwatch, record how many seconds it takes your bot to move 6 feet—that's how many seconds you should run the motors to place the bot close to the halfway point.

- *Number of rotations*: Determine the circumference of the bot's wheels (the distance around the tire) in inches. Divide 72 inches (6 feet = 72 inches) by the wheel circumference and that will tell you how many rotations to program the bot's motors to spin to place the bot halfway across the room.

- *Number of degrees of rotation*: Gently push the robot across the floor 6 feet and, using the Brick's View option of the feedback panels in the configuration pane, record how many degrees of motor rotation the move takes.

For the purposes of my SnapShotBot, I'm going to use the second method. I've measured a wheel and determined that the wheel's circumference is 7.069 inches–let's just round that to 7 inches, okay? When I divide 72 inches by 7 inches, the number I get is 10.3. I'm going to round this number down to 10—don't worry, just getting it close to the middle of the room will be enough, so you don't have to be exact. So when I program my bot to move to the center of the room, I'm going to set the motors for a duration of 10 rotations.

Task 2

Okay, now that the bot is in the center of the room, let's take a look at Task 2, "Turn Left to face library." You already know how to do this task, from Chapter 4. You can refer to Chapter 4 after you build your bot to find the instructions for manually turning your bot 90 degrees and obtaining the proper angle to turn one of the motors, but here's a quick summary:

1. Turn on the Intelligent Brick.

2. Use the Brick's right or left button to scroll to the **View** option and then press the orange select button.

3. Use the right or left button to find **Motor degrees** and then press the orange select button.

4. Select a port to monitor (I'm choosing Port B for the wheel on the right side of the Brick) and press the orange select button.

5. Place the SnapShotBot on a flat surface, and press the orange select button to reset the counter.

6. Twist and turn the SnapShotBot left 90 degrees so that *only* the right-side wheel turns.

7. Write down the result displayed on the LCD screen. (For the record, I got -464 degrees.)

8. Press the orange select button to reset the counter.

9. Twist and turn the SnapShotBot right 90 degrees so that *only* the left-side wheel turns.

10. Write down the result on the LCD screen. (For this turn, I got -460 degrees.)

The first turn your bot will make is a left turn. But later your bot will also make a right turn, so be sure to record both results (left and right turn). Record these values somewhere on your Design Journal page. (Of course, you'll perform these steps *after* you've built the robot.)

Task 3

Task 3 is for your bot to take a picture, so let's give this a little thought. We've already allocated two motors to control the right and left wheels. So, we'll use the third motor to build a device that can press the button on a disposable camera. Can you picture the robot in the middle of the room, facing the library? The robot is low to the ground, so I'll probably want to angle the camera up a little bit so it can take a better picture—I'll have to remember to put that in my Mindstorm section. I'll also need to make some sort of holder for the camera. At this point, Task 3 is simple enough—I'll just need to plan on something to hold the camera and something that will allow the motor to press the button.

Task 4

Task 4 is "Move forward until black obsidian ring is detected and stop." From the Robot Description of the obsidian stone ring, we know that it's a different color than the stone used in the rest of the floor. This is a perfect test of our Light Sensor. The Light Sensor can detect changes in color, so we can add the Light Sensor to our bot and program it to detect the color of the regular floor. We can also program the Light Sensor to try to detect a change in the sensor reading as the bot begins to move forward towards the ring. When the sensor reading drops (black will give a lower reading than the brown-stone color), we'll instruct the bot to stop.

This is a good place to stop and do a few experiments with the Light Sensor. After you build your SnapShotBot, you're going to set up a test environment. So, right now you need to figure out where you're going to perform your test. Possible locations are a living room floor (wood floor or carpet), a garage floor, or even a tile floor—as long as the floor isn't black or a very dark color, you shouldn't have any trouble. Once you determine your test floor, find a piece of black paper (or a piece of paper that is much darker than your floor color). Now, here's what I want you to do:

1. Turn on the Intelligent Brick.

2. Use the Brick's right or left button to scroll to the **View** option and then press the orange select button.

3. Use the right or left button to find the **Reflected Light** option and then press the orange select button.

4. Use the right or left button to select the port used by your Light Sensor and then press the orange select button—the LED light on the Light Sensor should turn on.

5. Point the Light Sensor near your test floor's surface. A good result can be achieved by holding it no more than 2 to 3 centimeters above the surface.

6. Write down the result displayed on the LCD screen for the "normal surface."

7. Place the black (or dark) paper under the Light Sensor at the same distance and notice the value changes.

8. Write down the new result displayed on the LCD screen for the "obsidian surface."

Record the results of your test somewhere on your Design Journal page. Write **Normal Floor** and the number that was displayed for it, and then write **Dark Paper** and the number for it, too. You'll need these numbers when you begin to program your bot.

Okay, so now your bot is near the basket. The next four tasks are simply steps to take to get the bot around the basket and heading back in the direction from which it came.

Task 5

Task 5 starts the journey around the basket by having the bot turn right, move forward a little bit, and then stop. But what do we mean by "a little bit?"

Well, we know that the black obsidian ring surrounding the basket is about two feet wide and two feet long (refer to Figure 10-2). And earlier in the chapter, you found out that the circumference of the wheels is roughly seven inches. We also know that the bot should be near the center of the ring, so let's figure out how many rotations we need it to make to get safely around the basket.

As shown in Figure 10-4, after the bot turns right, it needs to move only about one foot forward (to Point A). One foot is 12 inches, so we divide that by the circumference of our wheels (approximately 7 inches) and that tells us we should program the bot's motors to spin 1.7 rotations to place it close to Point A. On the back of your Design Journal page, sketch Figure 10-4 and write down the rotation values you calculate—between the bot and Point A, write **Rotations:** and the number that you calculated.

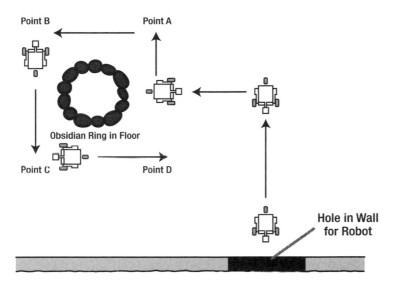

Figure 10-4. *The SnapShotBot needs to go around the basket.*

Task 6

Task 6 states "Turn left, move forward short distance and stop." Again, what is a "short distance?" Well, in Figure 10-4 we can see that the distance from Point A to Point B is 2 feet, or 24 inches. Once again, divide 24 inches by the wheel's 7-inch circumference and we get 3.5 rotations. On your map, write down **Rotations:** and the number calculated for the motors to spin between Point A and Point B.

Task 7

Task 7 is identical to Task 6. This will get you from Point B to Point C. Write **Rotations:** on your map and then write the number calculated for the motors to spin between Point B and Point C (3.5). Just to be safe, if you like, you can add in another few rotations to make certain the bot gets completely around the basket. Now you have the proper number of rotations to get your bot to Point A, then from Point A to Point B, and finally from Point B to Point C (or slightly beyond Point C).

Task 8

Starting at Point C, your bot simply needs to make a left turn and move back to the center of the room. If everything has been done properly, your SnapShotBot will have encircled the basket with the two pieces of twine that will be used to pull the basket.

Task 9

Okay, so let's pretend that the SnapShotBot is moving back to the center of the room. You, as a team member, will be looking through the small opening in the wall. As soon as you see the SnapShotBot, you need a method for telling it to stop, turn right, and come back to you. Won't the Sound Sensor work perfectly here? Task 9 is "Stop when Sound Sensor is triggered," and this task will be easy to include—we'll need to remember to include the Sound Sensor in our Mindstorm section later in the chapter.

Task 10

Task 10 is our final task: "Turn right and move forward to library exit." Once the bot has stopped (triggered by the Sound Sensor), it will turn 90 degrees to the right. You recorded the number of degrees needed to make a right turn earlier, remember? After the bot has turned, it should be facing the opening in the wall. Start the bot moving forward and just wait for it to come back to you—that's it!

What About the Twine?

Now, you may have noticed there's no mention of the twine in the Task List. I intentionally left it out because it's not really a bot task (well, other than to pull the string). We'll need to include some sort of beam or component where we can tie two pieces of twine to the SnapShotBot. When the bot returns to you after completing Task 10, you'll use the two ends of twine that you held on to (while the bot was moving in the library) and the two ends of twine tied to the bot and you'll PULL! As you pull on the twine, the twine will catch on the basket and allow you to pull the basket towards you!

This was a *long* Task List, but this bot has a lot of things to do. We're not done just yet, though. Hopefully, as you were thinking about the tasks involved, you came up with some limitations or constraints that you will need to keep in mind as you begin building.

Limitations and Constraints

Your bot has one primary job—go around the basket while holding the twine and return to the team. There are no obstacles in the way (other than the basket itself), and all you've got to worry about are the walls and tables. If you can just navigate your bot around the basket, you're home free. The few limitations I came up with are shown in Figure 10-5.

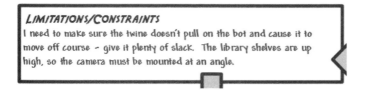

LIMITATIONS/CONSTRAINTS
I need to make sure the twine doesn't pull on the bot and cause it to move off course - give it plenty of slack. The library shelves are up high, so the camera must be mounted at an angle.

Figure 10-5. *The SnapShotBot does have a few limitations to consider.*

As for taking a photograph, however, there is a small limitation to consider. Your bot will most likely be fairly low to the ground. (A tall bot is more likely to tip over or possibly be wobbly, but I don't want to put any limits on what your SnapShotBot will look like. If you choose to build a taller bot, you may find that you have an additional constraint or two to work around, but that's all part of the fun, right?)

For my little bot, if I simply sit the camera on top of a flat spot, the final picture will be of mostly the lower part of the library wall. I want to get as large of a picture as possible, showing as much of the books and scrolls as I can manage. Because of this limitation, I'm fairly certain I'll have to angle the camera back a little bit so that it's pointing slightly upwards. Just imagine you are the bot, down low on the floor. Look up to the middle of the wall, and that's the angle that you'll want to use to mount the camera.

One minor constraint that I also added involves the twine that will be tied to the bot. Imagine a dog on a leash. If you hold the leash tight, the dog will not be able to continue moving away from you. The same goes with your robot. You'll need to keep feeding out a lot of additional twine so the bot never gets stopped. There's also a risk of the bot moving a little off course if the twine ever gets tight. So, my best recommendation to you is to provide a *lot* of slack to your bot by paying attention to the tightness of the twine and never letting it get tight.

Did you come up with any additional constraints? If so, write them down in your Limitations/Constraints section and keep them in mind during the building and programming of your bot.

Mindstorm

Most likely, you've already got an image in your mind of what your SnapShotBot will look like. Feel free to look at Chapter 11 if you'd like to see my final version of the SnapShotBot. My guess is that my version doesn't look like what you're imagining. Am I right? Perfect!

For this bot, feel free to use my steps to build the SnapShotBot, but maybe you're feeling good about your design skills at this point and want to build your own version first. Give it a try! If you get stuck, take some of my ideas. The goal is for you to try to build your own version of this bot. And the Mindstorm section of your Design Journal page is the ideal place to begin putting down your ideas before you begin to build.

In Figure 10-6, you can view my ideas for my bot in the Mindstorm section of my Design Journal page.

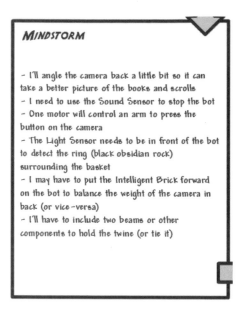

MINDSTORM

~ I'll angle the camera back a little bit so it can take a better picture of the books and scrolls
~ I need to use the Sound Sensor to stop the bot
~ One motor will control an arm to press the button on the camera
~ The Light Sensor needs to be in front of the bot to detect the ring (black obsidian rock) surrounding the basket
~ I may have to put the Intelligent Brick forward on the bot to balance the weight of the camera in back (or vice-versa)
~ I'll have to include two beams or other components to hold the twine (or tie it)

Figure 10-6. *The Mindstorm section for my SnapShotBot*

The first Mindstorm item was mentioned in the previous section: "I'll angle the camera back a little bit so it can take a better picture of the books and scrolls." Because the books and scrolls are stacked along the left wall (see Figure 10-2) and the bot is so low to the ground, I'll angle the camera back and it will be able to take a picture that doesn't include most of the floor. As stated earlier, if the camera is just facing directly forward, the final picture will contain a large portion of the floor and lower wall; this might be okay to you, so feel free to place your camera any way you like.

Again, I'm not going to cover every item on my Mindstorm list, but I would like to cover two more that I feel are important. First, "The Light Sensor needs to be in front of the bot to detect the ring (black obsidian rock) surrounding the basket." This is easy to understand. If you place the Light Sensor on the back of your bot, there is a chance that your bot might hit the basket before stopping at the black ring. Placing the Light Sensor at the front of the bot allows the bot to detect the black ring early and stop before most of the robot body crosses inside the ring (and possibly collides with the basket).

Second, "I may have to put the Intelligent Brick forward on the bot to balance the weight of the camera in back (or vice versa)." This is based on my experiences with building small bots with the Mindstorms NXT kit. Too often, I've found that some of my bots tend to have too much weight in the front or back or on a side. Because of this, some bots are unbalanced, increasing the risk of tipping over. I'll try to remember as I build my bot to place the Brick and the camera (and its motor) on opposite sides of my bot. I might choose to put the camera in front and the Brick in back, or vice versa. I haven't decided yet on this point and will probably wait until I begin to build.

Now, take your Mindstorm ideas and your Task List and the Robot Description and pull them all together by creating some rough sketches—these will help you when you start to build. When you have an idea in your mind, putting it down on paper will help you start snapping pieces together in a logical manner to achieve that mental image. So let's finish up with the Sketches section of your Design Journal page.

Sketches

Alright, I'm warning you again to keep the snickering to a minimum! My sketches aren't the best, but I think you'll get the idea. Take a look at Figure 10-7 to see my rough sketches of the (soon-to-be-built) SnapShotBot.

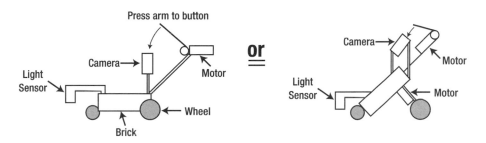

Figure 10-7. *I'm using basic shapes to represent parts of my SnapShotBot.*

Notice that I'm not drawing with extreme detail. Yes, this is partially because I'm not the best artist. But more importantly, it's because I don't need to draw every beam and connector and sensor to develop a working shape and concept of where everything will go. Wheels are circles, the Brick is a rectangle, sensors are smaller rectangles, and motors . . . well, the motors just look weird. Sorry.

After you complete your sketches, there's no point in waiting, so start building. Take everything you've written and drawn on your Design Journal page and build *your* version of the SnapShotBot . . . or whatever name you have given it.

In Chapter 11, you'll find the step-by-step instructions for building my version of the SnapShotBot. Feel free to steal ideas from it or just ignore it all and make your version bigger (or smaller), better, faster (or slower), and as unique as you can imagine.

SnapShotBot—Build It

Go ahead and take a look at one version of the SnapShotBot in Figure 11-1. It's a weird-looking little bot, but, then again, I *like* strange-looking robots . . . and this one definitely qualifies. As you can see, the Light Sensor is located at the front. I've also placed the camera towards the back of the bot at an angle. The weight of the Brick is sufficient to keep the bot from tipping over, thankfully.

There are a few other items that you might be interested in, as well. I've used one of the plastic balls that come with the basic Lego Mindstorms NXT kit as the front wheel. You'll see this trick used on a lot of NXT bots because the ball-wheel rolls easily and allows bots to turn a little more smoothly than does a rubber wheel. I could have used something similar to the pivot wheel found on the ExploroBot, but I wanted to try this option out. You'll also notice during the building process that I use a lot of the longer beams (11 and 15 holes) to provide reinforcement and strength to the camera housing. Since the housing is angled back and is a little top-heavy, I rely on these types of support beams a lot—it's a personal building style that works for me.

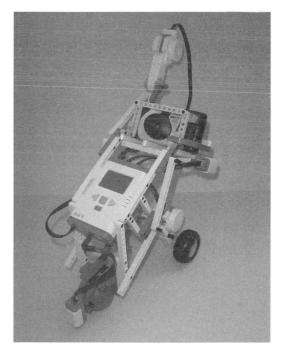

Figure 11-1. *One possible version of a SnapShotBot*

Jump In

I had no trouble getting my basic design for the SnapShotBot. Using my sketches from Chapter 10, I knew that I wanted my bot to have two rear-wheels to drive this heavier bot. I intentionally placed the camera at the top of the bot because I wanted it to have the best view (even with the angle) to take a picture.

One special note here: I purchased a disposable camera for this bot, but I could just have easily built the camera cage (that's what I'm calling it, okay?) to hold my digital camera. It wouldn't have been as wide, but it would definitely have been taller to keep the digital camera from falling out. You may have to play around with the camera cage a bit to get it to fit the camera you decide to use. Keep the camera nearby as you build so you don't have to guess about the dimensions of the cage. A few extra pieces here and there will allow the bot to hold your camera firmly.

If I later decide to use my digital camera, I can reprogram the bot to take numerous photos. If I were to send my bot into an unknown area with the risk that it might not come back, I'd probably rather use a disposable camera so I wouldn't lose my expensive digital one. But for now, all I need my bot to do is go in and take one photo.

Follow along with my instructions to build my version *or* build your own version and feel free to compare your design to mine—you may find an idea or two that you can use with your own bot.

■**Note** I really would like to see your version of the SnapShotBot, so take a picture and e-mail it to me. My e-mail address is in the Introduction.

Okay, let's go build the SnapShotBot!

Step by Step

I've divided the SnapShotBot building instructions into three sections. The first section contains the basic body—the Intelligent Brick and two wheel motors. The second section adds the ball-wheel assembly, the Light Sensor, and reinforcement beams. The third section completes the SnapShotBot by adding the camera cage, one motor to push the camera's button, and more reinforcement beams. Build these three sections and wire them up, and your SnapShotBot will be complete and ready for programming.

As with previous chapters, I'll add comments to sections where a little help might be needed. And remember, if you see an image with text and arrows, pay attention because the text and arrows are probably pointing to a placement of a part (or parts) that otherwise might not be immediately noticeable in the picture.

And, finally, I'll add new parts to an image to let you know what parts are needed in an upcoming step.

First Section: Basic Body

Figures 11-2 through 11-16 show the steps and components used to build the basic body and wheels, as well as a few pieces needed before you begin the second section to add the ball-wheel assembly and Light Sensor. Start with the pieces you see in Figure 11-2.

Figure 11-2. *Starting pieces for the SnapShotBot*

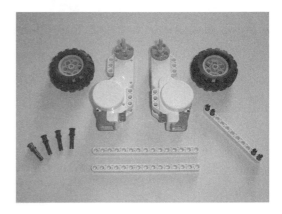

Figure 11-3. *Place the axle rods with half-bushings in the motors and insert the four small black connectors in the 11-hole beam as shown.*

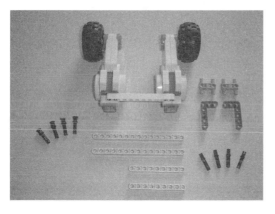

Figure 11-4. *Connect the two motors with the 11-hole beam.*

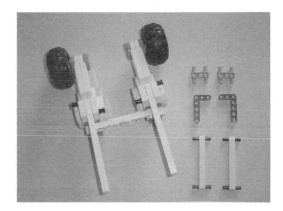

Figure 11-5. *Use two pins to connect a 15-hole beam to each motor as shown.*

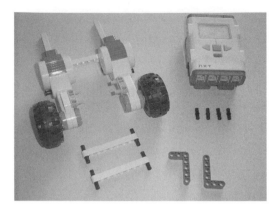

Figure 11-6. *Flip the Brick over and insert the two gray components into the motors as shown.*

Figure 11-7. *Use the two 9-hole beams to reinforce the connection between the motors, and put two small black connectors in the side of the Brick as shown.*

Figure 11-8. *Put two more small black connectors in the Brick as shown and place the two L-shaped components.*

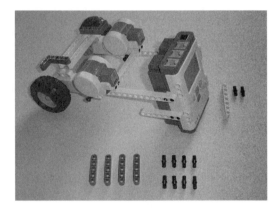

Figure 11-9. *Connect the motor assembly to the Brick and then connect one of the 7-hole beams using two small black connectors.*

■**Note** These two L-shaped components are where I will tie the two pieces of twine.

Figure 11-10. *Flip the Brick to the other side and connect the other 7-hole beam using two small black connectors.*

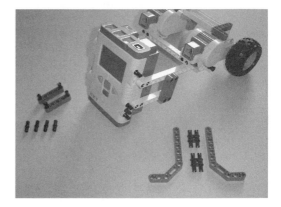

Figure 11-11. *Use the two gray 5-hole beams to reinforce the legs, and place the four small black connectors in the Brick as shown.*

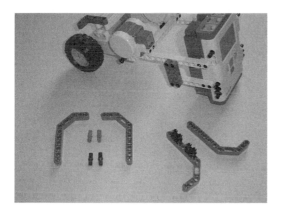

Figure 11-12. *Flip the Brick to the other side and reinforce the legs using the other two gray 5-hole beams, and place the other four small black connectors.*

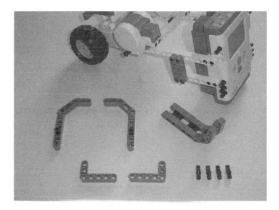

Figure 11-13. *Assemble the gray components— pay attention to the position of the small blue connectors and the small black connectors.*

Figure 11-14. *Connect the gray components and place two small black connectors in each L-shaped component.*

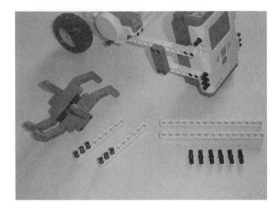

Figure 11-15. *Place the L-shaped component and three small black connectors in each 9-hole beam.*

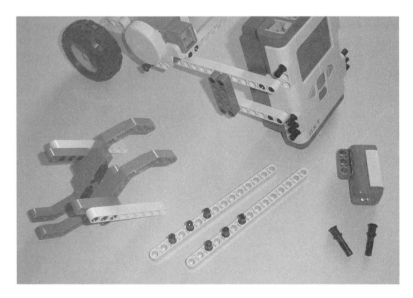

Figure 11-16. *Connect the 9-hole beams as shown and place three small black connectors in each 15-hole beam.*

Now it's time for the ball-wheel assembly and Light Sensor . . .

Second Section: Ball-Wheel Assembly and Light Sensor

Figures 11-17 through 11-28 show you how to complete the main body. When finished, you'll have a fully functional rolling bot body that could be customized with other parts and sensors to perform other duties. Okay, let's move forward.

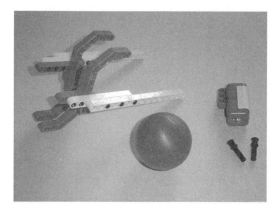

Figure 11-17. *Start with a plastic ball, the Light Sensor, and the assembly shown.*

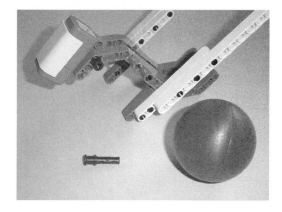

Figure 11-18. *Connect the Light Sensor using one of the black pins as shown. Notice the rear hole on the Light Sensor is visible and the pin does not go through it.*

Figure 11-19. *On the other side of the assembly, use the other black pin to connect the Light Sensor.*

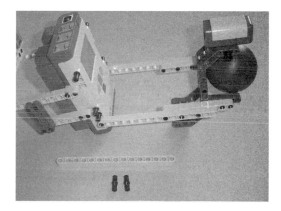

Figure 11-20. *Connect the ball-wheel assembly to the Brick as shown. It will swivel for now, and that's okay.*

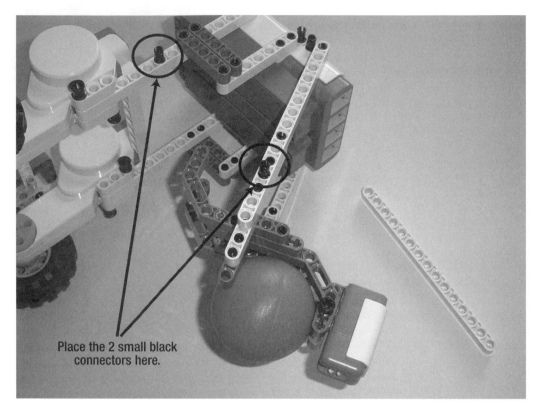

Place the 2 small black connectors here.

Figure 11-21. *Place the two small black connectors as shown.*

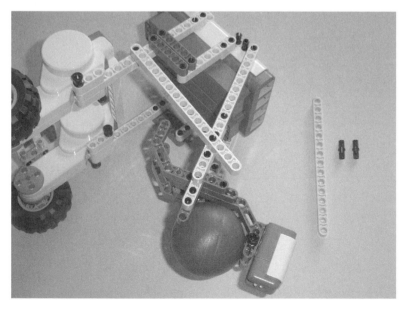

Figure 11-22. *Use the 15-hole beam to reinforce the ball-wheel assembly.*

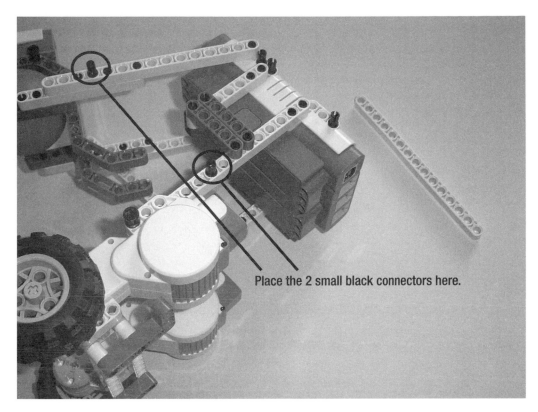

Place the 2 small black connectors here.

Figure 11-23. *Turn the Brick over and place the two small black connectors as shown.*

Figure 11-24. *Use the 15-hole beam to reinforce the ball-wheel assembly.*

Figure 11-25. *The rolling main body so far*

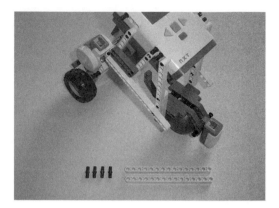

Figure 11-26. *These 15-hole beams will hold the camera cage.*

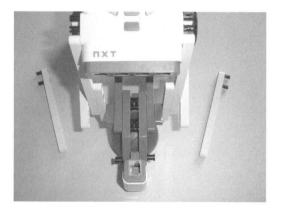

Figure 11-27. *Connect the small black connectors as shown.*

Figure 11-28. *Place the 15-hole beams on the side of the Brick.*

At this point, you have a three-wheel rolling bot. There are plenty of places to connect other motors, parts, and sensors to customize this bot. But we need to finish the SnapShotBot, so let's move on to the camera cage and motor.

Third Section: Camera Cage and Motor

We're almost finished. We need to assemble the camera cage and design a method for pushing the camera's button. Figures 11-29 through 11-61 cover the completion of this bot.

Figure 11-29 shows the pieces needed to start building the camera cage.

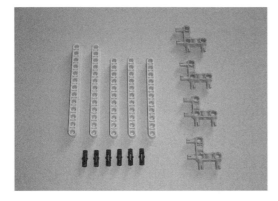

Figure 11-29. *Start with these components for the camera cage.*

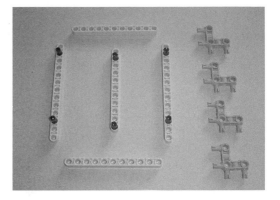

Figure 11-30. *Place the small black connectors as shown.*

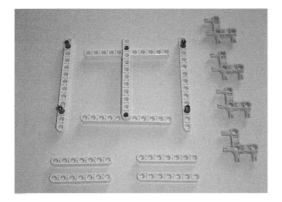

Figure 11-31. *Connect the 11-hole beam to the other 11-hole beams as shown.*

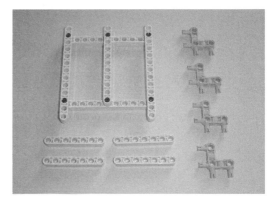

Figure 11-32. *Place the two 13-hole beams as shown.*

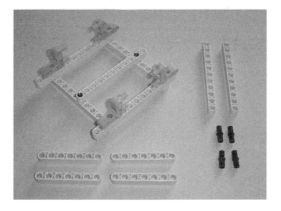

Figure 11-33. *Connect the four gray pins to the camera cage body.*

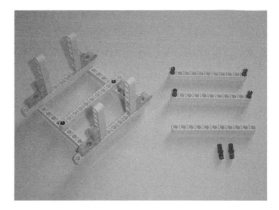

Figure 11-34. *Connect the four 7-hole beams to the gray pins and place two small black black connectors in the 11-hole beams.*

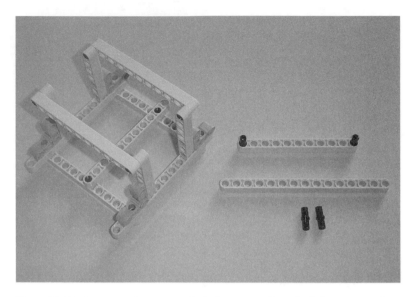

Figure 11-35. *Connect the two 11-hole beams to the 7-hole beams on the camera cage body and place two small black connectors in the other 11-hole beam.*

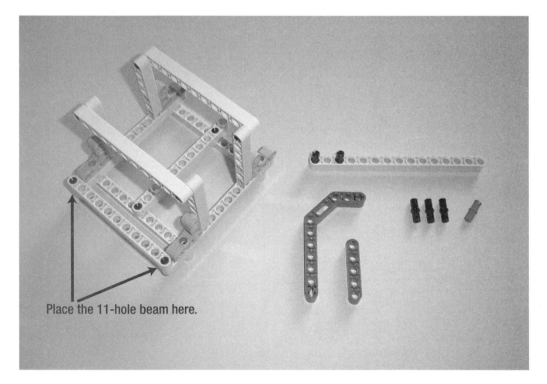

Place the 11-hole beam here.

Figure 11-36. *Place the 11-hole beam on the cage and two small black connectors in the 15-hole beam.*

Figure 11-37. *Connect the 15-hole beam to the cage to hold the motor.*

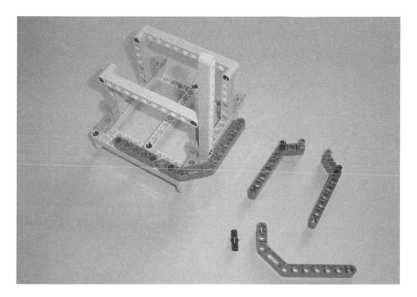

Figure 11-38. *Connect the two gray components to the cage as shown.*

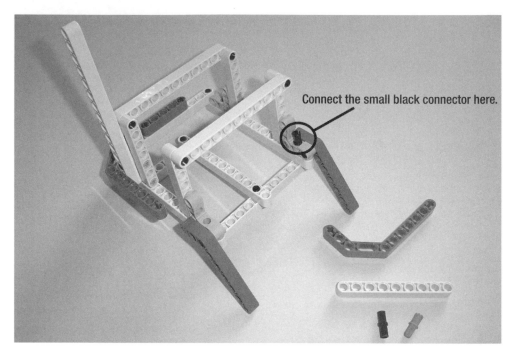

Figure 11-39. *Spin the cage around and connect the two gray legs. Also place the small black connector as shown.*

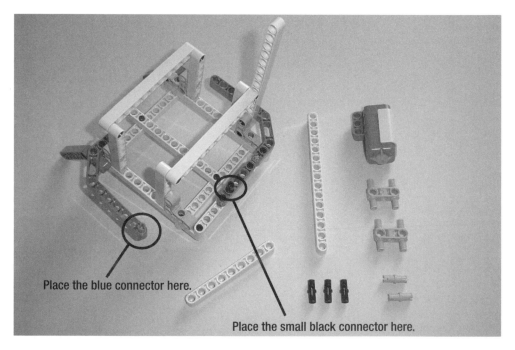

Figure 11-40. *Connect the gray component. Place the blue connector and the small black connector as shown.*

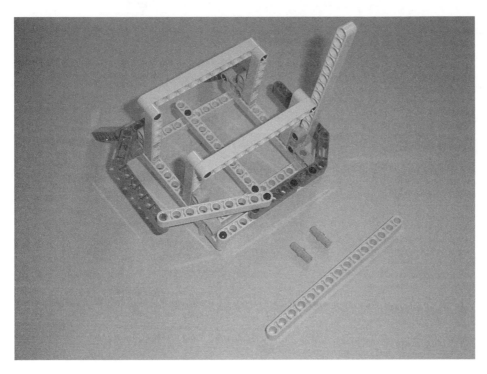

Figure 11-41. *Connect the 9-hole beam.*

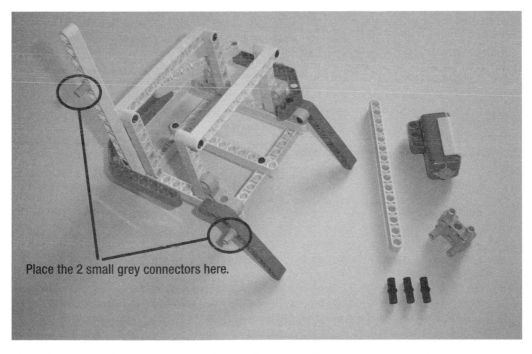

Place the 2 small grey connectors here.

Figure 11-42. *Spin the cage around and place the two small gray connectors as shown.*

Figure 11-43. *Connect the 15-hole beam to the cage and snap the two small gray pins together.*

Figure 11-44. *Connect the two small gray pins to the Sound Sensor.*

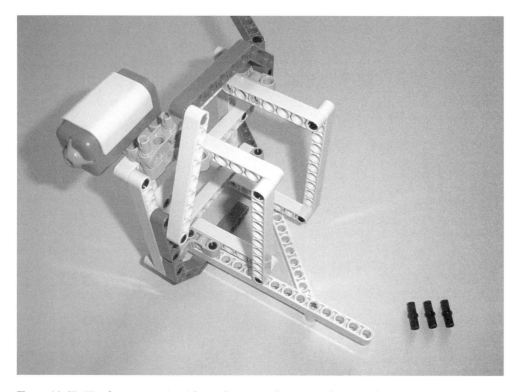

Figure 11-45. *Tip the cage on its side as shown and connect the Sound Sensor.*

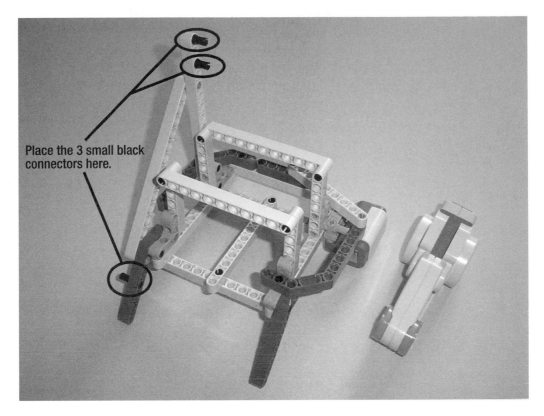

Place the 3 small black connectors here.

Figure 11-46. *Place the three small black connectors.*

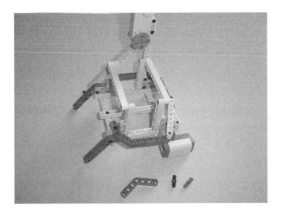

Figure 11-47. *Connect the motor to the 15-hole beam as shown.*

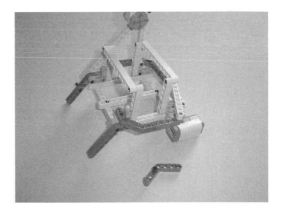

Figure 11-48. *Place the blue connector and small black connector in the gray component.*

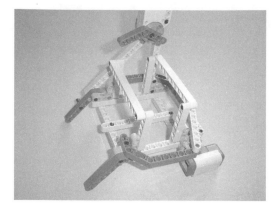

Figure 11-49. *Connect the gray component to the motor as shown. This is the arm that will press on the camera button.*

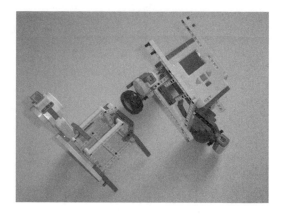

Figure 11-50. *Retrieve the main body so you can connect to the camera cage.*

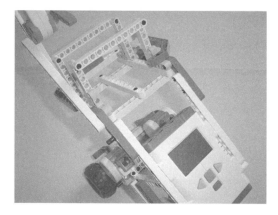

Figure 11-51. *Connect the camera cage assembly to the main body as shown.*

Figure 11-52. *A 13-hole beam and two long black connectors will be used for reinforcement.*

Figure 11-53. *Place the two long black connectors in the 13-hole beam as shown.*

Figure 11-54. *Connect the 13-hole beam to the main body.*

Figure 11-55. *A 15-hole beam and a black pin are used for reinforcement on the other side.*

Figure 11-56. *Insert the black pin in the 15-hole beam as shown.*

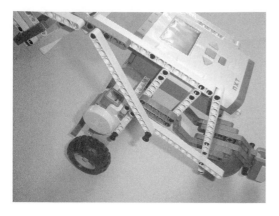

Figure 11-57. *Connect the 15-hole beam to the main body.*

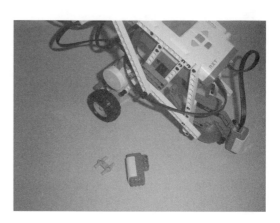

Figure 11-58. *The Sound Sensor and gray component will be needed.*

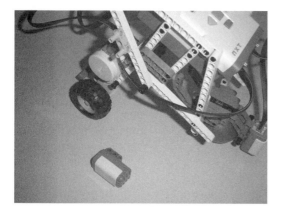

Figure 11-59. *Place the gray component as shown.*

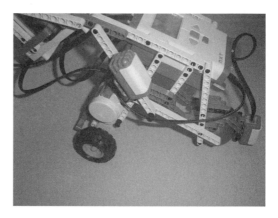

Figure 11-60. *Connect the Sound Sensor to the bot.*

Now, put your camera in the camera cage and position the arm that will press the button so that it is directly over the button, but not pressing down on it. In Figure 11-61 you can see that I've got the small arm almost touching the camera button.

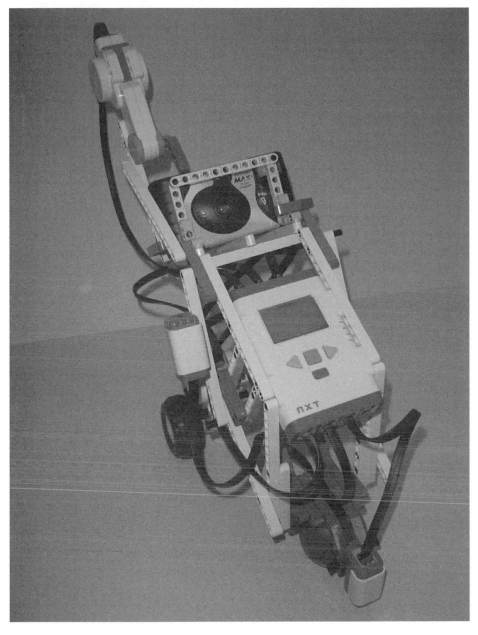

Figure 11-61. *The unwired SnapShotBot completed*

All that's left to do is wire it up and program it. Take another look at Figure 11-1 to see how I've wired up the bot. Now that you've completed your SnapShotBot, it's time to program it. Chapter 12 will walk you through the steps to program your little (or not-so-little) SnapShot-Bot so that it can enter the library, take a picture, circle around the basket, and let your team retrieve the key.

■ ■ ■

SnapShotBot—Program It

You might think that programming the SnapShotBot is a little more involved than the previous bots. Although the program might be a little larger in size, the truth is that you're already experienced with all the programming blocks you'll need.

For this chapter, I'm going to walk you through the programming using a slightly different method. When I program my bots, many times I create the program in full and then upload it to my bot for testing. From there, I add and remove blocks as needed. Although this is perfectly fine for many bots, for a large program this might not be the best way to test your bot. If you find a mistake early in the program, it can cause you to have to delete other portions of your program. And if you find a *really huge* mistake, you might find yourself deleting the program completely and having to start over.

So, let me show you another method for programming that involves building your program in small steps, uploading the program, then testing it. When you're done with this chapter, you should be able to decide for yourself when it might be beneficial to program in small steps or simply program the entire thing and then test and debug.

One Block at a Time

Get your SnapShotBot Design Journal page and open up the Lego Mindstorms NXT software. Type **SnapShotBot** into the blank text field labeled **Start New Program**, then click the **Go** button (see Figure 12-1).

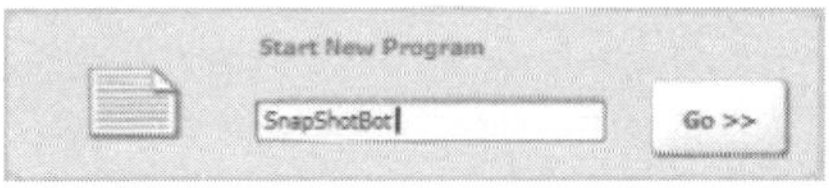

Figure 12-1. *Enter **SnapShotBot** for the new program name and click **Go**.*

■**Note** To have more work space visible on your screen, close down the RoboCenter area on the far right by clicking the small red X in the upper-right corner of the software.

In the SnapShotBot building instructions in Chapter 11, you might have noticed I placed the Touch Sensor on the back of the bot. I plan on using the Touch Sensor as a sort-of **Start**

button for my bot to get rolling. So, the first item you'll place in your program will be a simple
LOOP block (see Figure 12-2) that waits for the Touch Sensor to be triggered (pressed and then
released). Once the sensor is triggered, the remaining program will begin. (You could use a
WAIT block that breaks when the Touch Sensor is pressed, but I like to use the LOOP block
because I can later add blocks inside the LOOP if I want the bot to perform some other actions
while it's waiting.)

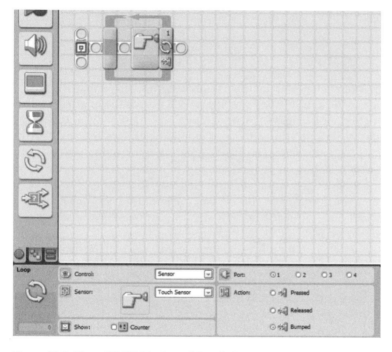

Figure 12-2. *Use a LOOP block and Touch Sensor trigger to start the bot.*

Now you can start on the actual programming blocks needed for the bot to perform the
actions in the Task List. Look at the Task List on your Design Journal page (turn back to Figure 10-3). Our first task is "Move forward to the center of room and stop." If you'll think back to
Chapter 10, we determined that to get halfway across the room, we needed to program our
motors to spin for ten rotations. Each rotation moves the bot approximately seven inches, so
when the motors spin for ten rotations, the bot will move forward approximately seventy
inches, or almost six feet. That'll be good enough to get the bot near the center of the room.

Place a MOVE block and configure it with a **Duration** of ten rotations for motors B and C. Be
aware that I've selected the direction for motors B and C as the down arrow (see Figure 12-3).
This is because the motors are reversed on my design—facing away from the back of the bot.
Because of this, forward motion for the bot means having these motors spin in the "reverse"
direction. If your bot differs, configure your motor directions based on your own design.

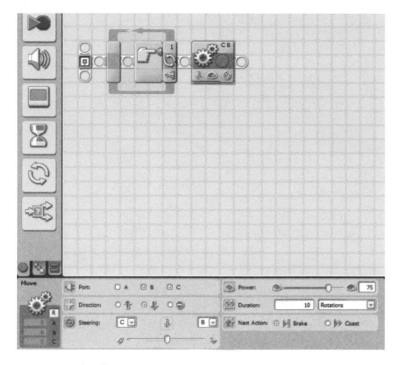

Figure 12-3. *Configure the MOVE block to move the bot forward, halfway into the room.*

Now it's time to test. I'm going to save the program (so I don't lose any of my work or the comments I've added) and upload it to my bot. When I run the program, the bot should wait until I press and release the Touch Sensor. After I trigger the sensor, the bot should move forward about six feet and stop. Here goes the test . . . and it worked, exactly as designed. (If your bot did anything differently, check your programming blocks and verify that the number of rotations is correct.)

Next on our Task List is "Turn Left to face library." Back in Chapter 10, I reminded you how to test your bot and obtain the number of degrees to turn for making a right and left turn. When I tested my bot, I obtained a value of -464 degrees when *only* the right-side wheel was turned (motor B). Some of you might have discovered the software does *not* allow you to enter a negative value for the duration. Don't let this concern you. The value was negative (–) to indicate the motor was turning in reverse. So what you'll do is configure the motor to spin in reverse (the down arrow) for 464 degrees—simple! Drop in your MOVE block and configure it as shown in Figure 12-4.

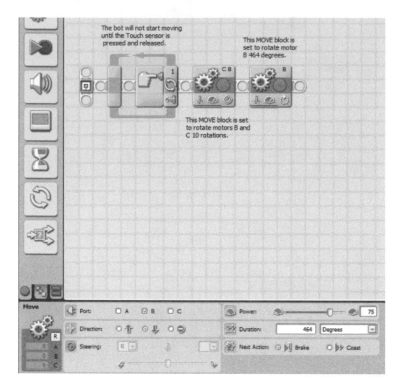

Figure 12-4. *This MOVE block will make the bot turn left.*

Now we test again. When I trigger the Touch Sensor, the bot moves forward about six feet. It then makes a left turn when motor B turns 464 degrees. So far, so good.

The Task List shows our next step is "Take picture." Before I configure motor A, however, I do want to add in a WAIT block. I'm worried that motor A might push the button on the camera just as the bot is coming to a stop—this would result in a blurred picture. I'll configure the WAIT block for 2 seconds (see Figure 12-5).

Next we need to configure motor A to turn and press the camera button. Because I don't know how far to turn it, this is where testing comes in. I dropped in a MOVE block and configured motor A to turn 45 degrees. During testing, I found this sometimes missed the button entirely. I reduced it to 20 degrees and tested again—same result. For my third test, I placed the arm directly on the button of the camera and configured the MOVE block for 10 degrees—it worked! The button pressed and a picture was taken (see Figure 12-6).

■**Note** Depending on the type of camera you're using, you'll probably have to perform a few different tests to determine the best way to press the camera button. When trying different motor settings, such as number of rotations or degrees, it's usually best to start big. Start with a large number of rotations or degrees—if it works, reduce it a little and try again. Keep reducing until you find the lowest setting that works. Your batteries will last much longer!

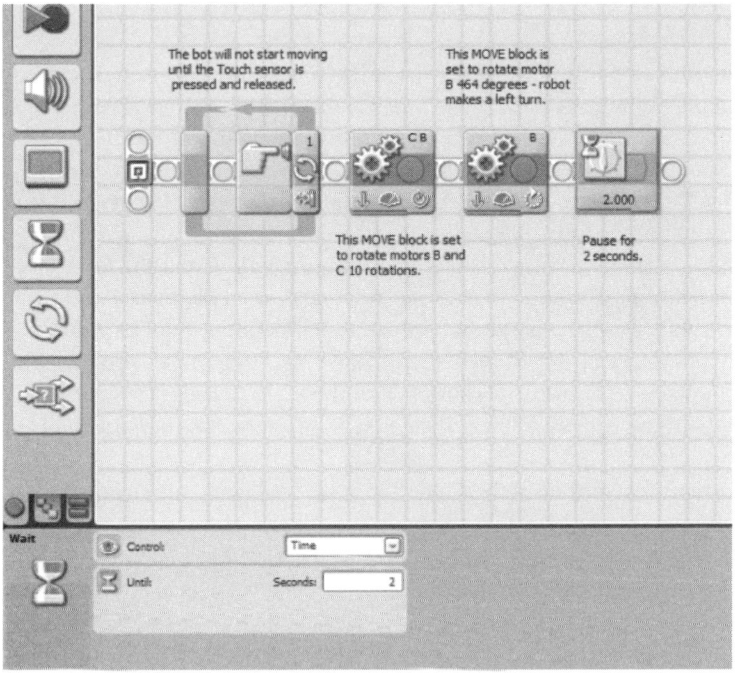

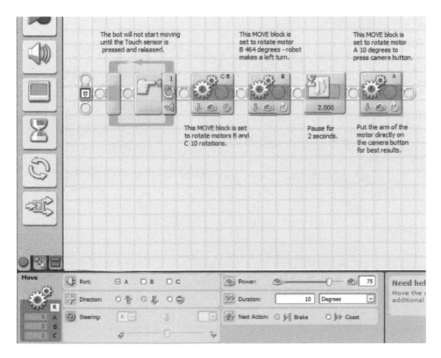

Figure 12-5. *A WAIT block allows the bot to stop moving before the picture is taken.*

Figure 12-6. *Using a MOVE block to take a photograph*

Finding the Basket

Okay, at this point, our little bot has made it to the center of the room, turned left, paused, and then taken the picture. Looking at the Task List, I see that my next step is "Move forward until black obsidian ring is detected and stop." I want my bot to start moving forward until its Light Sensor detects the black obsidian rock surrounding the basket. I also want the bot to move forward slowly so it doesn't get too close to the basket. When the Light Sensor detects a change in the reflected light, I want the bot to stop.

Back in Chapter 10, I told you how to test your Light Sensor to obtain a reading for a "normal surface" and an "obsidian surface." When I tested my "normal floor" (a light-colored wood floor), the Light Sensor returned a value of 25. When I placed the dark paper (black) under the Light Sensor, I got a value of 10. Your values will probably differ a bit. I'm going to program my Light Sensor to check for a value of 15 or less to be safe. When the Light Sensor is triggered (value of 15 or less), the bot will stop moving forward because it has detected the "obsidian surface."

Now, to keep the bot moving forward until the Light Sensor is triggered, you're going to need to use a LOOP block configured to test the Light Sensor. You can see the settings for the LOOP block in Figure 12-7.

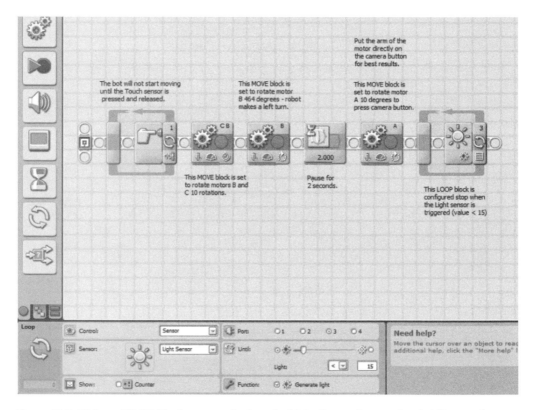

Figure 12-7. *Using a LOOP block to test whether the Light Sensor is over the obsidian surface*

To make the bot actually approach the basket, throw in a MOVE block. You'll configure this block a little differently than other LOOP blocks you configured for the earlier bots. With this MOVE block, instead of configuring motors B and C with a **Duration** of Unlimited, you'll have them move forward for one rotation of the wheels. After each rotation, the Light Sensor will check to see if it's over the "obsidian surface." If it isn't, the bot will move forward another rotation of the wheels, and the Light Sensor will check again. By doing it this way, you can make sure the bot doesn't rush forward quickly and cross too far over the obsidian ring (see Figure 12-8).

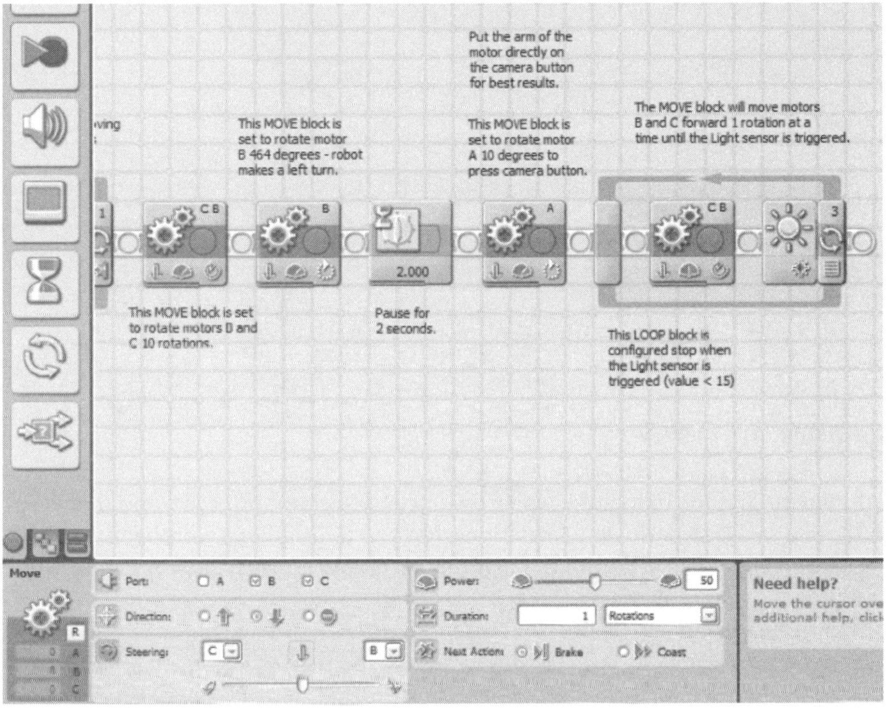

Figure 12-8. *Using a LOOP and MOVE block with the Light Sensor*

After the Light Sensor is triggered and the bot stops, the bot will need to go around the basket with the twine and prepare for the trip back.

Getting Around the Basket

Now the bot is in front of the basket. What's next? Look at the Task List: "Turn right, move forward short distance and stop."

Our first task will be to get the bot to turn right. Back in Chapter 10, I recorded the value as -460 degrees for a right turn. Remember, the negative sign (–) indicated that motor C was turning in reverse. So you'll insert a MOVE block that's configured to turn motor C in reverse for 460 degrees (see Figure 12-9).

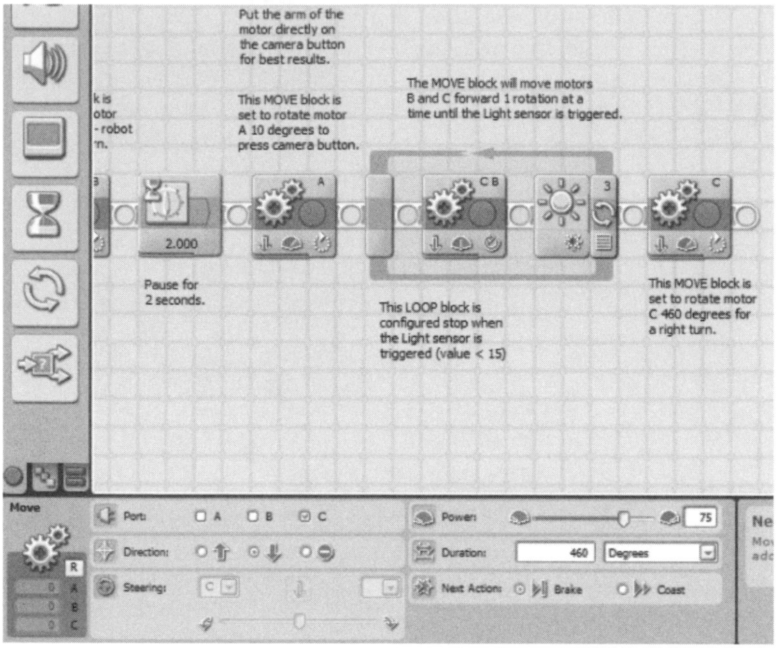

Figure 12-9. *A MOVE block will allow our bot to make a right turn.*

We determined in Chapter 10 that the "short distance" was about one foot, and that we would need motors B and C to perform 1.7 rotations, but you'll round that number up to 2. We'll insert a MOVE block (see Figure 12-10) that will get us to Point A (turn back to Figure 10-4 for the mini-map).

If you examine the mini-map in Figure 10-4, you'll notice that once the bot reaches Point A, it will make three left turns before heading back to its starting point. It will turn left (1) at Point A, move forward, and stop at Point B; turn left (2), move forward, and stop at Point C; turn left (3), then finally move forward, and stop at Point D. This is a perfect location to use a LOOP again. It allows us to reduce the number of programming blocks by performing the same actions three times. Those actions are "Turn Left and Move Forward a Short Distance." So let's place the LOOP first (see Figure 12-11).

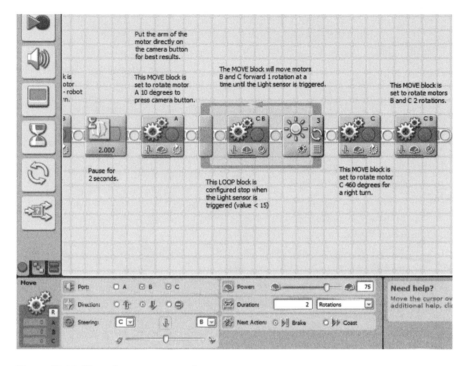

Figure 12-10. *Now the motors need to stop.*

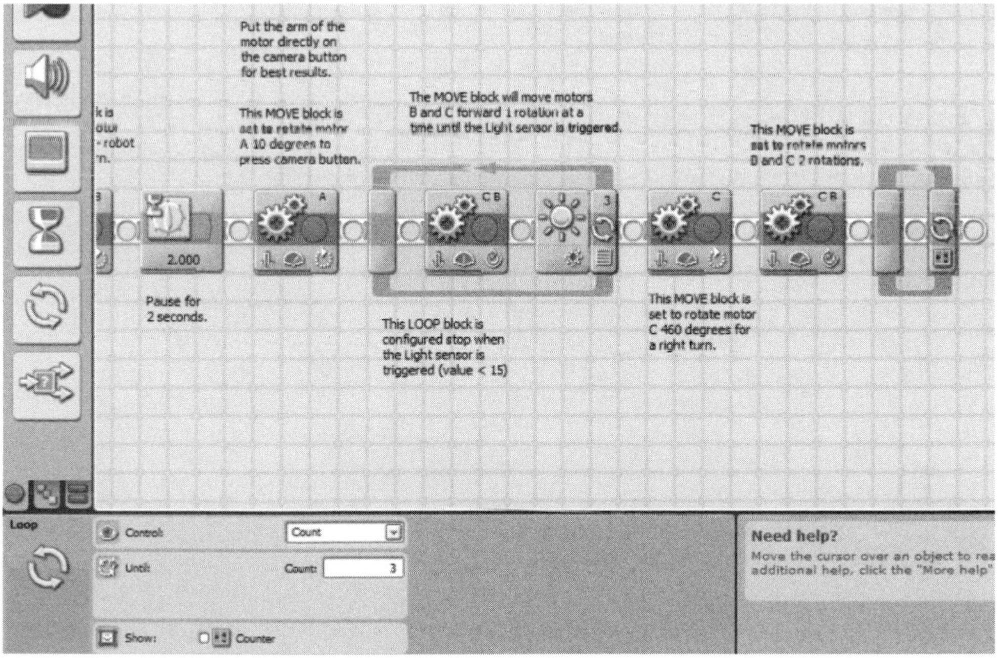

Figure 12-11. *The LOOP block gets the bot around the basket.*

The LOOP block in Figure 12-11 will run three times. Any blocks placed in it will also run three times before the LOOP block breaks and the program continues. What will happen three times? First, a left turn: a MOVE block will turn the bot left. Second, the bot will move forward approximately 2 or 3 feet. Back in Chapter 10, we determined that 3.5 rotations would be needed to move our bot 2 feet. Let's round that number up to 4 rotations (28 inches), which should give us plenty of room for our bot to navigate around the basket. So, you'll first place the MOVE block for a left turn (see Figure 12-12).

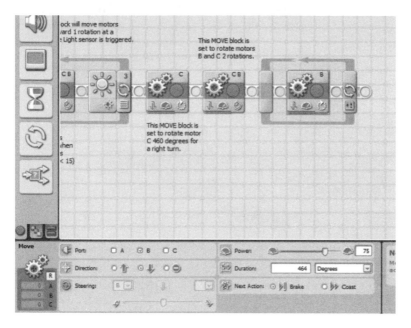

Figure 12-12. *This MOVE block turns the bot left.*

Next, place the MOVE block to move the bot forward 28 inches (see Figure 12-13).

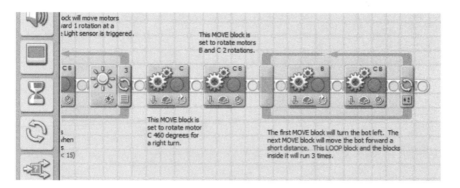

Figure 12-13. *This MOVE block moves the bot forward a short distance.*

Now you need to test your bot. At this point, let me describe my test environment and show you how to set up your own.

First, I'm running this test in my living room. I've cleared away a chair so I'll have plenty of room for my bot to run. In Figure 12-14, you can see how I've set up my test run. I've placed the "basket" (actually a plastic container with a remote control inside for weight) about six feet forward and three feet left from my bot's starting position. I've also placed my piece of dark paper to the right of the basket for the bot's Light Sensor to detect. If all goes well with my practice run, my bot should end up at Point D.

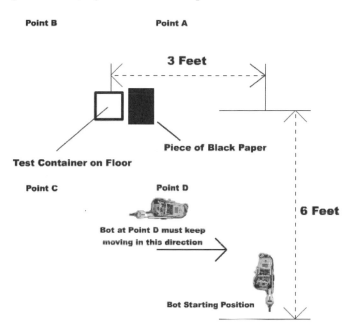

Figure 12-14. *Test environment for the SnapShotBot*

Because I've been testing my bot frequently, I wasn't surprised that my test run was successful. I knew from previous tests that my bot would enter the library, turn left, take the picture, and move forward until the Light Sensor was triggered. Getting the bot around the basket using a series of three left turns and forward movements worked perfectly. My bot ended up roughly in the area I've labeled Point D, pointed right and ready to finish its return.

Getting the Bot Home

The hard part is done. All that's left at this point is getting the bot back to you. There are numerous ways to do this, but the one I've selected uses the Sound Sensor again. If you'll look again at Figure 12-14, my bot is stopped at Point D, pointed to the right (back towards the dotted line where the bot first started its motion into the library). What I plan on doing is programming my bot to continue moving forward (moving to the right in Figure 12-14) until I "see" it. What I mean by "see" is that in the real library, the team will be looking through the hole in the wall. When the bot first enters the library and turns left towards the basket, the team will lose sight of the bot. Only when the bot returns and continues to move away from the basket will the team see the bot again. What I plan on doing is simply yelling "*Stop!*" The Sound Sensor will detect the noise, and I'll program the bot to stop, turn right, and come back to the hole in the wall. Simple!

First, you add a LOOP that will break when the Sound Sensor is triggered (see Figure 12-15).

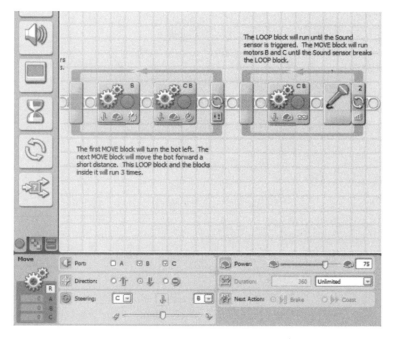

Figure 12-15. *Add in a LOOP block with the Sound Sensor configured.*

Next, you add in a MOVE block that will keep motors B and C moving until the Sound Sensor is triggered (see Figure 12-16).

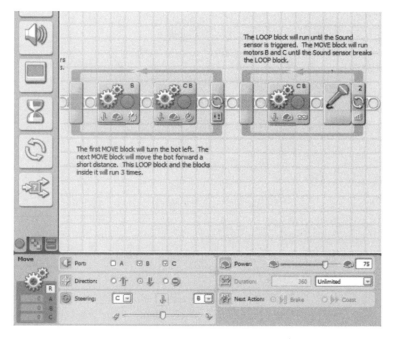

Figure 12-16. *The MOVE block will run the motors until the LOOP is broken by the Sound Sensor.*

Once again, we test. I had to adjust the Sound Sensor's sensitivity after my first run. I had it initially set to a value of 50, but I increased that to 80. I believe the sound of the motors spinning was loud enough to trigger the Sound Sensor, so once the bot started rolling, it immediately stopped. Only after I increased the value to 80 did the bot keep rolling until my voice (and loud "*Stop!*") broke the LOOP block and the bot stopped.

The next task is "Turn right and move forward to library exit." That should be easy enough. Drop in a MOVE block and configure it for a right turn (see Figure 12-17).

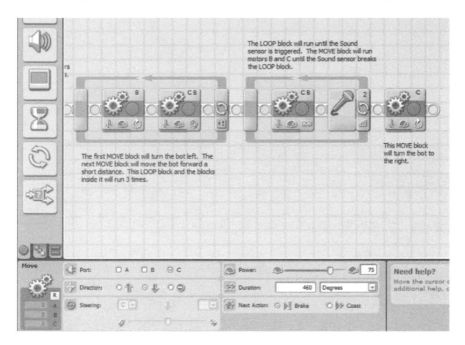

Figure 12-17. *This MOVE block turns the bot right.*

Use one final LOOP block to run motors B and C continuously. You'll simply reach in, grab the bot and turn it off . . . Oh, and get the picture developed. Drop in the LOOP block first (see Figure 12-18).

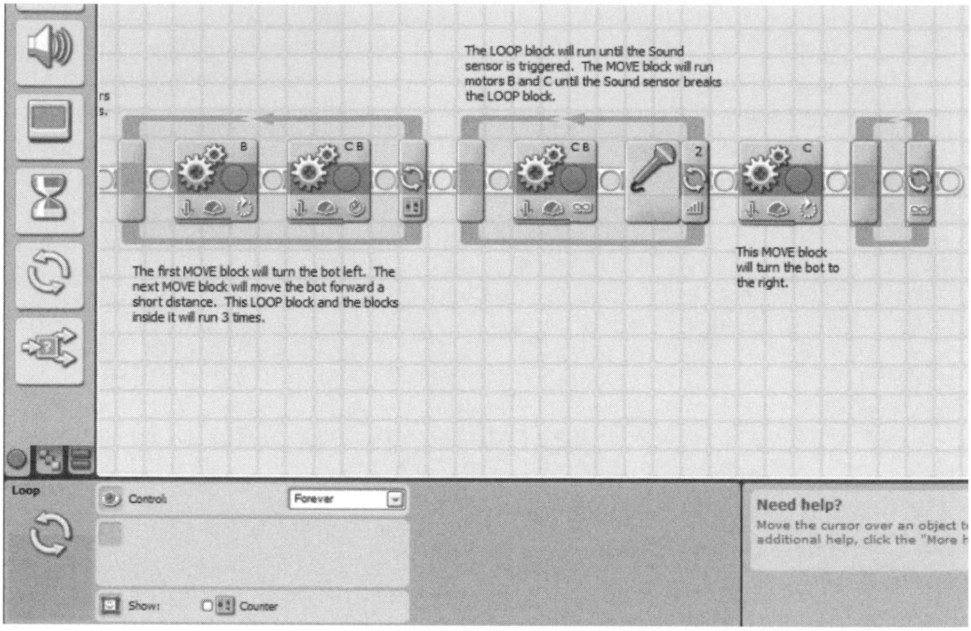

Figure 12-18. *This LOOP block will run the motors continuously.*

Then drop in the final MOVE block, configured to run motors B and C for an Unlimited duration (see Figure 12-19).

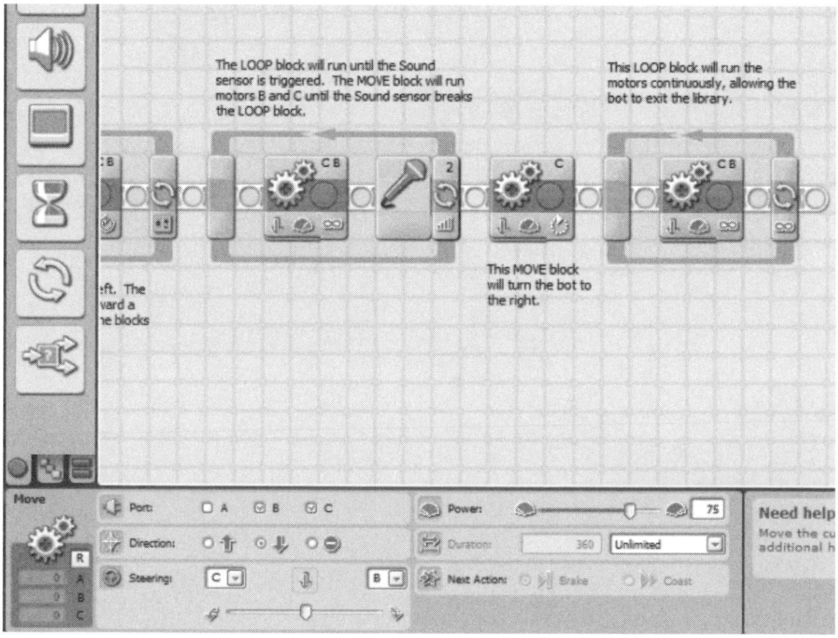

Figure 12-19. *This MOVE block runs motors B and C.*

That's it! Upload the program and test it. And test it again. Once you're confident that your SnapShotBot is running perfectly, set up your test environment one more time for the final test. Place the basket, the dark paper, and the bot in their starting positions. If you're using a regular camera or disposable camera, be sure you've wound the camera before sending the bot off. Place the arm that will press the camera's button directly above the button. Get two rolls of string (or twine) and tie one end of each roll to the SnapShotBot. I included two L-shaped beams on the back of my SnapShotBot where I could tie my strings. Remember to give plenty of slack on the string. Even better—have someone help you hold one of the rolls so you can both watch the strings and keep the tension off. When you're ready, press and release the Touch Sensor and watch your SnapShotBot begin its job. As it rolls in, be sure to feed out plenty of string—you don't want the string to get tight and pull the bot off course. When the bot turns to take the photograph, feed some more string as it moves towards the basket.

As the bot moves around the basket, you'll continue to feed the bot more string. Start watching for it to return, and when you see it, yell "*Stop!*" The bot should turn (don't forget to keep feeding more string) and head in your direction. If you've given the bot plenty of string, it should come right back to you. Grab the bot and turn it off.

Now, cut the two string ends from your bot and cut the string from the two rolls. Take all four string ends and place them together in your hand. Start pulling very slowly. Keep pulling slowly until you feel some resistance. When you feel the string tighten a little, pull even more slowly. At this point, the string should be pulling the basket towards you. Keep pulling until you've got the basket (and the key!) in your hands.

Congratulations! You've got the key and the team can continue exploring King Ixtua's tomb.

CHAPTER 13

■ ■ ■

Get In, Grab It, Get Out

Location: Southwest Guatemala

Weather Conditions: 84 degrees Fahrenheit, Humidity 48%, Rain 0%

Day 4: Outside King Ixtua's Library, 8:43 AM

Evan laughed as he watched his uncle slowly pull the twine. His uncle kept trying to grab the basket, but it was still four or five feet away. Evan could tell his uncle was anxious to retrieve the key.

"And I've got it!" Uncle Phillip yelled, his voice echoing down the hallway.

Uncle Phillip stood, turned, and faced the rest of the team, holding the basket above his head.

"Is the pa'aachi inside?" asked Grace, nervousness in her voice. Without the key, the team would be unable to continue its exploration of the tomb.

Evan watched as a smile slowly appeared on his uncle's face.

Uncle Phillip reached into the basket and pulled out an unusually shaped object. He turned it over in his hands, letting Max, Grace, and Evan get a good look.

Made of animal bone, the key was over a foot in length. The key was shaped like a walrus tusk, with one end almost two inches in diameter and the other end a small, dull point. Its surface was covered with carved Mayan glyphs, and the key had a dozen notches cut into it.

Max began taking photographs of the key. "Can you turn it over, please?" He took another photo and then lowered the camera. "I hate to rush things, but can we maybe try it out?" he asked.

Uncle Phillip laughed. "I was thinking the exact same thing. Let's do it," he replied.

The Throne Room

Uncle Phillip inserted the key into the hole in the floor. When nothing happened, he twisted the key clockwise. From behind the wooden door, the team heard a loud SNAP!

"I think that did it," said Evan.

"I think you're right," replied Uncle Phillip with a smile. "And if I'm right about what is behind that door, we're almost to the king's burial chamber. Max, take a photo of this, please."

Evan watched as Max photographed Uncle Phillip pushing against the large wooden door. He expected a loud creaking sound, but the door opened smoothly.

After the door was open, Uncle Phillip peered into the darkness, shining his weak flashlight around. "Grace, would you bring me those portable lights?"

Grace picked up two of the small battery-powered lights and handed them to Uncle Phillip. "The manuscript states the throne room is safe. No traps," she said.

"Let's light up the room first," Uncle Phillip said. "Just in case."

Evan watched as his uncle placed the two portable lights on the floor, just inside the room, and turned them on. The lights flickered for a few seconds and then flooded the room with a bright white light.

"Okay, Max. Let me have a few of those bags of sand," said Uncle Phillip.

Evan had wondered about the six bags that Max had carried in earlier. He had seen Max filling them with sand earlier. He watched as his uncle tossed a bag into the room, followed by another and then another. After Uncle Phillip had tossed all six bags, he took a step into the room. "Give me just a minute," he said. "Wait until I give the all clear."

"Be careful, Uncle Phillip," said Evan, stepping closer to the door to watch his uncle.

"He'll be fine, Evan," said Grace. "The manuscript says that when Tupaxu built this tomb, King Ixtua requested that no traps be built in his throne room. He didn't want anyone hurt or trapped inside."

Evan continued to watch as his uncle walked slowly around the room, examining the corners, floor, and walls. "So is there anything special about the throne room?" asked Evan.

Grace shrugged her shoulders. "The manuscript doesn't give us any detail about the room other than it was designed to look just like the throne room the king used when he was alive."

"But many of the Mayan throne rooms that have been found also contain a secret passage to the burial chamber," added Max. "This throne room is the last room sketched in the manuscript. The burial chamber wasn't included. I'm betting that we'll find the burial chamber connected to this room."

Evan smiled. "That would be awesome to find," he said. "My friends will never believe me when I tell them what I've been doing this summer."

Max raised the camera to his eye. "Smile, Evan," he said as the camera flashed. "We'll take some more before you go home."

Before Max could reply, Uncle Phillip appeared in the doorway. "Okay, everyone come on in. Don't touch anything just yet," he said. "Max, I need you to take plenty of pictures and examine the king's throne. Grace, I need you to examine the door leading to the library and help me with a pedestal in the room. And Evan, I may have another special project for you."

Locate the Burial Chamber

One hour after the team had entered and examined the throne room, Uncle Phillip made an announcement. "Okay, team meeting in the tent. Let's go," he said.

As the team assembled and pulled up chairs, Grace placed a large piece of posterboard on the table.

"Okay, looking at Grace's drawing here, I'll give you my initial thoughts," said Uncle Phillip.

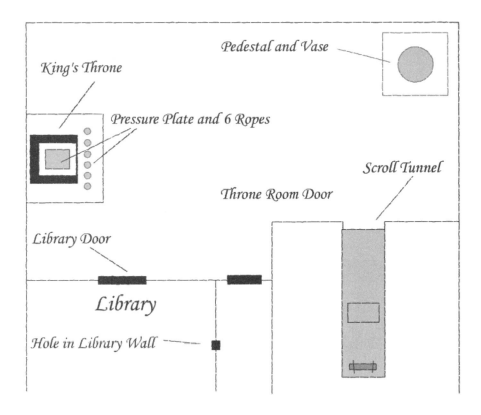

Figure 13-1. *Grace's sketch of the throne room*

"Since the manuscript doesn't give us any information on this room, we need to look at what we do have," said Uncle Phillip. "There do not appear to be any doors other than the library door and the door we used to enter. Max examined the throne and there does appear to be a pressure plate that triggers if someone sits down. There are also six small, thick ropes coming up from holes in the floor in front of the throne. There is a very large vase on a pedestal in the opposite corner of the room. Grace and I did not find any traps or similar pressure plates on this pedestal or under the vase. And, finally, there is a tunnel in one wall, about 12 feet deep, with a scroll at the end. Any thoughts? Grace?"

"I think the burial chamber is under the pedestal. If we don't figure out how to open it correctly, though, my guess is that a trap will trigger and close off the chamber permanently," Grace replied.

Max nodded. "The scroll in the tunnel is probably important in some way, too."

Uncle Phillip turned to Evan. "Evan, do you have any ideas?"

Evan looked at Grace's sketch of the room and smiled. "Those six ropes have to be important, too. When I was looking at them, my instinct was to pull them," he replied.

Uncle Phillip smiled at Evan. "I felt the same way. You almost can't resist pulling on them." He leaned back, crossed his arms, and looked at each of the team members. "Well, would anyone like to hear my guess?"

Evan, Grace, and Max all nodded and smiled together.

Uncle Phillip pointed first to the scroll. "We need to get the scroll. I believe I see three pressure plates in the tunnel that will trigger if anything heavier than a monkey, or a robot, crosses over the plates," he said with a smile and a nod to Evan. "The tunnel is large enough for a person to crawl down it, but I think that's a trick. If the pressure plates are triggered, the burial chamber will probably be lost to us for good."

"What about using a long pole with a hook on the end to grab the scroll?" asked Max.

"I thought of that, too," said Uncle Phillip. "My only concern is that Tupaxu might have thought of that as well. He was very smart. He probably designed the tunnel so that last pressure plate *must* be triggered when the scroll is lifted. It's probably more sensitive to weight and would guarantee that a small monkey was in the tunnel and not a human."

Max looked at Evan. "Have we told you how glad we are that you brought that robotics kit with you?" he asked.

Evan smiled. "I can probably get something built to get the scroll," he replied.

"Good," said Uncle Phillip. "Because I believe that scroll will have instructions on how to locate and enter the burial chamber. I think that someone will need to sit on the throne, triggering the pressure plate. Once the plate is triggered, my guess is that one of those ropes will need to be pulled. All the other ropes will probably trigger a trap that will also make the burial chamber inaccessible."

"But what if sitting on the throne triggers the trap?" asked Grace. "Maybe Tupaxu designed the throne only for King Ixtua to sit on?"

Uncle Phillip nodded. "You might be right. That's why the scroll is so important. I still think it will tell us exactly what we need to do."

Max and Grace nodded in agreement.

"Evan, why don't you and Max go and take a closer look at the tunnel. Take any measurements you need, okay? Grace and I will be in the library if you need us. This is important, so take whatever time you need. There is no rush on this one," Uncle Phillip said.

Max stood up and stretched. "Ready?" he asked Evan.

Evan took a deep breath and let it out slowly. "Okay," he said. "Let's go."

Scroll Challenge

"Two feet tall, two feet wide," said Max, measuring the height and width of the tunnel entrance.

Evan wrote down the information in his Design Journal. "That gives me plenty of room for a robot."

Max pointed his flashlight down the tunnel. "The measurements for the scroll will have to be estimates. What do you think? Does the scroll look about a foot in length?" he asked. "Looks about three or four inches from the back wall, too."

Evan peered down the tunnel. "Yeah, that's about right. And maybe four or five inches above the tunnel floor?"

Max nodded. "I wish we could be exact, but let's make it four inches to be safe," he replied. "I think your uncle is right. That does look like a pressure plate in front of the scroll."

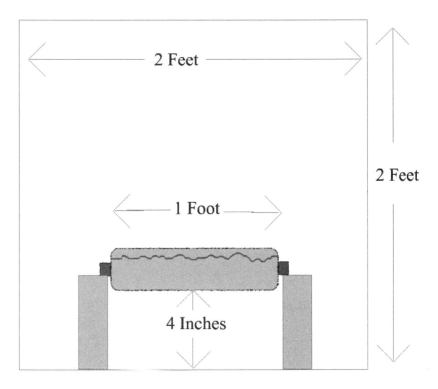

Figure 13-2. *Evan's drawing of the scroll at the end of the tunnel*

"Any idea how much a spider monkey would weigh?" asked Evan.

"No idea, but we'll find out. I guess you can't make your robot too heavy, huh?"

Evan shook his head. "I'll definitely have to keep the weight in mind."

Max smiled and turned off his flashlight. "If I were a monkey, I'd just get in, grab it, and get out," he said. "Fast and simple."

"Well, the motors are fast. But I don't think moving quickly is the right idea. It'd be too easy to make a mistake," said Evan. "As for grabbing the scroll, that's the tricky part, I think."

"Can I make a suggestion?" asked Max.

Evan nodded. "Sure."

"Whatever you build, it doesn't need to be fancy. From what I've seen of your other bots, this one should be fairly basic. Maybe just a simple lifting mechanism to get the scroll off those legs and then bring it back," Max said.

"You're right," said Evan. "But it can't move too fast or it might knock the scroll off the legs. Well, I'm done here."

"Okay. Let's go see your uncle," said Max.

Max's Solution

"I like Max's idea," said Evan, eating his lunch back at the tent. "I'll have to figure out how to build a lifting mechanism to support the scroll, but I definitely think it'll work."

Uncle Phillip turned to Max. "Maybe two arms?" he asked. "One on the left and one on the right?"

Max shook his head. "I was thinking of something even simpler, like a single lifting crane. Just something to get under the scroll, lift it up, and then haul it back," he replied. "But it's really Evan's decision. He's the one who has to build it."

Evan listened to the ideas being discussed. He knew that the scroll was important. The bot had to function properly or the expedition would probably be over.

"Can you give me three or four hours? That should be enough time to develop something," Evan said.

"Evan, you take all the time you need," said Uncle Phillip. "I don't like putting this kind of pressure on you, so you let me know when you're ready. So far, your little bots have worked perfectly. I have no doubt that whatever you design for the tunnel, it will get that scroll. We'll all be in the library inventorying all the artifacts, so take your time." Uncle Phillip grabbed Evan's shoulder and squeezed it, then turned and left.

Evan pulled out his Design Journal and began to write.

Story continues in Chapter 17 . . .

■ ■ ■

CHAPTER 14

GrabberBot—Planning and Design

Taking the suggestion from Chapter 13, this bot doesn't need to be quick but it does need to be simple. All we need is for the bot to move to the end of the tunnel, avoid knocking the scroll off its support legs, grab the scroll securely, and return to the tunnel entrance.

With those requirements in mind, let's move forward and develop a solution to this challenge.

GrabberBot Planning and Design

If you'd like to skip ahead to Chapter 15 and take a look at my final solution for the GrabberBot, feel free. Right now, I can imagine numerous bots that could be built to retrieve that scroll, and I'm sure you can, too. Get out a blank Design Journal page and a pen—your goal for this challenge is to develop an alternative to my GrabberBot.

■**Note** There are two blank Design Journal pages left in the back of this book (if you used one each for Chapters 2, 6, and 10). If you need more pages, feel free to make photocopies of the Design Journal page or visit the Source Code area of the Apress Web site to download the page in PDF format.

In the Robot Name box, write **GrabberBot** or create your own name; some other names I considered included SnatchBot and BringItBackBot. After you've got your bot name picked out, it's time to think about the bot's description.

The Robot Description

A robot like this one—one that has just two or three jobs to perform—might seem fairly simple to describe. With many bots, the description is so simple that you might wonder if it's even worth spending the time writing it out. I've built plenty of bots without any written description; I just knew what I wanted it to do and I started building.

But don't let this bot fool you. There are some things about this bot that are a little tricky and deserve some attention. Take a look at my Robot Description in Figure 14-1. I might have run into some trouble if I had just started building without considering all the things involved in retrieving the scroll.

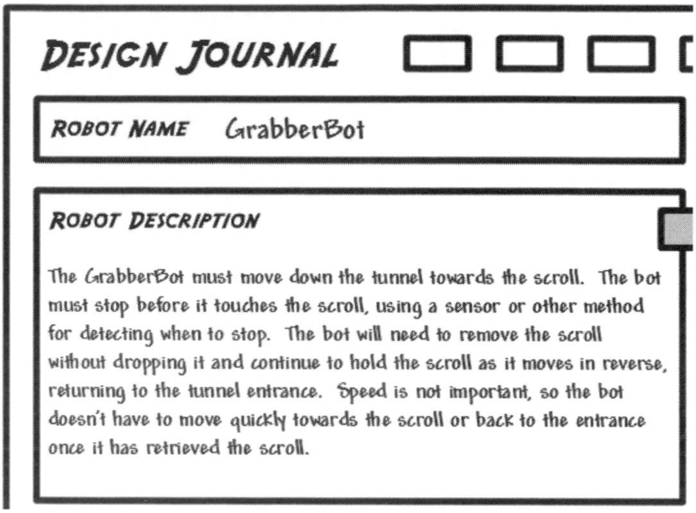

Figure 14-1. *The GrabberBot Robot Description revealed a couple of tricky items.*

Where would I have encountered trouble? Well, when I just start building randomly, I sometimes find that I have to tear it apart and start over because I didn't take an external factor into consideration. With this bot, it is likely that I *would have* thought about a method for the robot to detect the end of the tunnel. But because I would have skipped the other parts of the Design Journal page, I *might not have* considered the limitations on the bot and where to place a sensor so that it didn't interfere with its primary task of grabbing the scroll. That's one of the risks of just snapping pieces together without a plan.

By using the Design Journal page and completing all the sections, I reduce the risk of starting to build and then having to start over when I run into a design that doesn't quite work the way it should.

Let's focus on one of my Robot Description sentences: "The bot will need to remove the scroll without dropping it and continue to hold the scroll as it moves in reverse, returning to the tunnel entrance." This should get you thinking about what's involved for the bot to "hold" the scroll. Will it hold it like a hand would hold an object, with fingers wrapped around the scroll? Could it somehow simply pinch the scroll and pull it away? If so, how could you make certain the scroll didn't come loose during the return trip? Will it come at the scroll from below or from above?

Your Robot Description should force you to start asking your own questions. And it's the answers to these questions that will help you start developing a picture in your mind of what the final bot will look like.

After I completed my Robot Description, I realized that my Task List was going to be very short, too. But a short Robot Description or Task List does not mean the design of your bot will be easy. Sometimes the difficulty is in the building of your bot, sometimes in the programming of it, and sometimes in both. I'll finish up my Design Journal page before I get too excited about the simplicity of the bot's description.

The Task List

My Task List is shown in Figure 14-2. How does it compare to your own?

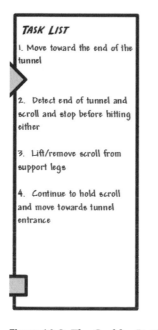

TASK LIST

1. Move toward the end of the tunnel

2. Detect end of tunnel and scroll and stop before hitting either

3. Lift/remove scroll from support legs

4. Continue to hold scroll and move towards tunnel entrance

Figure 14-2. *The GrabberBot Task List may be short, but each item is important.*

Let's go through each of the four tasks in detail and develop some ideas. These ideas can be used in the Mindstorm section, as long as they don't violate any of the limitations or constraints in the next section of your Design Journal page.

The first task is "Move toward the end of the tunnel." Simple enough. If we ignore the shape of our bot for now and just concentrate on this task, what attributes of the robot can we consider? Well, one item is the bot's speed. As it moves down the tunnel, do we want it moving fast or slow or somewhere in between? Personally, I don't want to wait forever, so I might plan on sending the bot down the tunnel at a high rate of speed until it gets close to the end of the tunnel. When it nears the scroll, I'd prefer that it slowly approach it, to avoid knocking it off the support legs.

The best part of moving down the tunnel is that the robot needs to move in a straight line only. No turns and no special zigzagging is needed—this bot will go straight to the scroll and then straight back to me.

The next task, "Detect end of tunnel and scroll and stop before hitting either," is a little more complicated. I could use the Sound Sensor and program the bot to stop when I yell "stop!" but this could be less accurate than using one of the other sensors. I'll probably get more accurate results if I choose to use the Touch Sensor or Ultrasonic Sensor; it really depends on whether I want to actually touch the scroll or wall (Touch Sensor) or detect the proximity of the scroll or wall (Ultrasonic Sensor).

The third task is "Lift/remove scroll from support legs." The scroll is sitting about four inches above the tunnel floor on two small support legs. If I accidentally knock the scroll off, I suppose I could build another bot to go down the tunnel and pick it up. But failure isn't an option for this bot (okay, sometimes it is, but let's think positive). I believe it will be safer to lift the scroll up, coming at it from underneath. If I create something to reach forward (like a hand) I might accidentally push the scroll off the pedestal. I could also create a mechanism that reaches down from above the scroll, but again, there is a slight chance I might cause the scroll to roll forward or backward and fall off the supports.

My final task, "Continue to hold scroll and move towards tunnel entrance," will only work if I've successfully grabbed the scroll and can hold it securely. If my bot has the scroll held securely, I can reverse the direction of the bot and have it move back towards the tunnel entrance. For speed, I'll probably have it move at a medium speed or slower; a fast-moving bot might get to me quicker, but I can afford to let it move slowly if it means not losing the scroll.

By examining my Task List in a little more detail, I've been able to start brainstorming (excuse me, *mindstorming*) about the size and speed of my bot and the components to use in it. But before I continue, I need to examine any constraints my bot might encounter.

Limitations and Constraints

Considering that the GrabberBot is heading down another tunnel, I know of at least two limitations for my bot: size and weight. All of the limitations for my bot are shown in Figure 14-3, in my Limitations/Constraints box.

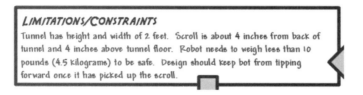

LIMITATIONS/CONSTRAINTS
Tunnel has height and width of 2 feet. Scroll is about 4 inches from back of tunnel and 4 inches above tunnel floor. Robot needs to weigh less than 10 pounds (4.5 kilograms) to be safe. Design should keep bot from tipping forward once it has picked up the scroll.

Figure 14-3. *The limitations for the GrabberBot must be taken into consideration.*

Obviously, my bot must be no taller than two feet and its width should not exceed two feet, either. The bot's weight, on the other hand, could be an issue.

A quick Internet search revealed that a full grown spider monkey averages about 6 to 10 pounds (2.7 to 4.5 kilograms). If I can keep my bot's weight below that number, I should be okay—the pressure plates shouldn't trigger like they would if a grown person were to crawl down the tunnel.

My final constraint is related to the position of the scroll. The scroll is four inches from the rear of the tunnel and about four inches above the tunnel floor. Whatever method I use to pick up the scroll must take those measurements into consideration.

If I can design my bot so that it doesn't violate any of those limitations, everything should be good.

And now, taking into consideration the Robot Description, the short Task List, and the Limitations/Constraints, are you ready to begin mindstorming?

Mindstorm

I know my Task List was short, but the Mindstorm section of my Design Journal page is much longer. Take a look at Figure 14-4.

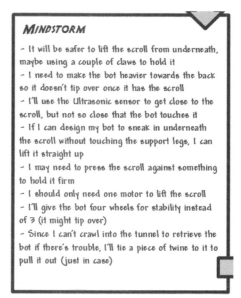

MINDSTORM

- It will be safer to lift the scroll from underneath, maybe using a couple of claws to hold it
- I need to make the bot heavier towards the back so it doesn't tip over once it has the scroll
- I'll use the Ultrasonic sensor to get close to the scroll, but not so close that the bot touches it
- If I can design my bot to sneak in underneath the scroll without touching the support legs, I can lift it straight up
- I may need to press the scroll against something to hold it firm
- I should only need one motor to lift the scroll
- I'll give the bot four wheels for stability instead of 3 (it might tip over)
- Since I can't crawl into the tunnel to retrieve the bot if there's trouble, I'll tie a piece of twine to it to pull it out (just in case)

Figure 14-4. *The Mindstorm section for my GrabberBot isn't short at all.*

The first Mindstorm item, "It will be safer to lift the scroll from underneath, maybe using a couple of claws to hold it," relates to how my bot will approach the scroll. Earlier in the chapter I mentioned that my bot could reach down and grab the scroll, reach forward and grab it, or reach from underneath. I still believe that the safest approach is to somehow get my bot under the scroll and somehow lift an arm or trap or other mechanism to surround the scroll and lift it directly up off the support legs.

Try this little test: take a couple of tin cans (vegetable soup, for example) and sit them about six or seven inches apart. On top of the cans, place something scroll-shaped—maybe a tube of toothpaste or cookie dough or paper towel roll. Now close your eyes. Have someone direct your hand to the "scroll" using *only* these verbal commands: forward, backward, stop, up, down, left, right, and grab—don't cheat! Don't use your fingers unless you plan on designing your bot with fingers (and I doubt you'll have enough motors to do this). Try different approaches to lifting the "scroll" off the tin cans. Which worked better? For me, an open palm coming in under the "scroll" is the easiest—if I avoid touching the tin cans, all I have to do is raise my hand ("UP!") and the scroll will sit on my palm.

Another Mindstorm item that I think will be very important is "I'll use the Ultrasonic Sensor to get close to the scroll, but not so close that the bot touches it." Take a look at Figure 14-5. This is how I'm visualizing approaching the scroll.

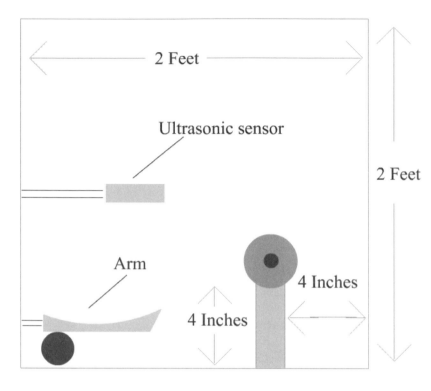

Figure 14-5. *Side view of the bot approaching the scroll*

What I'm considering doing is having the Ultrasonic Sensor above the scroll and some sort of arm mechanism below the scroll. As the bot moves towards the scroll, I'll configure the Ultrasonic Sensor to stop the bot at a certain distance from the wall. That distance will be determined through testing, but the idea is that it will stop the bot when the arm is directly underneath the scroll. The bot stops, the arm lifts up, and the scroll is captured.

Remember, we're just mindstorming right now, so I'm not getting too detailed in my drawing or design just yet. Testing might prove later that this method doesn't work—that's a risk, but that's why I'm spending time thinking about this bot before I start building.

The last Mindstorm item I want to cover is "I may need to press the scroll against something to hold it firm." If I can get the bot to successfully lift the scroll, there is a chance that when the bot begins to move in reverse, the scroll might roll off the arm. What I'd like to do (and I'll test this) is to have the arm lift the scroll up against some beams or other NXT components—this should hold the scroll firmly while the bot moves. Again, I'll have to test this and it might not work.

The rest of my Mindstorm items are fairly self-explanatory. A four-wheel bot will be more stable than a three-wheel bot; a bot that's heavy in the rear won't tip forward when it picks up the scroll; one motor should provide sufficient lifting power; and, something that occurred to me after I designed the SnapShotBot, tying a string to my bot will allow me to pull it out if the bot gets into trouble. If the scroll falls off the support legs, I don't know what will happen, but the best-case scenario for that happening would be to simply build another bot that goes down the tunnel and retrieves the fallen scroll. But let's not let that happen, okay?

Well, we're done with the Mindstorm section of our Design Journal, and there's only one section left before we begin to build.

Sketches

As you saw in Chapter 10 in Figure 10-7, I don't use detailed images of things like sensors and wheels. I don't like to spend time drawing components in detail when I can use a rough sketch to get my point across. I do the same thing when sketching my ideas for the shape of my bots. While completing my Design Journal page, I began to build some rough pictures in my mind of what I want my bot to look like. So take a look at Figure 14-6 and remember not to laugh too loud or you'll disturb your neighbors.

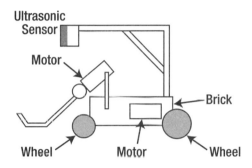

Figure 14-6. *Once again, basic shapes are used to represent parts of my GrabberBot.*

Again, I'm not drawing every sensor, wheel, beam, and connector piece. I just want to use basic shapes to represent those items. The brick is easy—rectangle. Wheels are circles. Motors are still weird looking, but I label them so I remember what they are.

When I'm done, I've got a good idea of where to start building. And that's exactly what I'm ready to do. Let's move on to Chapter 15 to get the GrabberBot built and ready to retrieve that scroll.

CHAPTER 15

■ ■ ■

GrabberBot—Build It

The final design of my GrabberBot has a lot of potential modifications. I realized after I completed the design that if I removed the Ultrasonic Sensor and the upper beams, I would be left with a nice base unit that could be used in future designs. But that's not what this chapter is about. This chapter gives you the building instructions for constructing a bot that can move down the tunnel and successfully retrieve the scroll.

If you've built your own version of the GrabberBot, congratulations. How does it compare to my design (see Figure 15-1)? I hope you're beginning to see that there are an unlimited number of designs for successful completion of these challenges. The only limits are your imagination and the parts in your kit.

Figure 15-1. *One version of a GrabberBot*

Note E-mail me a picture of your version of the GrabberBot—I'd love to see it. You can find my e-mail in the Introduction at the start of the book.

Now, on to the GrabberBot's building instructions.

The GrabberBot's building instructions are divided into three sections. The first section consists of the main body (Brick, three motors, four wheels). The second section adds the lifting arm mechanism, and the third section adds the Ultrasonic Sensor, Touch Sensor, and various support beams. After you've built the GrabberBot, Chapter 16 will provide you with the programming instructions.

Just like previous building instruction chapters, comments will be provided for sections that might be a little tricky. Some images will include text and arrows to point out special areas of construction where you need to focus your attention.

First Section: Main Body

Figures 15-2 through 15-24 walk you through the steps for constructing the main body. Start with the motor and components you see in Figure 15-2.

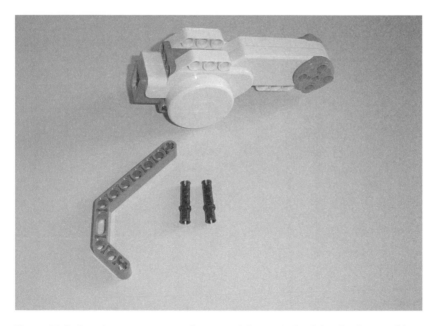

Figure 15-2. *Starting components for one of the main body's wheel assemblies*

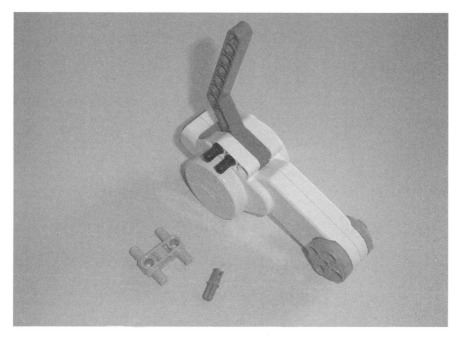

Figure 15-3. *Place the long black connectors in the motor as shown to secure the angled gray component.*

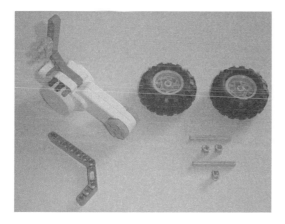

Figure 15-4. *Insert the gray pin and small blue connector as shown.*

Figure 15-5. *Insert the axle rod into the motor and slide the bushing on. Connect the other angled gray component as shown.*

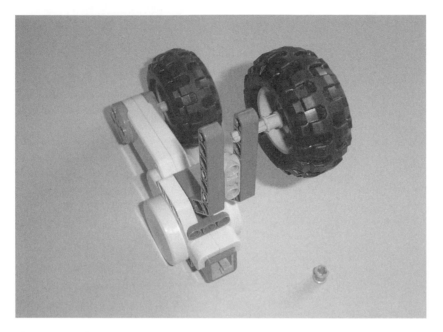

Figure 15-6. *Place one tire on the axle rod. Insert the other tire into the angled gray connector as shown.*

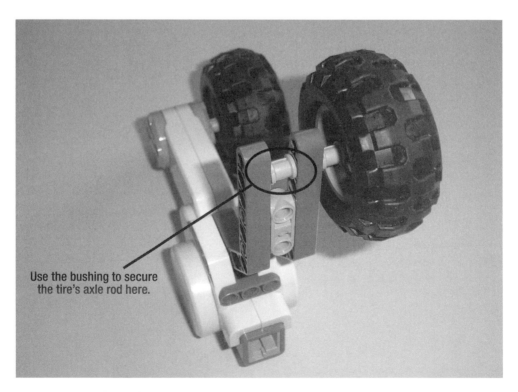

Use the bushing to secure the tire's axle rod here.

Figure 15-7. *Use the bushing to secure the tire's axle rod as shown.*

Now you'll perform the same steps to make the opposite wheel assembly.

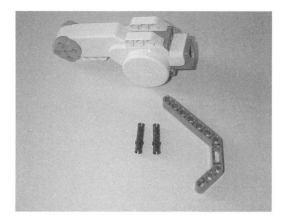

Figure 15-8. *Starting components for the main body's other wheel assembly*

Figure 15-9. *Place the long black connectors in the motor as shown to secure the angled gray component.*

Figure 15-10. *Insert the gray pin and small blue connector as shown.*

Figure 15-11. *Insert the axle rod into the motor and slide the bushing on. Connect the other angled gray component as shown.*

Figure 15-12. *Place one tire on the axle rod. Insert the other tire into the angled gray connector as shown.*

Just like Figure 15-7, use the bushing to secure the tire's axle rod in the angled gray component for Figure 15-13.

Figure 15-13. *Use the bushing to secure the tire's axle rod as shown.*

Now that you've completed the left and right wheel assemblies, it's time to configure the Brick (see Figures 15-14 through 15-16).

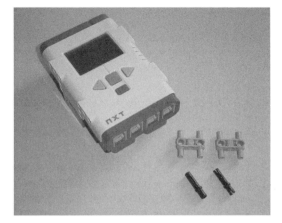

Figure 15-14. *The Brick and components are needed to create the main body.*

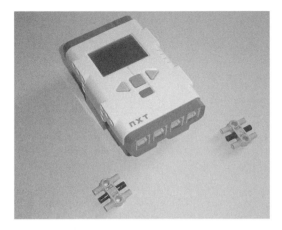

Figure 15-15. *Insert the long black connectors into the gray pins.*

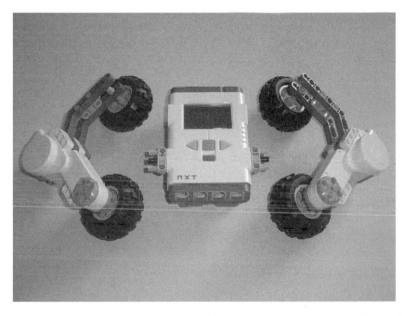

Figure 15-16. *Insert the gray pins (and long black connectors) into the Brick.*

Next, you'll connect the wheel assemblies to the Brick (see Figures 15-17 through 15-24).

Figure 15-17. *Connect the right and left wheel assemblies to the Brick.*

Figure 15-18. *Place the four small black connectors in the 15-hole beam.*

Figure 15-19. *Connect the 15-hole beam to the back of the motors to secure them and place the two small black connectors in the 11-hole beams.*

Place the two 11-hole beams on the back side of the 15-hole beam as shown here.

Figure 15-20. *Connect the two gray pins to the motor and place the two 11-hole beams as shown.*

Figure 15-21. *Place the two 7-hole beams on the back of the motor as shown.*

Figure 15-22. *Connect the motor to the main body as shown.*

Figure 15-23. *Insert the four small black connectors into the beams as shown.*

Figure 15-24. *Connect the 11-hole beam to the motor mount as shown.*

That's all for the main body. Up next is the lifting mechanism.

Second Section: Lifting Arm Mechanism

Figures 15-25 through 15-33 show you how to build the lifting arm mechanism and connect it to the main body. Start with the components shown in Figure 15-25.

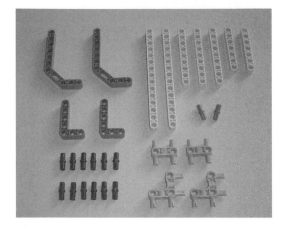

Figure 15-25. *The components used to make the lifting arm mechanism*

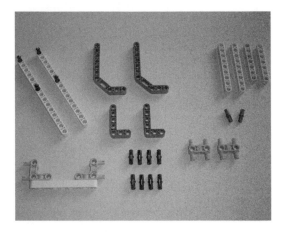

Figure 15-26. *Put the four small black connectors in the 15-hole beams and place the two gray pins in the 9-hole beam.*

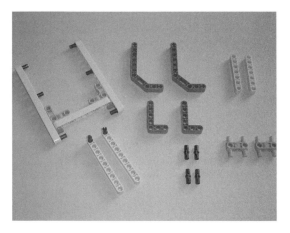

Figure 15-27. *Connect the 15-hole beams to the 9-hole beam. Insert the small black connectors as shown.*

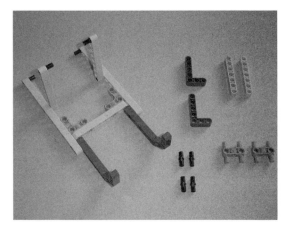

Figure 15-28. *Connect the two 9-hole beams and the two angled gray beams to the main lifting mechanism as shown.*

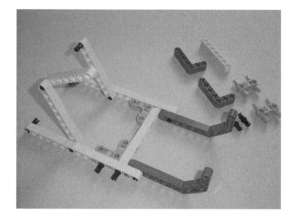

Figure 15-29. *On one side, insert two small black connectors and connect one 7-hole beam as shown.*

Figure 15-30. *On the other side, insert two more small black connectors and connect the remaining 7-hole beam as shown.*

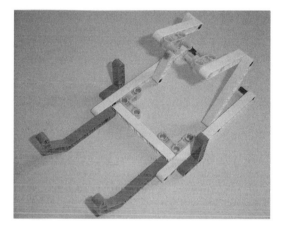

Figure 15-31. *Connect the two L-shaped beams and the two gray pins as shown.*

Figure 15-32. *The lifting arm connects to the main body.*

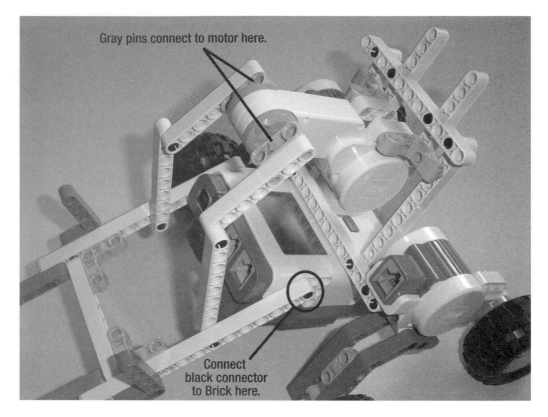

Gray pins connect to motor here.

Connect
black connector
to Brick here.

Figure 15-33. *The two gray pins go in the motor as shown and the two small black connectors connect to the Brick.*

Now you have the basis of the GrabberBot. All that's left is to place the Ultrasonic Sensor and the beams that the lifting arm will pin the scroll against.

Third Section: Sensors and Various Beams

You're almost done. The GrabberBot needs the Ultrasonic Sensor to detect the wall and some beams. I decided to use the Touch Sensor again as a **Start** button. Figures 15-34 through 15-54 show you how to complete the bot.

Start with the components shown in Figure 15-34.

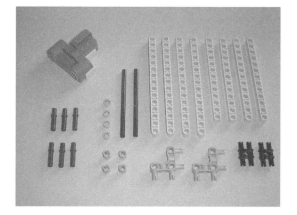

Figure 15-34. *Final components for the GrabberBot*

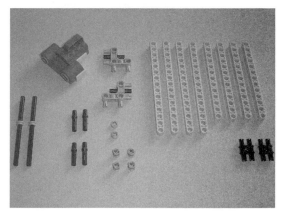

Figure 15-35. *Insert two small bushings on the axle rods and two long black connectors in the gray pins as shown.*

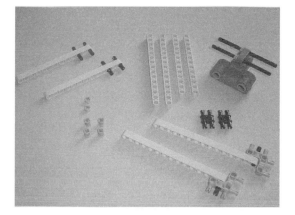

Figure 15-36. *Place four long black connectors in the 13-hole beams. Connect two gray pins to the 15-hole beams and insert the axle rods in the Ultrasonic Sensor.*

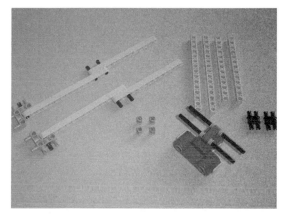

Figure 15-37. *Connect the 13-hole beams to the 15-hole beams. Place the other two small bushings on the axle rods as shown.*

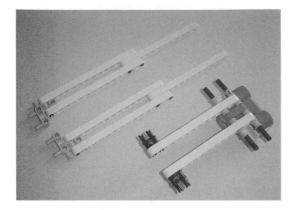

Figure 15-38. *Connect the 15-hole beams and the 13-hole beams as shown. Place the black pins in the 13-hole beams and four bushings on the axle rods.*

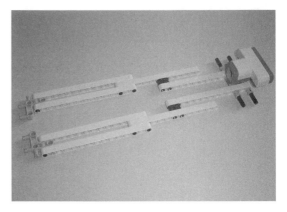

Figure 15-39. *Connect everything together as shown to make the long Ultrasonic Sensor neck.*

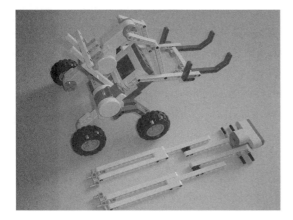

Figure 15-40. *The Ultrasonic Sensor and neck will connect to the main body.*

Figure 15-41. *Connect the Ultrasonic Sensor and neck to the 11-hole beam on the main body as shown.*

Figure 15-42. *These 15-hole beams will connect to the motors for reinforcement.*

Figure 15-43. *Place the small black connectors in the 15-hole beams as shown.*

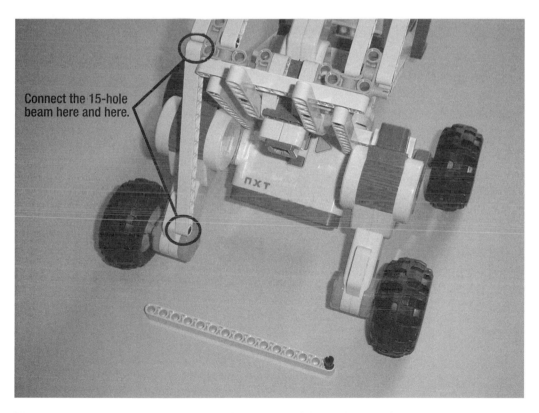

Connect the 15-hole beam here and here.

Figure 15-44. *Connect a 15-hole beam to the motor and the neck assembly as shown.*

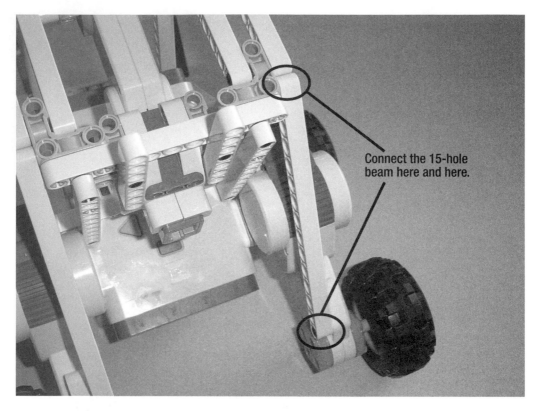

Connect the 15-hole beam here and here.

Figure 15-45. *Use the other 15-hole beam and connect it to the motor and neck assembly.*

Figure 15-46. *The Touch Sensor will function as a **Start** button.*

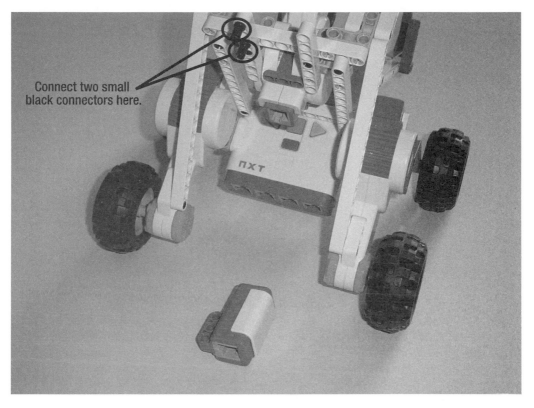

Figure 15-47. *Place the two small black connectors as shown.*

Figure 15-48. *Connect the Touch Sensor.*

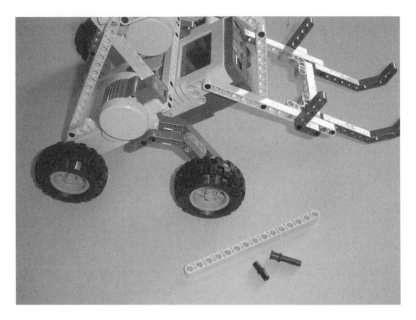

Figure 15-49. *This 15-hole beam will provide strength to the GrabberBot neck.*

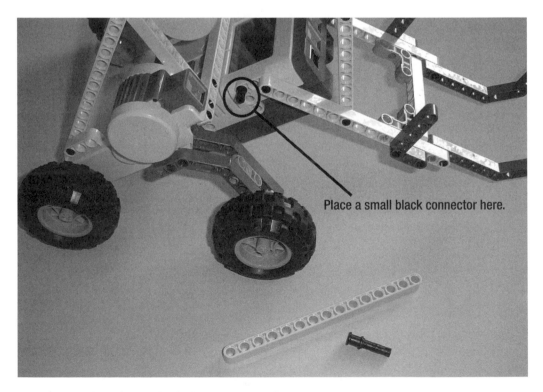

Place a small black connector here.

Figure 15-50. *Place the small black connector as shown.*

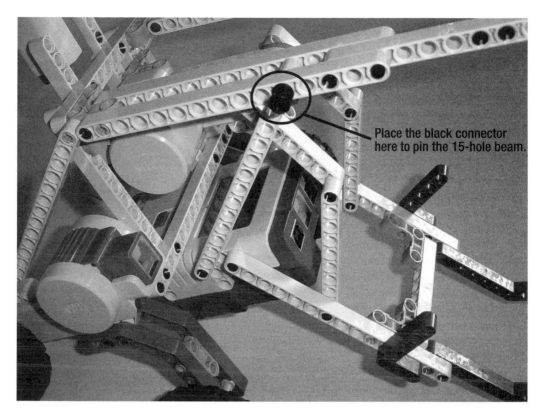

Place the black connector here to pin the 15-hole beam.

Figure 15-51. *Connect the 15-hole beam and use the black connector to pin it.*

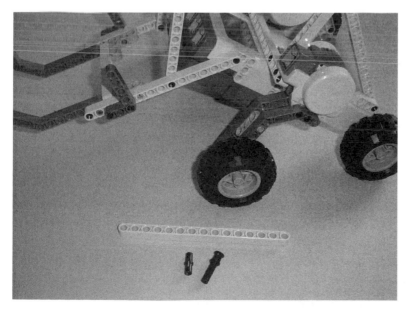

Figure 15-52. *On the other side, use another 15-hole beam for reinforcement for the neck.*

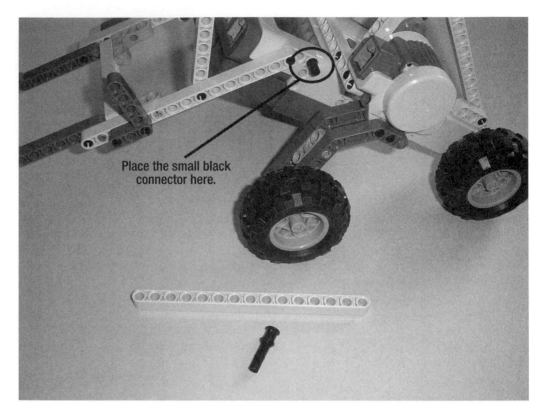

Figure 15-53. *Place the small black connector as shown.*

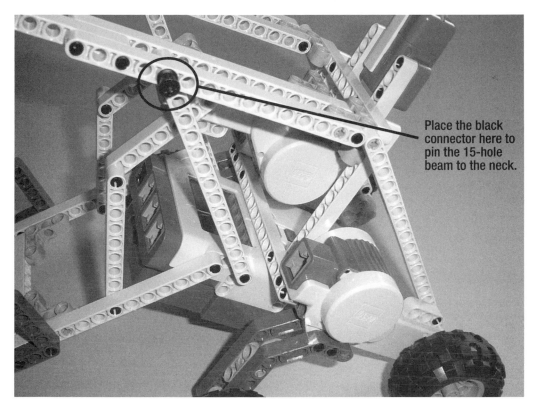

Place the black connector here to pin the 15-hole beam to the neck.

Figure 15-54. *Connect the 15-hole beam and use the black connector to pin it.*

Now your GrabberBot needs to be wired up and programmed. Take a look at Figure 15-55 to see how I've wired up the bot.

Figure 15-55. *The wired-up and ready-to-be-programmed GrabberBot*

Chapter 16 will show you how to program the GrabberBot so it can head down the tunnel and grab the scroll.

■ ■ ■

GrabberBot—Program It

During the programming of the GrabberBot, I'm not going to tell you to use any particular method for programming—I'm leaving that up to you. You might choose to open up the NXT software and start dropping blocks until you've got the program completed; then you'll upload the program, test it, and debug it if you find any problems. Or you might use the method described in Chapter 12, moving forward with your program only after you've successfully placed a block and then tested that the bot does what it's supposed to do.

Or you can follow along with the method I'll present in this chapter, which is a slight variation on the second method. I'll place a block, configure it, upload it to my bot, and then test it. If the bot doesn't perform as anticipated, I'll reexamine the block and its configuration settings and see whether I've made a mistake. In some instances, such as the placement of a WAIT block, I might place two blocks and then test—the WAIT blocks are sometimes so simple I choose to test them at the same time as a more advanced block.

Whichever method you choose, take notes of your successes, but ESPECIALLY your failures. Try to determine where you made your mistakes—were you in a hurry and missed something important? Did you choose the wrong programming block for the job? If you pay attention to your mistakes and learn why you made them and how you solved them, your bot programming skills will definitely improve.

Down the Tunnel . . . Again . . .

If you're following along with the method I've chosen, open up the Lego Mindstorms NXT software, type **GrabberBot** into the blank text field labeled **Start New Program**, and then click the **Go** button (see Figure 16-1).

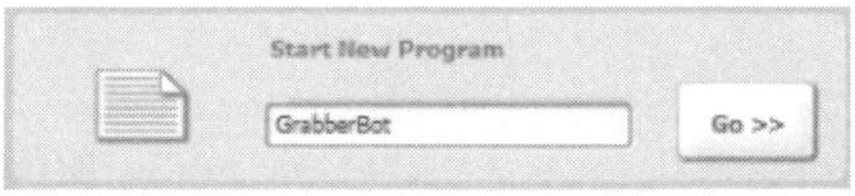

Figure 16-1. *Enter GrabberBot for the program name and click Go.*

Note If the RoboCenter area is visible on the far right of your screen, click the small red X in the upper-right corner of the software, and it will free up more visible workspace on your screen.

Just like with the SnapShotBot in Chapter 11, I have placed the Touch Sensor on the back of the bot to use as a **Start** button for the GrabberBot. I've found that if I don't need the Touch Sensor for a bot design, I can include it as the **Start** button, and it keeps me from having to press any buttons on the Brick—and sometimes the location or orientation of the Brick can make pressing its buttons difficult. By placing the Touch Sensor in an easy-to-reach location, I don't have to worry about accidentally bumping my bot when I pull my hand away quickly after pressing the orange **Run** button. (Some programmers put a 5- or 10-second WAIT block at the beginning of their programs so they can press the orange **Run** button on the Brick and still have time to place their bot correctly before it begins to run—that works, too.)

The first block I'll place in my program (again) is a LOOP block (see Figure 16-2) configured to detect the press and release of the Touch Sensor. When the button is pressed and released, the loop will break and the remaining programming blocks will begin to run.

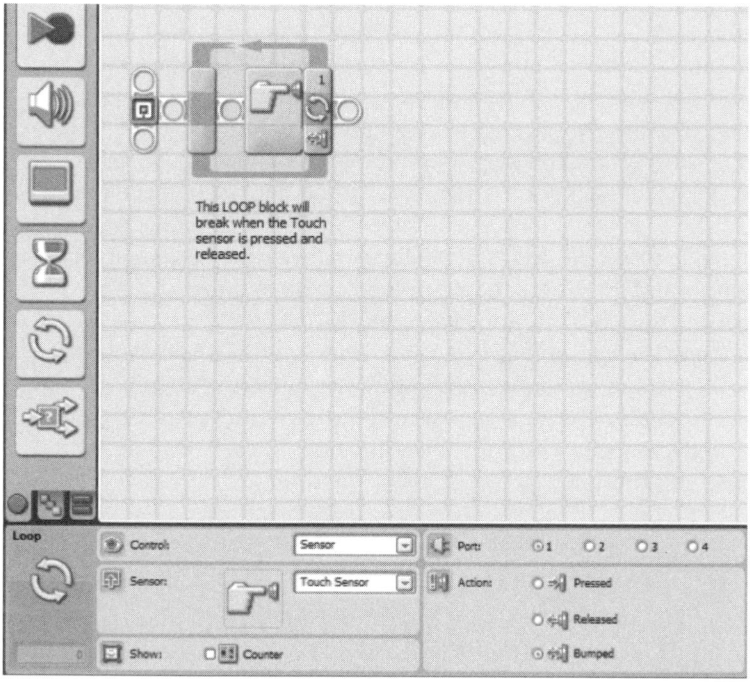

Figure 16-2. *A LOOP block and Touch Sensor trigger are used to start the GrabberBot.*

Look back at my Task List (turn back to Figure 14-2). My first task is "Move toward the end of the tunnel." There are actually two movements here, though. The first is the bot moving toward the scroll and stopping a safe distance away to begin detecting the wall. The second movement is toward the scroll (at a slower pace) and letting the Ultrasonic Sensor detect the wall and the proper place for the GrabberBot to stop to grab the scroll.

Right now, I need to perform the first movement, but I still haven't told you how I plan on programming the bot to keep from moving too far (and accidentally bumping the scroll). Look at Figure 16-3.

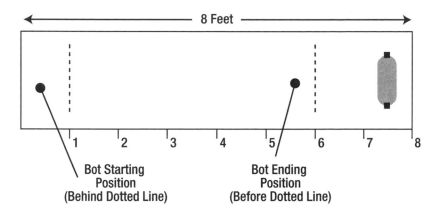

Figure 16-3. *Determining the correct distance for the GrabberBot*

In this figure, I've labeled the GrabberBot's starting position as being behind an imaginary line that is at the 1-foot mark inside the tunnel. My bot is slightly longer than 1 foot, but my calculations will be based on the FRONT wheels being behind this line. The tunnel is 8 feet deep, and the scroll is 4 inches from the back wall of the tunnel. I have placed another imaginary line at the 6-foot mark. If I can program my bot to stop before it reaches the 6-foot point shown in Figure 16-3, it should be a safe enough distance away not to accidentally bump the scroll.

The method I'm going to use for accomplishing this is more exact than the method you saw for the SnapShotBot in Chapter 12. In Chapter 10, I divided distances to travel by the circumference of the wheel (7 inches) and rounded the numbers up or down. The distances the SnapShotBot traveled weren't as exact as I need for my GrabberBot to travel. So I need a different method for fine-tuning the distances my GrabberBot will move. There's a little math involved (sorry), but I don't think you'll have trouble following along—but do grab a calculator. (Unlike your school teacher, I allow calculators!)

Let's start off with a simple observation. The wheels of your Grabberbot are 7 inches in circumference. This means that when the wheel makes one complete rotation on the ground, it will have traveled 7 inches. Are you with me so far? Now it just so happens that when a wheel spins completely around for 1 rotation, it has also spun 360 degrees. When you travel around a circle and return to your starting point, you have made a trip of 360 degrees, got it? Okay, so if the wheel spins for half a rotation, how many degrees has it traveled? Did you answer 180 degrees? What about a quarter of a rotation? The answer is 90 degrees.

Now, let's move our bot around a little more. If your bot moves forward for 8 rotations, how many degrees has it traveled? To find the answer, you simply multiple 360 (degrees) by 8 (number of rotations) and the answer is 2880. If you wanted to configure a MOVE block to spin your robot for 8 rotations, you could also program it to spin for 2880 degrees—it will move the same distance. Test it!

And the best part about converting rotations to degrees is that you don't have to round your number of rotations off—if you want your bot to move 2.25 rotations, you simply multiply 360 by 2.25 and the answer is 810 degrees!

And the math works both ways, by the way. If you have a bot you want to move forward 3432 degrees, how can you determine how many rotations to program it? Just do the reverse—divide the number of degrees of movement by 360, and the answer will be the number of rotations you need to program your bot to move. So, 3432 degrees divided by 360 equals 9.5 rotations (round your numbers to one decimal place, but don't worry—for most of your bots, this should be accurate enough).

So, before moving forward, let's make sure you understand two simple rules:

1. To convert rotations to degrees, simply *multiply* the number of rotations by 360, and the answer is the equivalent number of degrees.

2. To convert degrees to rotations, simply *divide* the number of degrees by 360, and the answer is the equivalent number of rotations.

So, how will I use this information to guide my GrabberBot to the proper location? Well, if the GrabberBot wants to move from the 1-foot mark to the 6-foot mark, it will need to move *NO MORE THAN* 5 feet, right?

I know that 5 feet is the equivalent of 60 inches (there are 12 inches in 1 foot, so for 5 feet, I simply multiply 5 by 12 to get 60). Since one wheel rotation is 7 inches, if I divide 60 inches by 7 inches, this will give me the number of rotations a wheel will spin if it travels 5 feet. The answer is 8.6 rotations. Now comes the math—Rule #1 tells me all I need to do to convert 8.6 rotations to degrees is multiply it by 360. When I do this, I get an answer of 3096 degrees. When I program my first MOVE block, I will tell my GrabberBot to move forward 3096 degrees, and I know that it should be stopped on or behind that second imaginary line in Figure 16-3.

Before I continue, are you now aware that robotics does involve some mathematics? Would you believe that more advanced robots will require even more advanced math skills? Since I let you use a calculator, please allow me to encourage you to not ignore your math and science studies, okay? If you like designing robots and hope to work your way up to more advanced designs, you'll need to concentrate in school on ALL your subjects (including History)! Okay, enough lecturing—back to the programming.

So now I can place that first MOVE block (see Figure 16-4). Notice I've configured it to spin 3096 degrees, which is equivalent to 5 feet.

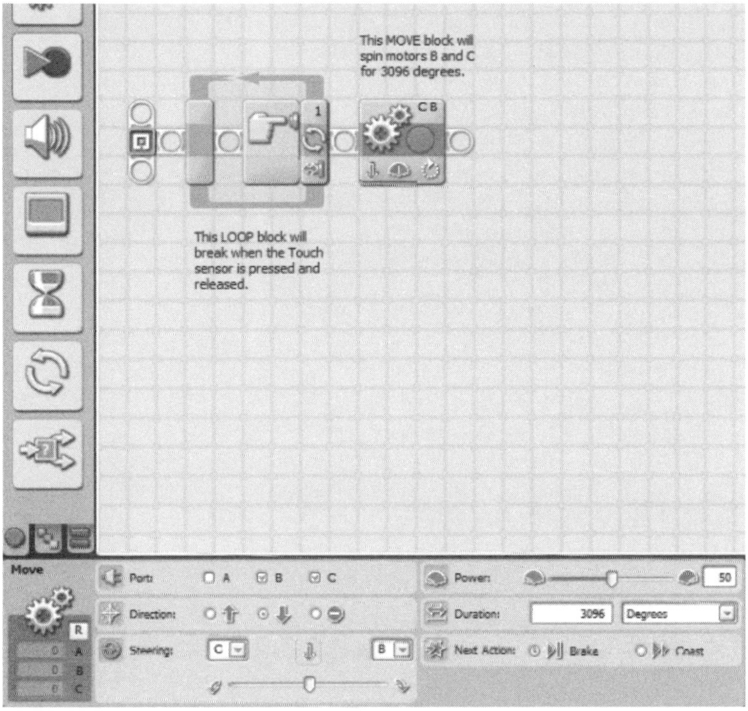

Figure 16-4. *This MOVE block controls the GrabberBot's movement down the tunnel.*

What if my calculations were a little off? Well, I did round the number of rotations from 8.5714 (when I divided 60 inches by 7 inches earlier), so could this make my GrabberBot possibly bump the scroll? If you look again at Figure 16-3, you'll notice that I've got another foot-and-a-half of distance before the scroll, so I should be safe. That's why I intentionally chose to stop the bot at the 6-foot mark and not the 7-foot position.

Now I'm going to upload my program and test it. I have a measuring tape, and I want to make sure that my bot moves forward about 5 feet and no more. I test it and . . . it works. I press the **Start** button (Touch Sensor), and the bot moves forward almost exactly 5 feet from its starting point. Excellent.

Because I need to take a deep breath at this point (and maybe you do, too), I'm going to have my bot pause for 10 seconds. I'm doing this because as I mentioned in Chapter 14, if I find that my bot isn't lined up exactly where I want it, I could use the string that I'm going to tie to the rear of my bot and pull it back. It's not the best solution, but I really want my bot to make one attempt on the scroll, and I want it to be successful. So I'll add in a WAIT block, which will let me look down the tunnel and make certain the bot is pointed directly forward and that the arm mechanism will fit smoothly underneath the scroll's supporting legs (see Figure 16-5).

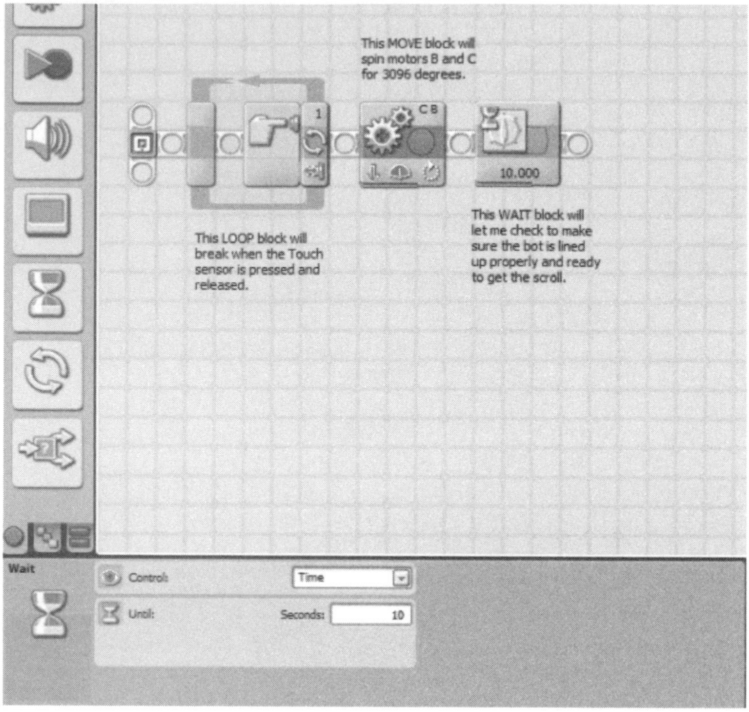

Figure 16-5. *A WAIT block will let me check to make sure the GrabberBot is ready to get the scroll.*

I'll tie a string to the rear of my bot, but hopefully I won't have to use it. The WAIT block is just a safety precaution that I've decided to add—feel free to leave it out if you feel your bot is ready to move forward and grab the scroll.

Approaching the Scroll

Now, the next movement for my GrabberBot is a little trickier. I've got to have the bot crawl forward, very slowly, and try and detect the back wall. Why the back wall, you may ask? Well, my GrabberBot is designed so that its arm mechanism will come in UNDER the scroll and lift up. It's small and I've designed it to fit between the two support legs. What I do NOT know is how close I need for the Ultrasonic Sensor to be to the back wall. If you take a look at my final GrabberBot design (refer back to Figure 15-55), you'll notice that the Ultrasonic Sensor sticks out a little further than the arm mechanism. What I'll do is test this over and over until I find the best position for the Ultrasonic Sensor to trigger—this position will be when the lifting arm is directly under the scroll, the best position for it to get a good lift-off of the scroll. It could be 4 inches from the wall or less than 1 inch—I won't know until I test it.

And since I need to test it, this is probably the best place for me to explain my test environment, which is shown in Figure 16-6.

Figure 16-6. *Photograph of the "scroll" and support legs*

What I've done for my test environment is measure out 8 feet from a wall in my living room. I place some obstacles to represent the tunnel walls (okay, they are couch cushions—use what you have). I measure 4 inches from the wall and place two small tin cans about 6 inches part—these are the support legs for my scroll. And finally, for the scroll, I sit on top of the cans a small, fuzzy paint roller. Simple, but it all works great.

Now, before I begin testing, I need to program my bot to slowly approach the scroll. To do this, I'm going to use a LOOP block that will break when the Ultrasonic Sensor is triggered. So I first drop in that LOOP block (see Figure 16-7).

For now, I've configured the Ultrasonic Sensor to trigger when it gets about 8 inches from the back wall (or other obstacle).

Next, I'll drop in a MOVE block (see Figure 16-8).

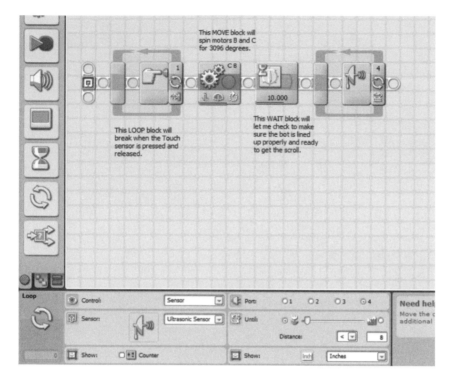

Figure 16-7. *The LOOP block will break when the Ultrasonic Sensor is triggered.*

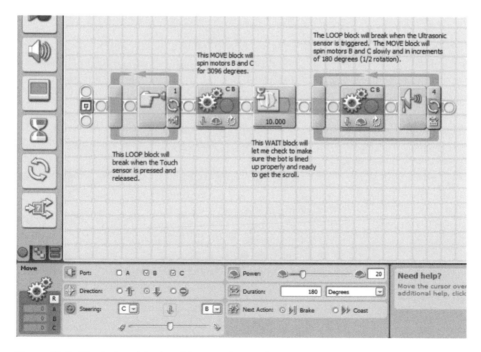

Figure 16-8. *The MOVE block will move the bot forward slowly for a short distance.*

I'm going to have the motors B and C spin slowly (**Power** is set to 20), and a just a little bit at a time. The bot will move forward a short distance (.5 rotation or 180 degrees), and the Ultrasonic Sensor will see whether the wall is within 8 inches. If not, the bot will move forward again. It will keep doing this until the Ultrasonic Sensor breaks the loop.

Finally, I want to add a WAIT block to allow the bot to fully stop (see Figure 16-9). It gives me time to pull the bot back with the string if I discover the bot is approaching the scroll at an incorrect angle.

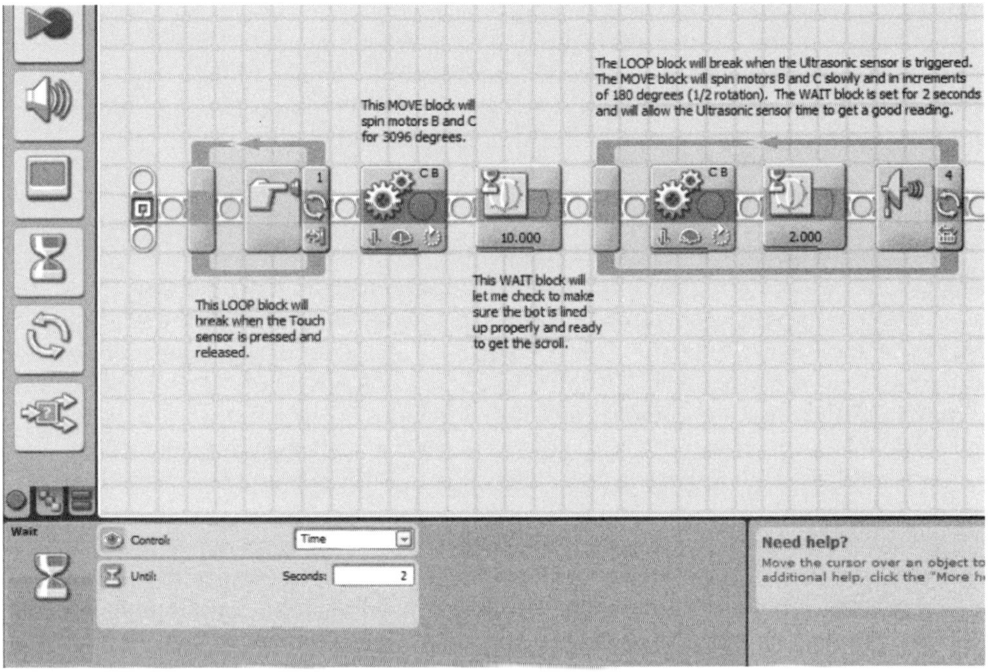

Figure 16-9. *The WAIT block allows the Ultrasonic Sensor to get a good reading.*

And now I upload the program and test. Below are my results—it took me four tests to determine the proper configuration of the Ultrasonic Sensor:

Test 1: Ultrasonic Sensor configured for < 8 inches—arm not under the scroll.

Test 2: Ultrasonic Sensor configured for < 6 inches—arm almost under the scroll.

Test 3: Ultrasonic Sensor configured for < 5 inches—arm almost but not completely under the scroll.

Test 4: Ultrasonic Sensor configured for < 4 inches—arm underneath the scroll.

■**Note** Every Ultrasonic Sensor is different, and your Ultrasonic Sensor will have a slightly different sensitivity than my Ultrasonic Sensor. Because of this, you need to test your bot and record your own results. The final value for my Ultrasonic Sensor (< 4 inches) may or may not work with your GrabberBot! Although the Ultrasonic Sensor is fairly accurate, always test with your own values, not the ones I am using—just to be safe!

At this point, my bot will now move down the tunnel and stop about 2 feet in front of the scroll. It then begins to move slowly toward the scroll (stopping and pausing every 3 inches) until the Ultrasonic Sensor detects the wall and triggers the bot to stop. Now my little bot's lifting arm is directly under the scroll and ready to lift it up and return it to me.

Acquiring the Scroll

When my GrabberBot lifts the scroll off its support legs, I intend for it to pin the scroll against the beams above the arm mechanism (flip back to Figure 15-55). By holding the scroll against these beams, it is less likely that the scroll will roll or fall out of the arm mechanism on its return trip.

Now, to do this, I will need motor A to apply continuous upward pressure against the scroll. To do this, I will simply put a MOVE block into a LOOP set to loop Forever. But if I have the LOOP block configured this way, it will never break. How will the bot be given instructions to return with the scroll?

The solution to this involves *parallel processes*. What are parallel processes? They are simply programming commands (blocks) your bot will execute simultaneously. For example, you could program a bot with a MOVE block that has motors B and C moving the bot randomly around the room, never stopping. At the same time, you could program the bot to also have motor A rotating the Sound Sensor back and forth, listening for sound input. So far, all of the bots I've shown you how to program involve one block running at a time (like a WAIT block or a LOOP block). When one block finishes, the next block starts.

In order to program my bot to do two things at once, I will create another path (beam) where I'll place programming blocks that will run simultaneously. But before I do this, I'll finish the program as if motor A already has the scroll pinned. And when I'm finished, I will then go back and add in that second sequence beam that will contain the blocks for motor A.

Okay, so if I assume that my GrabberBot already has the scroll pinned, all that's left is for the bot to move backward and return to the end of the tunnel. I'll do this by adding in a MOVE block for motors B and C (see Figure 16-10). I don't want the bot to return too quickly, so I'm also going to program it for a slower speed (**Power** set to 40).

Now I upload the program and verify that the bot will reverse direction. The bot worked fine, so now I'm going to add in the necessary blocks for the bot to grab the scroll—for this I'll be adding a parallel process as mentioned earlier.

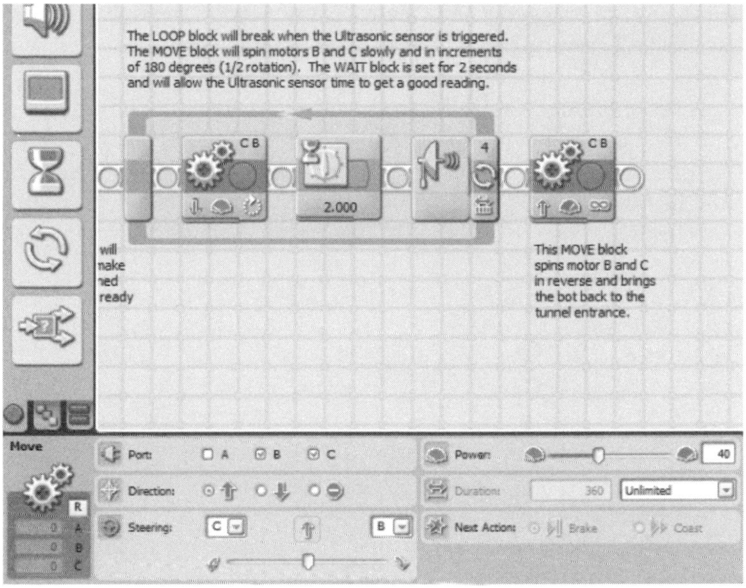

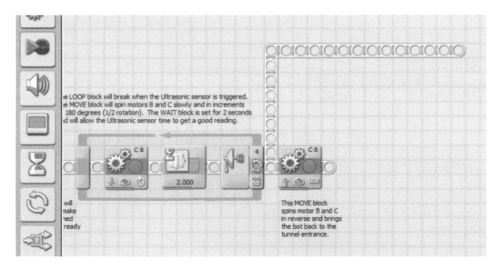

Figure 16-10. *A MOVE block is used to bring the bot back to the tunnel entrance.*

Fortunately, the NXT programming language allows us to do this by simply creating another beam that breaks off of the main beam. To do this, simply hold down the Shift key (the mouse pointer will change to a funny little symbol) and click where you want this new beam to start. Then drag up (or down) and you'll see a new beam starting. When you click once, you can make a bend in the beam and move it in a new direction. Double-click where you want to place the end of the new beam. I want the parallel action to occur at the same time as the MOVE block that returns the bot to the tunnel entrance. So I have to start this new beam just before that MOVE block's position (see Figure 16-11).

Figure 16-11. *Place the start of the new beam before the MOVE block.*

As you can see in Figure 16-11, I've dragged a new beam up and over (to the right) to allow me some space to place new blocks. I can still place blocks on the original beam, as you'll see later in Figure 16-13.

At this point in the program, my bot's arm is under the scroll, and I want it to lift up just enough to pin the scroll against the upper beams of my GrabberBot. I'll need to test motor A many times to determine the proper number of rotations or degrees to do this. But for now, I'll place a MOVE block to perform the lifting (see Figure 16-12). I configure it to lift slowly (**Power** is set to 30) and for an initial 180 degrees.

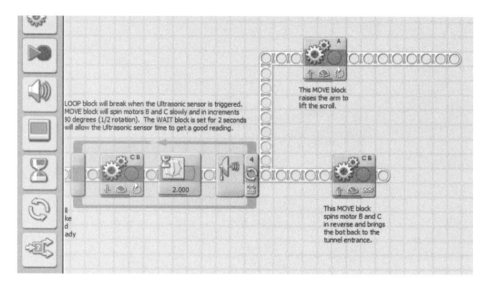

Figure 16-12. *The MOVE block will spin motor A to lift the scroll.*

Now I upload and test the program. And I encounter three problems. The first problem is that the 180 degrees I've configured motor A to spin is not enough (the scroll's weight may be the issue). I test it again and am able to determine that 270 degrees is the best setting to pin the scroll against the upper beams.

The second problem requires me to increase the **Power** setting from 30 to 60—I need this additional power to lift the weight of the scroll. Remember, TEST OFTEN!

The third problem requires a short explanation. When the program runs and the extra beam splits off (see Figure 16-11), the program will execute the first block in the upper beam and the first block in the original beam at the same time. What this means is that motor A will lift (the upper, new beam) at the same time as my MOVE block (in the lower, original beam) has motors B and C spin in reverse to return the bot. *Big problem!* The bot needs to first grab the scroll and then move in reverse.

To fix this, I'll simply add a WAIT block that will run at the same time as motor A is lifting. I do this because I want to give the bot time to lift the scroll and pin it before the bot begins to move. I'll put in a WAIT block configured for 5 seconds as shown in Figure 16-13 and another WAIT block configured for 10 seconds as shown in Figure 16-14. The 10-second WAIT block lets the robot pause before the lifting operation. The 5-second WAIT block allows the arm to close before the "reverse" MOVE block is executed and the robot returns with the scroll.

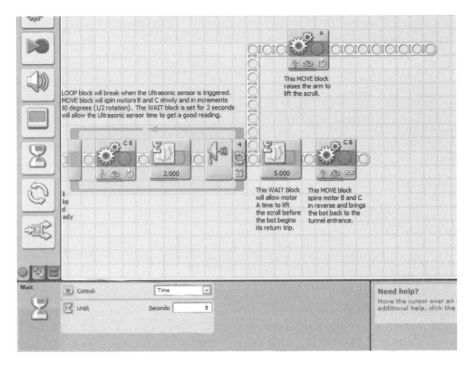

Figure 16-13. *The WAIT block will give motor A time to lift the scroll.*

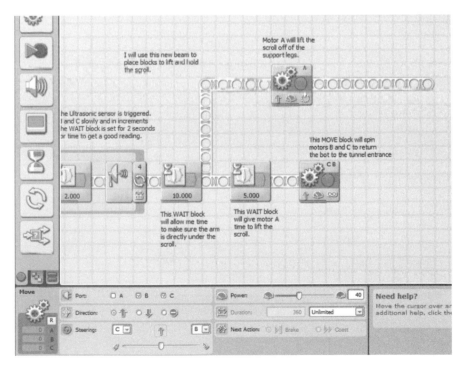

Figure 16-14. *An additional WAIT block allows the robot to get everything ready to move.*

And once again, I test my bot. Because I've been testing my bot often, usually after each major programming block is added, my bot doesn't require any additional changes. On its *VERY FIRST TEST*, this is what happens:

1. I push the **Start** button (Touch Sensor).

2. The bot moves forward toward the scroll about 5 feet and stops. It doesn't touch the tunnel sides at all (okay, cushions from my couch).

3. The bot moves 3 inches forward, the Ultrasonic Sensor tries to detect the wall and fails, and the bot moves forward another 3 inches.

4. The bot repeats step 3 about 6 times before the Ultrasonic Sensor is triggered.

5. Motor A spins, and the lifting arm raises the scroll and pins it against the upper beams of the GrabberBot.

6. A few seconds later, the bot begins moving backward and brings the scroll back to me.

PERFECT TEST!

Just to be sure, I perform two more tests with the GrabberBot, and they're successful. With three successful runs of the GrabberBot, I am fairly confident in my bot's ability to run down the tunnel, find the scroll, lift it off the support legs, and then return it to me.

Take your GrabberBot and test it until you are able to successfully retrieve the test scroll a few times. When you're ready, set up the scroll one final time and run the bot. If it works, congratulations!

You've got the scroll, and the team is one step closer to finding King Ixtua's burial chamber . . .

CHAPTER 17

■■■

Bravery, Wisdom, and Honor

Location: Southwest Guatemala

Weather Conditions: 89 degrees Fahrenheit, Humidity 52%, Rain 25%

Day 5: Inside King Ixtua's Throne Room, 10:12 AM

Evan's uncle had unrolled the small scroll with gloved hands, careful not to tear the thin parchment. After Max had finished photographing the Mayan writing on the scroll, Uncle Phillip had given the scroll to Grace for translation. That had been two hours earlier, and now Evan was sitting with his uncle and Max in the tent, waiting for Grace to complete her initial review of the scroll's contents.

Max had used the time to inventory all the film he had used photographing the excavation and exploration of the tomb. He told Evan that he had over 1,000 photographs and would probably take an additional 300 or more before the team left for Florida.

Uncle Phillip had been working on his laptop, creating a proposal to present to the government of Guatemala for further excavation and study. Evan was surprised at the amount of paperwork that his uncle had to file in order to request more time at the site.

And Evan had used the time to dismantle his GrabberBot.

But all that stopped when Grace entered the tent, carrying the scroll, a handful of paper sheets, and a large piece of posterboard. She walked over and placed it all on the table. "Well, I think we're ready," she said.

"What did you find," asked Uncle Phillip. "Did the scroll have the instructions we need?"

Grace nodded. "Even better," she said with a smile. "The scroll does tell us how to access the burial chamber. But it also tells us quite a bit about the burial chamber itself."

Uncle Phillip leaned back in his chair and stared at the tent's roof. "I was hoping for that," he replied. "It would be a shame to come this far and not get a glimpse of the burial chamber."

Max shook his head. "I was worried, too," he added. "The Tupaxu manuscript had no information on the burial chamber."

Evan looked at his uncle and then to Grace. "So, what's next?" he asked.

Uncle Phillip laughed and stood up. "Exactly right, Evan. Grace, what do we do?"

Grace pointed at a sheet of paper. "The scroll clearly states that to open the burial chamber, someone must be sitting on the throne. That pressure plate must be triggered. Once it is triggered, this rope must be pulled," she said, pointing at a small drawing she had made.

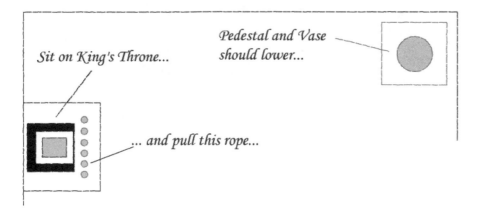

Figure 17-1. *Grace's sketch of the throne room*

"After the rope is pulled, this pedestal will lower and the burial chamber can be accessed," Grace added. "But, we'll need to be very careful with the burial chamber. I would suggest that we go open the burial chamber before we do anything else. I need to verify that the room matches the scroll's description first."

Uncle Phillip nodded. "I agree. Let's go open the chamber and see what we're facing. We've come this far with no mistakes, so there's no point in rushing forward too fast."

Evan stood with the others and followed his uncle back to the tomb.

The Burial Chamber

Uncle Phillip sat on the King's throne and waited. "Anyone hear or see anything unusual?" he asked.

Evan tried to listen for any strange noises that might indicate a trap had been triggered, but the chamber was silent.

Max shook his head. "I don't hear anything."

"I don't either," said Grace.

Uncle Phillip pointed to the throne room's entry door. "I'd like all of you to stand outside while I pull the rope. Just in case something goes wrong," he said.

Max, Grace, and Evan walked back to the corridor and waited.

"Okay, I'm pulling the rope now," Uncle Phillip said.

A few seconds passed. And then a grinding sound was heard by the team.

Grace pointed at the corner. "The pedestal is dropping," she said.

Evan watched as the pedestal began to lower. The large vase on the pedestal began to disappear down a large square hole. Another minute passed and then the grinding sound stopped.

"Congratulations, team!" said Uncle Phillip as he stood, a huge smile on his face. "Come on in and let's take a look at King Ixtua's burial chamber."

Evan followed Max and Grace as they crossed the room. Max had turned on his flashlight and handed it to Evan's uncle.

Uncle Phillip took the flashlight and got down on his stomach. "Come on, all of you get in here and take a look, too."

Evan got down on the floor next to his uncle. Grace and Max were next to them on the adjacent side of the square hole.

"Do you hear that?" asked Evan.

"Running water," replied Uncle Phillip, shining the flashlight into the hole.

"That was part of the major trap of the tomb," said Grace. "If we had triggered any of the earlier traps, the tomb was designed to flood. Look over there," she said and pointed.

Evan angled his head to look where Grace was pointing. The beam of light from the flashlight was reflected in a large stream of water running across the room. But what caught his eye was the large stone sarcophagus behind the stream of water. There wasn't much light from the flashlight, but what he could see amazed him.

Uncle Phillip handed the flashlight to Grace. "Okay, Grace, take a look around and verify what you can about the room. Max, take some photographs, but no one goes in until we discuss our plan, okay?"

Grace and Max nodded.

"Evan and I are going to go back to the tent and give you some room to move around. As soon as you're ready, come back and let's figure out our next step."

Evan tried to make sense of the things he saw in the burial chamber as he stood up. He had seen what he thought were some small figurines, and some sort of ramp leading to the sarcophagus.

Famous Figures

Max was finishing one of his uncle's famous grilled burgers when Max and Grace returned. They sat down at the table and began to eat the lunch Uncle Phillip had prepared.

A few minutes later, Uncle Phillip took a seat at the table with the team.

"Max, did you get enough photographs?" Uncle Phillip asked.

"Plenty," replied Max. "I'll take more once we get some better lighting down there, though."

"Most definitely," said Uncle Phillip. "Grace, were you able to verify the accuracy of the scroll?"

Grace nodded and finished chewing. "Yes, and I'm happy to report that it appears that the burial chamber has not been disturbed. It matches the scroll's description exactly, including measurements."

"That sounds like good news," said Evan.

Grace stood and pulled the posterboard over where the team could easily view it. "This is a drawing of the burial chamber with a few measurements I was able to translate."

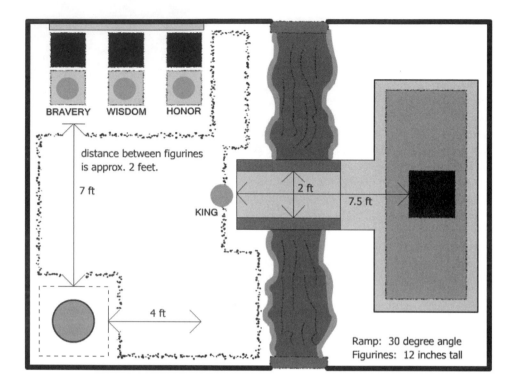

Figure 17-2. *Grace's sketch of the burial chamber*

Evan looked over the drawing. The sarcophagus was the largest item in the room, but it was the small objects that caught Evan's eye. He was certain there had to be at least one more challenge. "What are these circles?" he asked.

"Inside the chamber are four small statuettes. Each one is a carved wooden figure," said Grace. "This first one is U'laka. He was King Ixtua's bravest warrior. The next one is Raxu, considered to be the king's wisest friend. And this one is Ba'rii, Ixtua's most loyal military leader. Each figurine has a different Mayan glyph carved on it—Bravery, Wisdom, and Honor."

"What about this one," asked Max, pointing to a fourth circle on the drawing.

"That's a small figurine of King Ixtua," replied Grace.

"And the water flows under this ramp here?" asked Uncle Phillip.

"Yes. And the scroll says that if the trap in this room is triggered, the room will flood. And that's the bad part," Grace added. "The floor around the pedestal is one large pressure plate."

"So, there is one more challenge," said Uncle Phillip.

"Oh, yeah," said Grace. "And it's an interesting one."

The Final Challenge

Uncle Phillip patted Evan on the back. "It looks like Tupaxu wasn't kidding about using monkeys," he said. "It's a good thing he didn't know about robots, Evan."

Evan smiled. "Okay, can we go back through this one more time? I want to make sure I understand this completely," he said.

Grace took a seat next to him and pulled the posterboard closer. "Absolutely, Evan," she replied. "Let's take this in stages."

She pointed first at the pedestal. "It's safe to stand on the pedestal, but that's as far as you can go. This line I've drawn around the front part of the room is a large pressure plate. Anything heavier than eight or nine pounds will trigger the trap. The water exits here, and if the trap is triggered, the exit will seal up, making the room flood. So far, so good?" she asked.

"Got it," Evan replied.

"Okay, the next task. Your bot must move across the room to these three figurines. Each figurine must be placed on the black obsidian pressure plate behind it. But you have to be careful because there's a vertical pressure plate on the wall behind the pressure plates. If a figurine tips over and touches the plate, this will also trigger the trap."

Evan pointed at the drawing. "Do you have accurate measurements of these statues?" he asked.

Grace nodded. "Accurate from the pedestal to the figures, but I don't have exact measurements from the black pressure plates to the back wall."

Evan frowned. "Okay, I'll have to remember that."

Uncle Phillip smiled. "The good news, Evan, is that the figurines are in front of their respective triggers. At least you won't have to shuffle them around," he said.

"Okay," said Evan. "And after that?"

"Your bot will need to push this final figurine of King Ixtua up the ramp onto this black pressure plate on top of the King's sarcophagus. That will disable the floor's large pressure plate, and then we should be able to enter the burial chamber safely. And that's it."

Evan laughed. "This Tupaxu really didn't want just anyone getting to the King's burial chamber, did he?"

"Tupaxu honored his king's wishes and designed the tomb to require a trained monkey's assistance," said Max. "I'd say he did a great job, too."

Uncle Phillip took a seat across from Evan. "Well, Evan, do you think you could design us a little robot that can handle this challenge?"

Evan's Solution

"I already have an idea," said Evan. "But I also have a few questions."

"Shoot," said Uncle Phillip.

"Well, how loud is it in that chamber? Is the water making much noise?" asked Evan.

Grace shook her head. "It flows quickly, but there's no turbulence. What you heard was as loud as it gets," she replied.

"Are you thinking about using a Sound Sensor?" asked Max.

Evan nodded. "I might need to control some of the bot's actions using my voice. If it's too loud in the room, it might not work."

"Understandable," said Uncle Phillip. "We'll make sure that we make no noise in that chamber."

Max and Grace nodded.

"I also need to know the approximate weight of those figurines," said Evan.

"They're carved from the wood of the Irichu tree. It's not extremely heavy, but it's not a lightweight wood either. I'll get one of our guides to cut a piece of wood the approximate size and shape of a figurine and we'll weigh it for you," said Max.

Uncle Phillip turned to Max. "Anything else?"

Max shook his head. "Maybe later, but for now, I need to give this one some thought."

"You take all the time you need, Evan," said Uncle Philip. "Once again, we're not in any rush and we don't want to make any mistakes."

An hour later, Uncle Phillip brought in a small carved object and set it on the table. "It's ugly, but it's about the same height and diameter as the statuettes in the burial chamber."

Evan looked at the piece of wood. Someone had carved the rough shape of a bird in flight into a foot tall piece of wood.

"It's about four inches in diameter," said Uncle Phillip. "And it weighs about two pounds."

"Thanks, Uncle Phillip," said Evan. "That will help."

"Good luck, Evan. We've all got some other work to keep us busy, so just let us know when you're done," Uncle Phillip replied, walking out of the tent.

Evan picked up the piece of wood and stared at it. An idea began to form.

Story continues in Chapter 21 . . .

■ ■ ■

CHAPTER 18

PushBot—Planning and Design

The GrabberBot built in Chapter 15 performed its tasks by lifting and bringing the scroll back. The bot for this next challenge will perform its tasks by doing the opposite—pushing the figurines into their proper locations.

Why pushing? Well, lifting the figurines is definitely a possibility. And you might choose to attack the problem using a lifting motion again. But for the purposes of designing my bot, I've decided that I want to keep the figurines in contact with the floor to avoid dropping them as well as reduce the risk of tipping my bot over if the statues are heavy. With that in mind, let me walk you through the planning and design of my PushBot.

PushBot Planning and Design

In Chapter 19, you can view my final solution for the PushBot. I've got a dozen different ideas for how I plan on completing this challenge, and they all involve exerting a pushing force on the figurines. But I'm not going to lock myself into any particular design just yet. So get out a blank Design Journal page and a pen and follow along with me as I begin to design this new bot.

■**Note** There should be one blank Design Journal page left in the back of this book (if you used one each for Chapters 2, 6, 10, and 14). If you need more pages, feel free to make photocopies of the Design Journal page or visit the Source/Download section of the Apress Web site (http://www.apress.com) to download the page in PDF format.

In the Robot Name box, write **PushBot** or another name for your new bot; once you've decided on your bot name, move on to the description.

The Robot Description

This little bot has some repeatable actions to perform. There are a variety of ways for it to complete the challenge, but until we better understand some of the problems the bot will encounter, it will be difficult to be too specific on which sensors it will use. Because of this, I'm going to try and keep my description as generic as possible and avoid specifying what components might be used.

Take a look at my `Robot Description` in Figure 18-1. Keep in mind that I've got plenty of time to provide more specifics later on the Design Journal page.

DESIGN JOURNAL ☐ ☐ ☐ [

ROBOT NAME   PushBot

ROBOT DESCRIPTION

The PushBot will start from the pedestal and move towards the first figurine (left-most figurine). The bot must detect the figurine and not bump it or tip it into the back wall (pressure plate). The bot must push the figurine on to the black pressure plate without tipping the figurine. The bot will perform the same action for the remaining 2 figurines near back wall. When done, the bot must find and locate the figurine on the ramp. The bot must push the figurine up the ramp and place it on the black pressure plate on top of the sarcophagus.

Figure 18-1. *The PushBot description isn't specific yet.*

It's very generic, isn't it? I haven't specified how the bot will detect the figurines or how it will push the figurine. I haven't even decided how it will know when the figurine is on the black pressure plate. These are things I will definitely need to decide, but I don't have a complete picture yet of my bot in action.

As with the GrabberBot design process in Chapter 14, I want to complete the Design Journal page before I actually begin to do any kind of building or testing. Why try and begin designing when you haven't even begun to consider the limitations the bot will encounter? To be truthful, my mind is already considering various options, but again, I'm not going to start building until I'm done with the planning and design process.

Now, that doesn't prevent me from giving my robot's description a little more thought. Let me walk through a couple of my bot's description sentences in more detail.

Consider the very first sentence: "The PushBot will start from the pedestal and move toward the first figurine (leftmost figurine)." I might as well take advantage of the fact that I can point my bot in the direction of the first figurine, right? If I were unable to see the first figurine, I'd probably need to add a sentence such as "The PushBot must start from the pedestal and FIND the first figurine," but luckily I won't have to do this. I can see the figurines the bot will move, and I'll use this to my advantage to get the bot off to a good start.

Take a look at the second sentence: "The bot must detect the figurine and not bump it or tip it into the back wall (pressure plate)." Although I didn't specify it, for the bot to detect the figurine without touching it will force me to use the Ultrasonic Sensor. That's fine. I didn't specify the Ultrasonic Sensor in the description, but just considering the statement has already helped me to define how one sensor will work with my PushBot.

My next sentence is "The bot must push the figurine onto the black pressure plate without tipping the figurine." Well, since I know I'm going to push the figurine, I know my bot will need to move forward and actually touch the figurine. Now, imagine a figurine that's about 1 foot tall and has a small round base. If you want to push it along the floor, what do you think is the best location on the figurine to push so it won't tip over? The answer is obvious—the base. Pushing from the bottom of the figurine will reduce the risk of it tipping . . . but not completely. It is still possible that pushing at the bottom will make the figurine tip toward the bot. Don't believe me? Try it.

Place an object like a bottled drink or something similar in size to the figurine (about 1 foot tall and 3 to 4 inches in diameter). Push quickly at the bottom of the object and see whether it doesn't tip back toward your hand.

What does this tell me about using my bot to push an object? It tells me that I'll need my bot to push slowly. It also tells me that I might want to consider some sort of cage or other construction that will surround the object and prevent it from tipping forward or backward. But again, I don't need to consider the details just yet—I'll wait until the Mindstorm section before I start considering any details for accomplishing these tasks.

The remaining items for the bot's description are simply variations—find a figurine and push it. I'll need to do this for the two additional figurines near the wall and then for the figurine at the foot of the ramp.

What I need to do next is put the steps my bot will perform into the ordered Task List.

The Task List

I've broken down the PushBot's tasks in Figure 18-2.

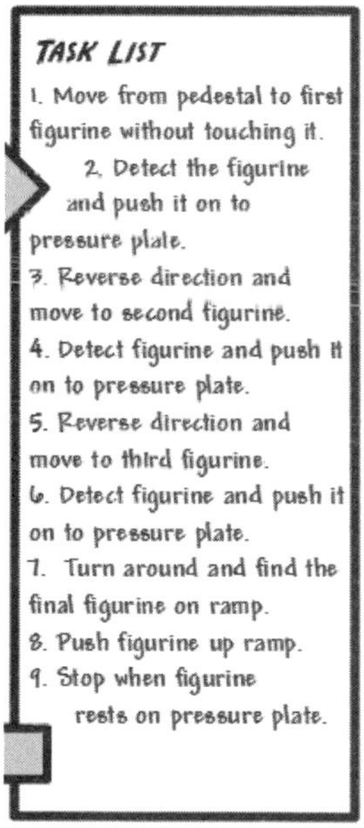

TASK LIST

1. Move from pedestal to first figurine without touching it.
   2. Detect the figurine and push it on to pressure plate.
3. Reverse direction and move to second figurine.
4. Detect figurine and push it on to pressure plate.
5. Reverse direction and move to third figurine.
6. Detect figurine and push it on to pressure plate.
7. Turn around and find the final figurine on ramp.
8. Push figurine up ramp.
9. Stop when figurine rests on pressure plate.

Figure 18-2. *The PushBot Task List has a lot of repetitive actions.*

I'm not going to cover every task in the list; as you can see, there's a lot of duplication of steps. This is a good thing, though. It should make programming the bot fairly straightforward when we get to Chapter 20. When you've got a bot that performs a lot of similar actions, you can look for ways to simplify the programming.

For now, though, let's look at a few of the tasks in more detail.

The first task is "Move from pedestal to first figurine without touching it." I know the distance from the edge of the pedestal to the first figurine. Just like I demonstrated in Chapter 16, I can program my bot later to move a specific distance forward before it begins trying to detect the figurine.

The next task, "Detect the figurine and push it onto pressure plate," is still a little vague. I mentioned earlier that the Ultrasonic Sensor would be useful to keep the bot from having to touch the figurine. But once the figurine is detected, I'll also need to somehow stop the bot from continuing to push the figurine beyond the pressure plate. I'm left with the Touch Sensor, the Light Sensor, and the Sound Sensor—any of these could possibly be configured to assist the bot with stopping properly. Right now, though, I don't need to decide which one. I'm going to put off making that decision until I begin to build.

The last task I want to cover is "Reverse direction and move to second figurine." This will involve some careful programming, but given that I know the measurements from one figurine to another, I should be able to program my bot to make the proper turns to put it in front of the two remaining figurines.

The other tasks in the Task List are, again, just variations of the same movements. After the bot has pushed the three figurines near the back wall, I'll have to get it placed properly so it can move up the ramp and push the final figurine.

With all the movements the bot will make, are there any obstacles to overcome? Let's consider those in the next section.

Limitations and Constraints

When I was considering the constraints my bot would be facing, I took another look at the burial chamber. But the bird's-eye view seen in Figure 17-2 doesn't tell the entire story. Take a look at Figure 18-3, and you'll see the constraints and limitations I believe my bot will encounter.

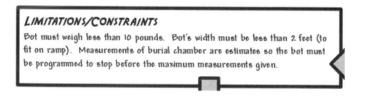

LIMITATIONS/CONSTRAINTS
Bot must weigh less than 10 pounds. Bot's width must be less than 2 feet (to fit on ramp). Measurements of burial chamber are estimates so the bot must be programmed to stop before the maximum measurements given.

Figure 18-3. *The constraints on the PushBot*

Because my bot will need to fit on the ramp, it will need to be less than 2 feet in width. While there doesn't appear to be a limitation on the bot's height, it will probably be safe to minimize the robot's height. Keeping the bot's components lower to the ground will reduce the risk of it tipping over when it moves up the ramp.

A very important observation from Figure 17-2 is that the measurements are not 100% exact. Take a good look at it, and you can see that many of the notes are estimates. It's difficult to measure the exact distance between the figurines, but by observation 2 feet appears to be a safe guess. I'll make sure my bot has plenty of room to turn and move so it doesn't accidentally bump one figurine while turning and/or pushing another figurine.

We know that the maximum weight of an adult spider monkey is approximately 10 pounds. None of my robots have exceeded that weight so far, but I'll need to be careful to keep this bot under that weight as well or the pressure plate on the floor will trigger the trap.

It might not seem like a lot of constraints, but every constraint puts more limitations on my bot's final design.

These will come into play when I begin the Mindstorm section of my Design Journal page in the next section.

Mindstorm

Now I can start putting down into words some of the images that are forming in my mind when I begin to think about the design of my PushBot. I've put my collection down on my Design Journal page, and you can see it in Figure 18-4.

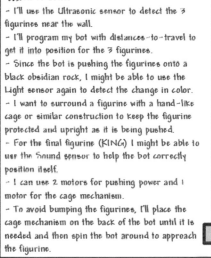

MINDSTORM

- I'll use the Ultrasonic sensor to detect the 3 figurines near the wall.
- I'll program my bot with distances-to-travel to get it into position for the 3 figurines.
- Since the bot is pushing the figurines onto a black obsidian rock, I might be able to use the Light sensor again to detect the change in color.
- I want to surround a figurine with a hand-like cage or similar construction to keep the figurine protected and upright as it is being pushed.
- For the final figurine (KING) I might be able to use the Sound sensor to help the bot correctly position itself.
- I can use 2 motors for pushing power and 1 motor for the cage mechanism.
- To avoid bumping the figurines, I'll place the cage mechanism on the back of the bot until it is needed and then spin the bot around to approach the figurine.

Figure 18-4. *The Mindstorm entries for the PushBot help us to start developing the final design.*

Let me go through some of the Mindstorm items and explain my reasoning behind them. The second one, "I'll program my bot with distances-to-travel to get it into position for the three figurines," will allow me to position the bot in front of each figurine without worrying about touching or tipping them over. As long as I program my bot to stop before the maximum distances shown in Figure 17-2, I should be safe. I'll have the bot back away from each figurine a good distance so it has plenty of room to safely turn and navigate to the next figurine.

The next Mindstorm item, "Since the bot is pushing the figurines onto a black obsidian rock, I might be able to use the Light Sensor again to detect the change in color," is a tried-and-true method I used with the SnapShotBot. The Light Sensor will be programmed to detect the change in color when the bot pushes a figurine onto the black pressure plate (black obsidian rock). This will require placing the Light Sensor on or very near the cage mechanism I intend to use so it detects the black pressure plate quickly.

Another `Mindstorm` item I find important is this one: "To avoid bumping the figurines, I'll place the cage mechanism on the back of the bot until it is needed and then spin the bot around to approach the figurine." What I'm envisioning is a grasping-type mechanism that will surround the figurine like a shell to protect it as it is being moved. This shell will need the ability to open and close; because of this, I think the shell will be fairly wide when it is fully open (but less than 2 feet—remember the constraints). I'm concerned that the cage mechanism might bump another figurine if the bot should turn left or right, so I'm going to try and place the mechanism on the back of the bot. When the Ultrasonic Sensor detects a figurine, the bot should stop (and possibly back up a little bit), spin around, and then approach the figurine slowly. And how will it know when to stop and close the cage on the figurine?

For the answer, consider the next `Mindstorm` item, "I might be able to use the Sound Sensor to help the bot correctly position itself near figurines." I used the Sound Sensor to tell the StringBot when to stop, so why can't I use it here? What I'll do is watch my bot approach the figurine (slowly). When it is in position, I'll yell "STOP!", and the bot will then close the cage and proceed with pushing the figurine forward until the Light Sensor is triggered by the black pressure plate.

I do this four times for four figurines, and the burial chamber is ready to be explored by the team. All that's left before I begin to build my PushBot is for me to consider the best placement for the sensors, motors, Brick, and cage mechanism. And this is where the final section of my Design Journal page comes into play.

Sketches

This is going to be a strange-shaped little robot. But, then again, all the bots have been a little unusual. (And admit it, that's the best thing about building robots—they're so unique!)

With this bot, it appears I'll be using EVERY sensor—Light, Ultrasonic, Sound, and Touch (for the **Start** button again—my favorite). I'll also be using all three motors and constructing some sort of cage mechanism.

I have some ideas on the placement of all these items, so take a look at Figure 18-5 and you'll see some of my initial thoughts on the PushBot's shape.

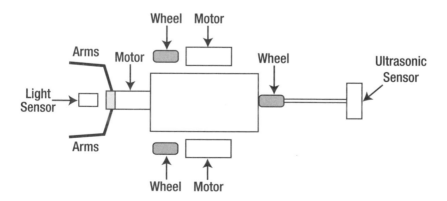

Figure 18-5. *Side view of the bot approaching the scroll*

I'll use basic shapes again to represent the motors, Brick, and sensors. I just want to start developing an idea so when I actually start building, I'll have a "target shape" to shoot for—my final design might not be exactly what is drawn, but the overall shape should be close.

And now that the sketches are done, it's time to start building and testing. In Chapter 19, I'll give you the steps to build my version of the PushBot.

CHAPTER 19

■■■

PushBot—Build It

It's time to build your final bot for the team. If you've chosen to build your own version of the PushBot, I'm confident it won't look like the one in Figure 19-1. My version of the PushBot has some unique features that I'll cover in this chapter, so if you'd like to build the version shown here, let's get started.

Figure 19-1. *The PushBot is a fun bot to experiment on.*

■**Note** If you've built a unique version of the PushBot, please e-mail me a picture. My e-mail address can be found in the Introduction near the beginning of the book.

Step by Step

I've divided the PushBot's building instructions into three sections. The first section covers the cage mechanism. The second section will show you how to assemble the wheels and neck/Ultrasonic Sensor assembly, and the third section gives you the steps to build the main body of the PushBot.

I'll continue to add comments for figures that might be a little tricky, as well as text and arrows to point out items that might be confusing.

First Section: Motor/Cage-Arm Mechanism

Figures 19-2 through 19-30 provide the steps for constructing the motor/cage-arm mechanism. Start with the motor and components you see in Figure 19-2.

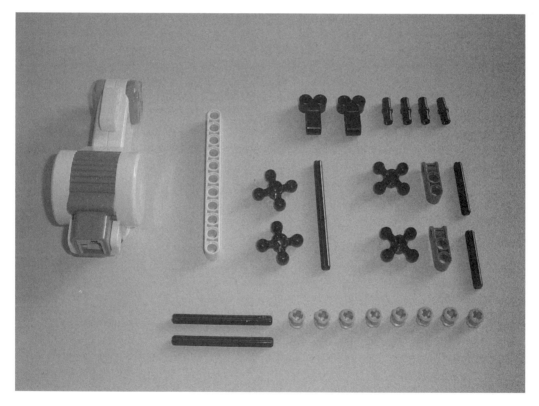

Figure 19-2. *These parts are used for the cage mechanism.*

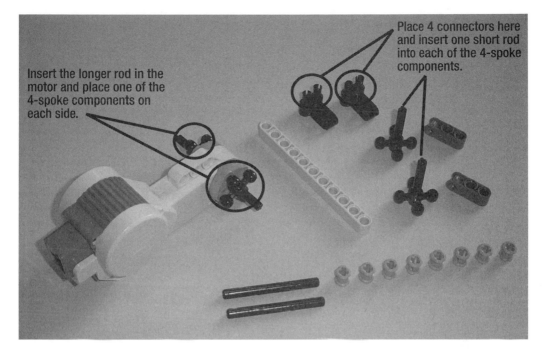

Figure 19-3. *Connect the components as described.*

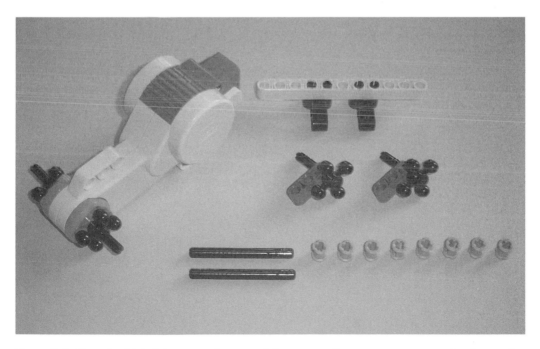

Figure 19-4. *Place the 11-hole beam as shown and the two small gray components on the short rods.*

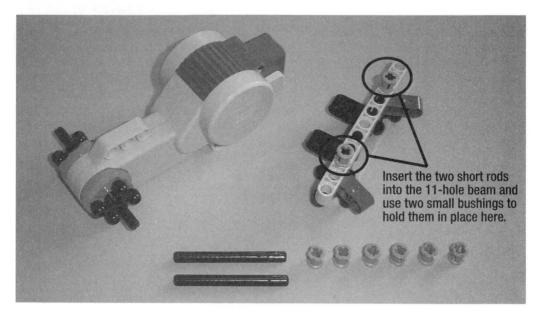

Figure 19-5. *Place the components as described here.*

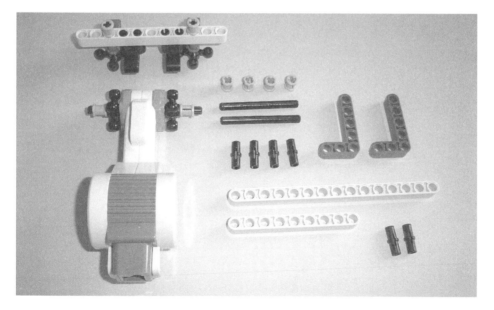

Figure 19-6. *Place two small bushings on the motor's axles.*

This next part can be tricky. You must insert the medium-length axles through the holes as shown in Figure 19-7 to secure the two pieces together. The two 4-spoke components on the motor are teeth that will spin the other two 4-spoke components on the cage-arm assembly. The easiest way to do this is to spin the two gray components labeled in Figure 19-7 away from the motor and then lower the cage-arm assembly.

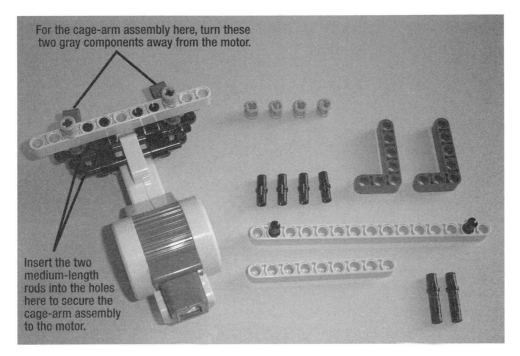

Figure 19-7. *Connect the cage-arm assembly to the motor as described here.*

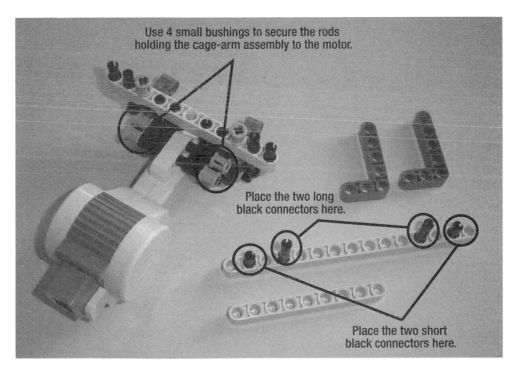

Figure 19-8. *Insert the black connectors into the 15-hole beam and use four small bushings to secure the rods that hold the cage-arm assembly to the motor.*

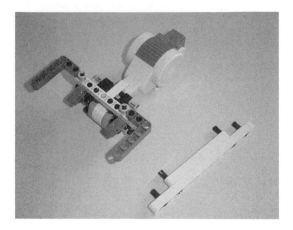

Figure 19-9. *Place the 9-hole beam on top of the 15-hole beam as shown.*

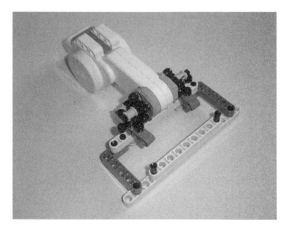

Figure 19-10. *Flip the motor/cage-arm assembly over and attach the 15-hole beam.*

Now, set this assembly aside for a moment. Figures 19-11 through 19-18 demonstrate how to build the actual cage.

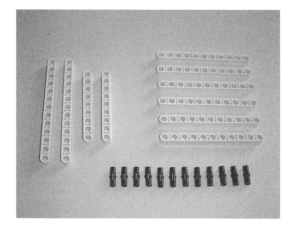

Figure 19-11. *Start with these components to build the cage's left and right side.*

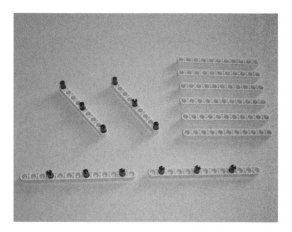

Figure 19-12. *Place the small black connectors in the beams as shown.*

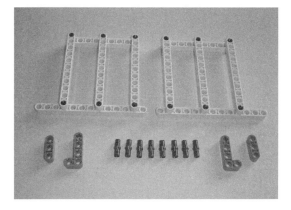

Figure 19-13. *Connect the six 11-hole beams as shown.*

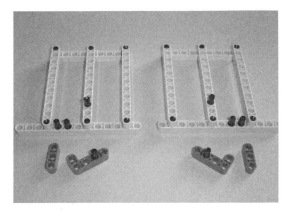

Figure 19-14. *Place the small black connectors in the components as shown.*

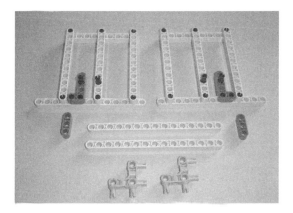

Figure 19-15. *Place the small L-shaped components as shown.*

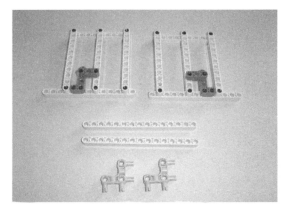

Figure 19-16. *Place the small 3-hole beams as shown.*

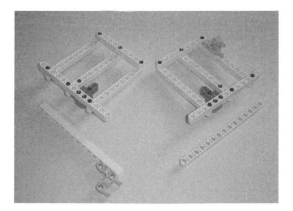

Figure 19-17. *Flip the cage assemblies over and connect the gray components as shown.*

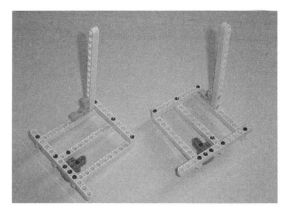

Figure 19-18. *The 15-hole beams attach to the cage assemblies.*

Figures 19-19 through 19-21 demonstrate how to build the vertical support bar (to support the figurines).

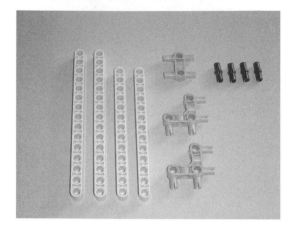

Figure 19-19. *Start with these components to build the vertical support bar.*

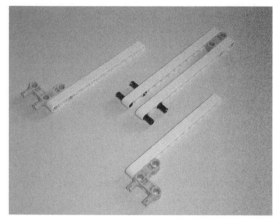

Figure 19-20. *Connect the components as shown.*

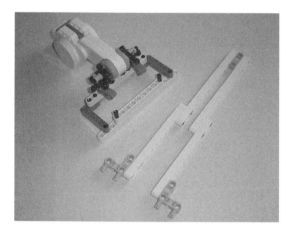

Figure 19-21. *The vertical support bar will connect to the motor/cage-arm assembly.*

Figure 19-22. *Insert the vertical support bar as shown.*

Next, you'll use four small black connectors to hold the left and right sides of the cage to the motor/cage-arm assembly (see Figure 19-23).

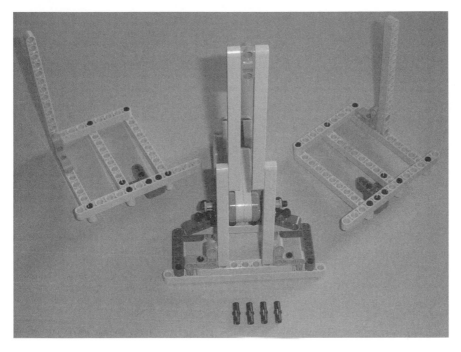

Figure 19-23. *The four small black connectors will help form the cage.*

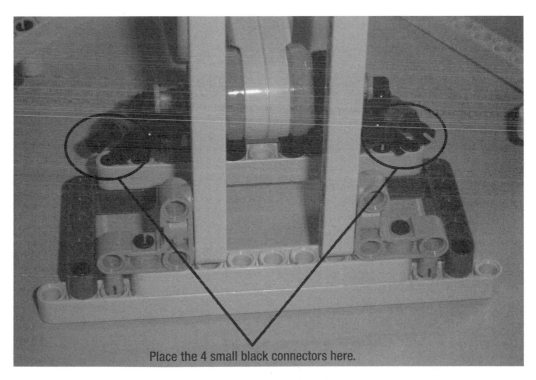

Place the 4 small black connectors here.

Figure 19-24. *Place the four small black connectors as described.*

Figure 19-25. *Connect the left and right sides of the cage as shown.*

Some final components will be added to the motor/cage-arm assembly in Figures 19-26 through 19-30.

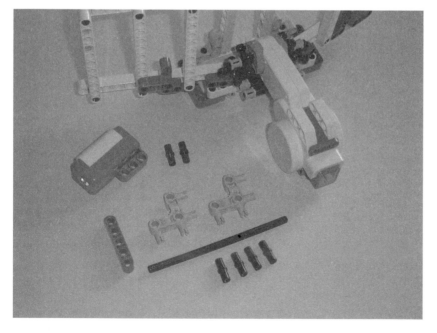

Figure 19-26. *These are the final pieces for the motor/cage-arm assembly.*

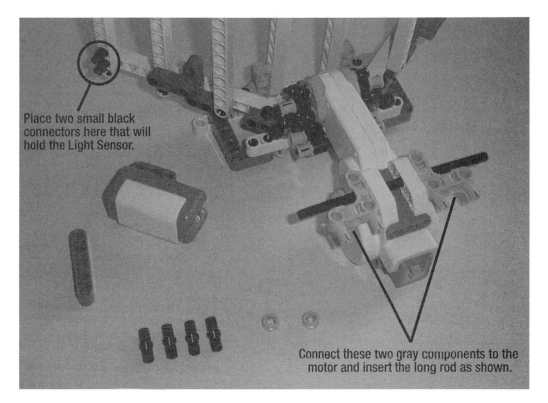

Place two small black connectors here that will hold the Light Sensor.

Connect these two gray components to the motor and insert the long rod as shown.

Figure 19-27. *Connect the components as described.*

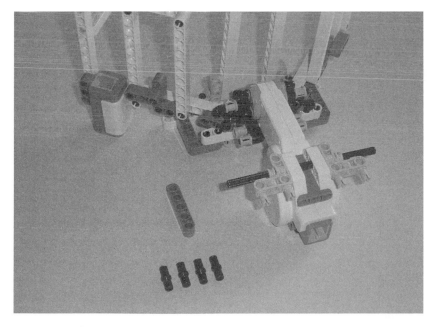

Figure 19-28. *Connect the Light Sensor and use two small bushings to secure the long rod.*

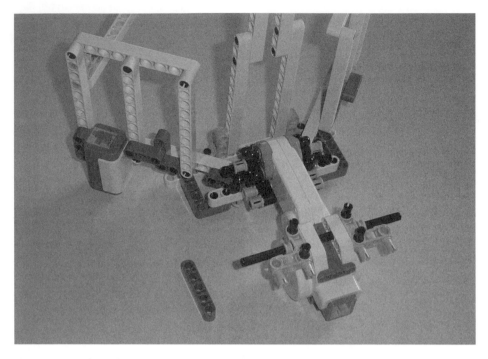

Figure 19-29. *Place the four small black connectors as shown.*

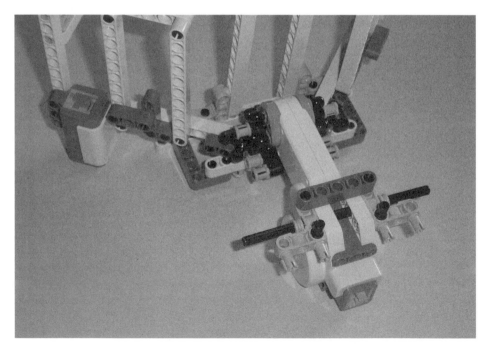

Figure 19-30. *Place the 5-hole beam as shown.*

Second Section: Wheels and Neck/Ultrasonic Sensor Assembly

Figures 19-31 through 19-42 demonstrate the construction of the wheels and the neck/Ultrasonic Sensor assembly.

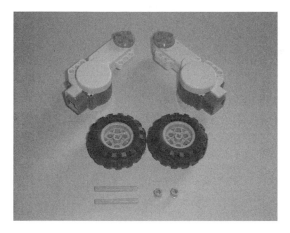

Figure 19-31. *Build the PushBot's wheels using these components.*

Figure 19-32. *Insert the rods into the motors and secure them with the small bushings.*

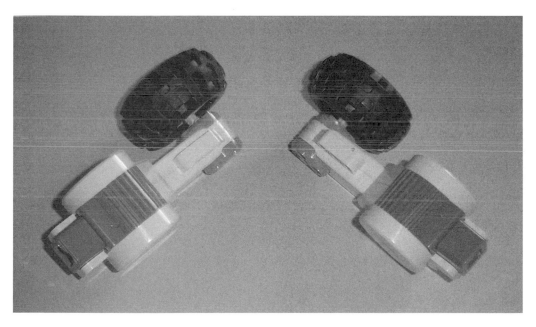

Figure 19-33 *Add a tire to each motor.*

Set the wheels aside for a moment and continue with the neck/Ultrasonic Sensor assembly.

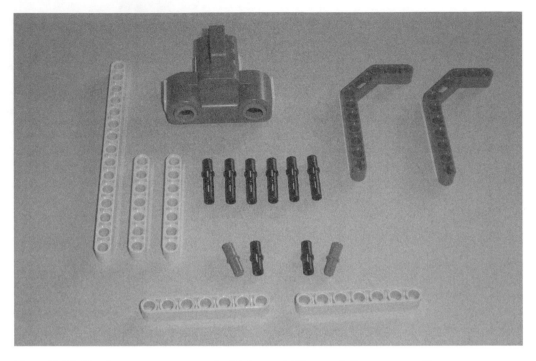

Figure 19-34. *Use these components to build the neck/Ultrasonic Sensor assembly.*

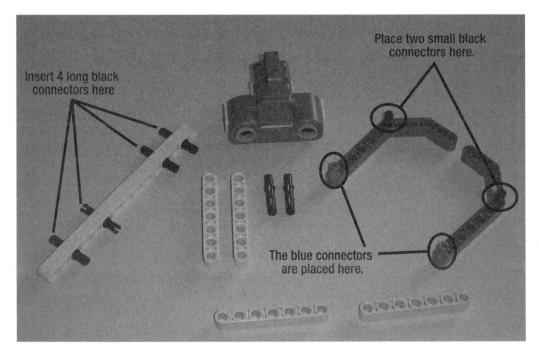

Figure 19-35. *Insert the black connectors and blue connectors as shown.*

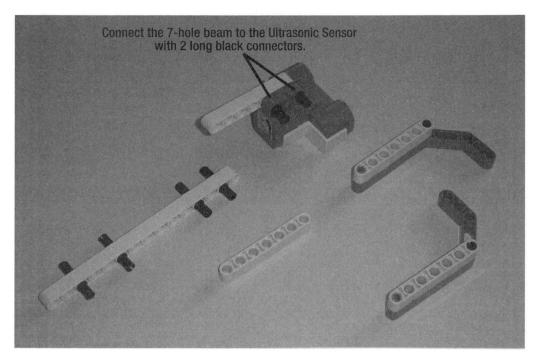

Figure 19-36. *Connect the two 7-hole beams as shown and connect one 7-hole beam to the Ultrasonic Sensor using two long black connectors.*

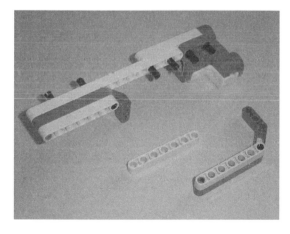

Figure 19-37. *Connect the components as shown here.*

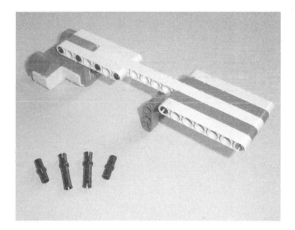

Figure 19-38. *Flip the neck assembly around and connect the other components.*

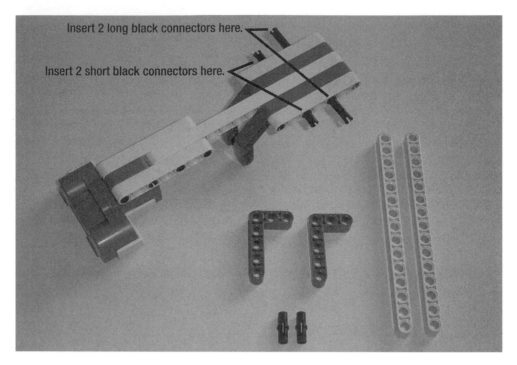

Figure 19-39. *Insert the black connectors as described.*

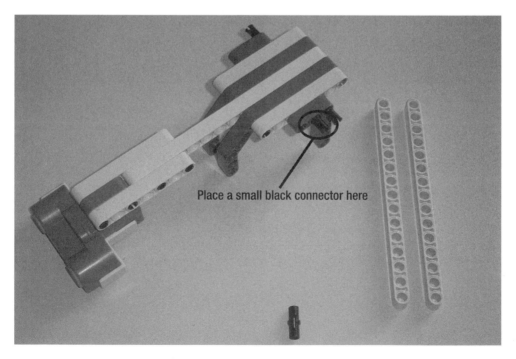

Figure 19-40. *Connect the L-shaped beams as shown and place one of the small black connectors as described.*

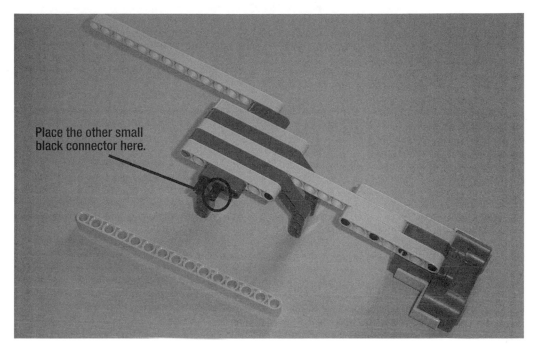

Place the other small black connector here.

Figure 19-41. *Spin the neck assembly around and place the other small black connector as described.*

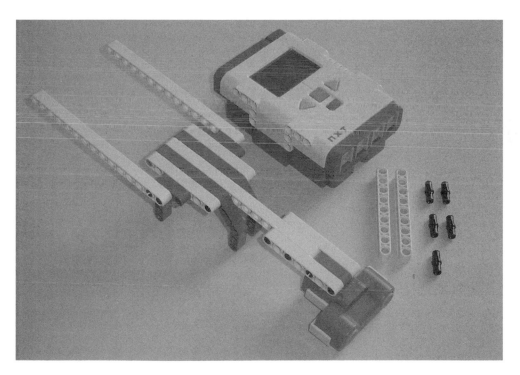

Figure 19-42. *Connect the 15-hole beam to the neck assembly and gather the other components shown.*

Third Section: Main Body

The PushBot is almost completed. Figures 19-43 through 19-66 demonstrate the steps needed to assemble the final bot.

Start with the neck/Ultrasonic Sensor assembly and Brick as shown in Figure 19-43. In Figure 19-43, the Brick's "top" (where the USB port is located) is to the right.

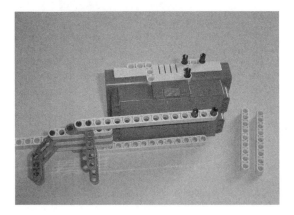

Figure 19-43. *Place the five small black connectors as shown.*

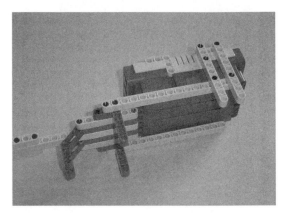

Figure 19-44. *Connect the two 9-hole beams as shown.*

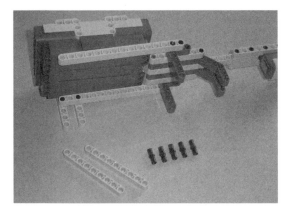

Figure 19-45. *Flip the Brick and neck/Ultrasonic Sensor assembly over.*

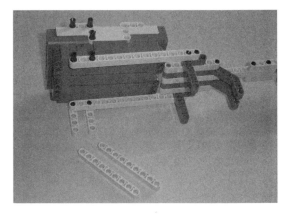

Figure 19-46. *Place the five small black connectors as shown.*

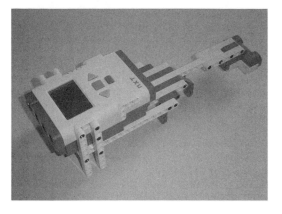

Figure 19-47. *Connect the two 9-hole beams as shown.*

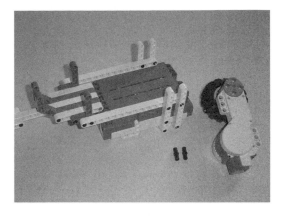

Figure 19-48. *Flip the Brick/neck assembly over.*

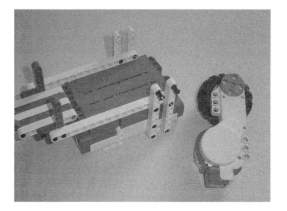

Figure 19-49. *Insert the two small black connectors in the 9-hole beams as shown.*

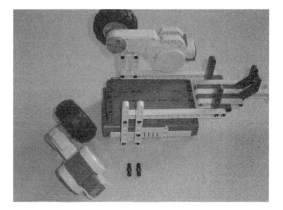

Figure 19-50. *Connect one wheel assembly as shown and then flip the Brick/neck assembly around.*

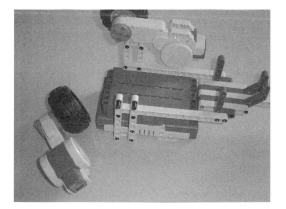

Figure 19-51. *Insert the two small black connectors in the 9-hole beams as shown.*

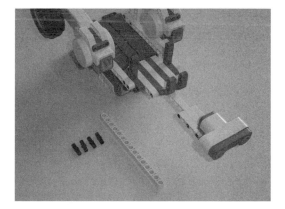

Figure 19-52. *Connect the remaining wheel assembly to the Brick/neck assembly.*

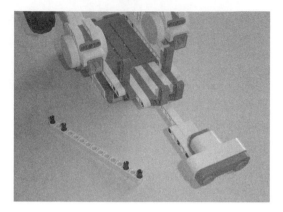

Figure 19-53. *Place the four small black connectors in the 15-hole beam.*

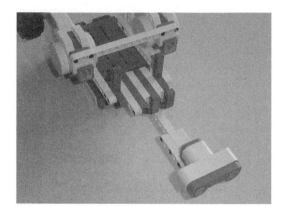

Figure 19-54. *Connect the 15-hole beam to the two motors for reinforcement.*

Figure 19-55. *Flip the Brick/neck assembly over and place a plastic ball as shown.*

Figure 19-56. *Gather the motor/cage-arm assembly and the Brick/neck assembly.*

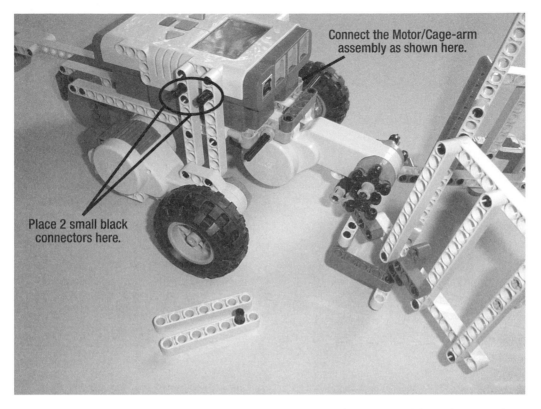

Figure 19-57. *Connect the motor/cage-arm assembly to the Brick/neck assembly as shown and place the small black connectors as described.*

Figure 19-58. *Place the 7-hole beam (with small black connector) as shown.*

Figure 19-59. *Place the 7-hole beam as shown.*

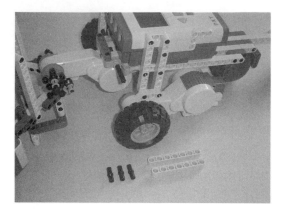

Figure 19-60. *Flip the bot around.*

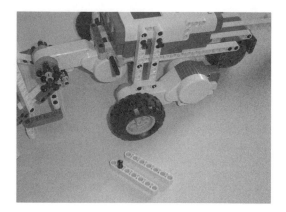

Figure 19-61. *Place the black connectors as shown.*

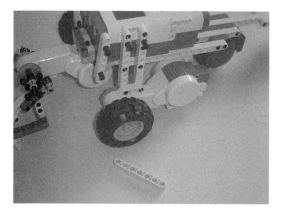

Figure 19-62. *Place the 7-hole beam (with small black connector) as shown.*

Figure 19-63. *Place the 7-hole beam as shown.*

Figure 19-64. *Gather the Sound Sensor and the Touch Sensor.*

Figure 19-65. *Place the two gray components as shown.*

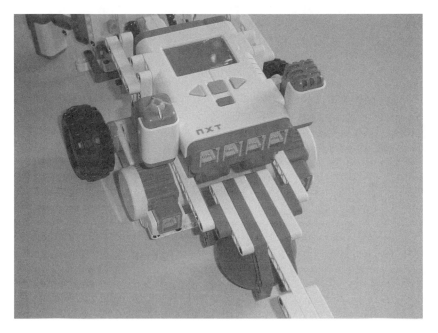

Figure 19-66. *Connect the Sound Sensor and Touch Sensor*

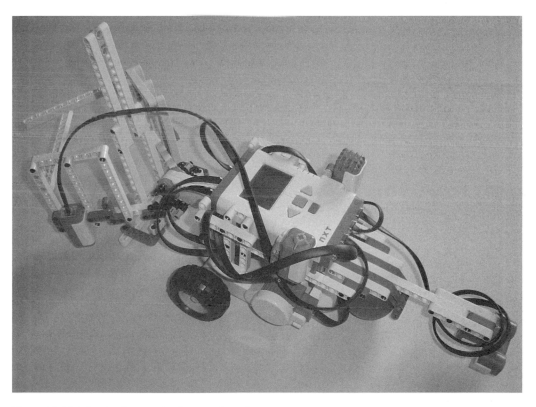

Figure 19-67. *The PushBot, wired up and ready to go*

In Chapter 20, I'll show you how I intend to program this PushBot to complete its tasks. Wire up this PushBot (or your own version) and continue reading. You're almost ready to send the bot into the burial chamber . . .

■ ■ ■

PushBot—Program It

The PushBot has a LOT to do! Because of this, I want to be absolutely certain that my program works, and I'll be testing it often. To make it easier on myself, I'm going to break down the program into three sections. The first section will cover getting the bot to the proper location in front of the first figurine. The second section will cover the programming blocks used to put the first three figurines into their proper locations. And the final section will be devoted to pushing the last figurine up the ramp and onto the Mayan sarcophagus.

If you've built your own version of the PushBot, your program will most likely not match mine exactly. It really depends on how you've built your bot to complete the challenge.

What I'll be doing in the next three sections is walking you through the programming of this last bot so the team can finally enter King Ixtua's burial chamber and see what it contains. So, without any further delay, let's get this bot programmed and ready to go.

Getting the PushBot into Position

In the Lego Mindstorms NXT software, I'll type **PushBot** in the blank text field labeled **Start New Program** and then click **Go** (see Figure 20-1).

Figure 20-1. *The beginning of the program for the PushBot*

■**Note** If the RoboCenter area is visible on the far right of your screen, click the small red X in the upper-right corner of the software, and it will free up more visible workspace on your screen.

Once again, I am using the Touch Sensor as a **Start** button for the PushBot. You can choose to use one of the Brick's buttons, but I like the simplicity of running the program and having it wait until I press the Touch Sensor. I've placed the Touch Sensor in an easy-to-reach place on top of the Brick.

The first block I've dropped in my program is a LOOP block (see Figure 20-2) that will wait for the Touch Sensor to trigger.

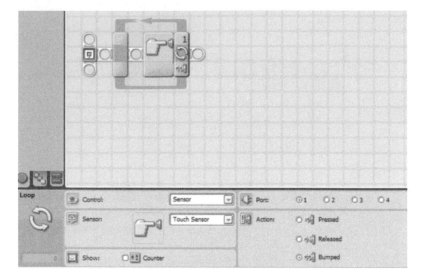

Figure 20-2. *This LOOP block will break when the Touch Sensor is triggered.*

The first task my bot must perform is "Move from pedestal to first figurine without touching it." I'm going to take advantage of the fact that I can place my PushBot initially on the floor and point it directly at the first figurine. After that, I have a couple of different methods available for getting the bot into position.

I know roughly the distance between the pedestal and the first figurine, so as long as I program the bot to stop before it touches the figurine, I should be safe. If you look back to Figure 17-2, you see that the estimated distance is 7 feet. I have measured my PushBot and it is just a little over 18 inches long (1.5 feet). Take a look at Figure 20-3. If I place my bot as shown and point it toward the first figurine, it will need to move forward 5.5 feet and then stop to avoid touching the figurine. So, for the first method, I could program a MOVE block with the correct number of rotations or degrees to move it 5.5 feet.

But I want to use the second method that relies on the Ultrasonic Sensor. Why do I want to do this? Well, if my measurements are off by just an inch or two, I might accidentally bump one of the figurines. I've noticed that when the batteries get low in my bot, sometimes strange things can happen with the motors. What I'd prefer is to use the Ultrasonic Sensor to detect the figurine and stop the bot a safe distance away. And to accomplish this, I'll simply program my bot to move slowly toward the figurine, constantly checking to see whether it detects an obstacle (figurine).

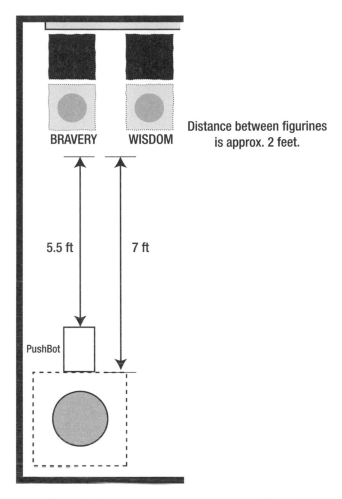

Figure 20-3. *The PushBot's initial movement will be 5.5 feet forward.*

In Figure 20-4, you'll see that I've dropped in a LOOP block that is configured to break when the Ultrasonic Sensor is triggered. Since I haven't tested yet, I'll set the Ultrasonic Sensor to be triggered when it detects an obstacle less than 12 inches away. Remember, this might change once I test the sensitivity of the Ultrasonic Sensor.

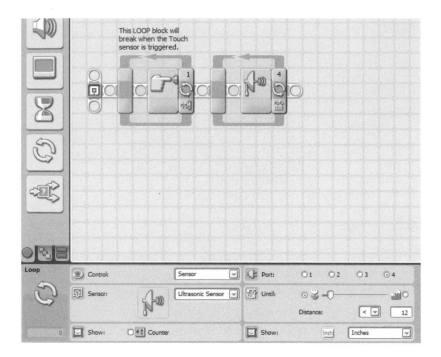

Figure 20-4. *This LOOP block will break when the Ultrasonic Sensor is triggered.*

Before I perform an initial test of my PushBot, I'll place a MOVE block inside the LOOP and tell it to spin motors B and C. I can choose to set the **Duration** of the motors either to Unlimited or for a specific number of degrees or rotations. I will test both methods to determine which is the safest way to approach the figurine. You can see the MOVE block in Figure 20-5, and this block is initially configured to spin for one rotation. I am doing this because I want the bot to move forward, the Ultrasonic Sensor to test for distance, and then the bot to move forward one rotation again; this will continue until the Ultrasonic Sensor is triggered. (I'll also test it with the motors spinning constantly until the Ultrasonic Sensor is triggered.)

I place a bottle of water about 9 feet away from the PushBot. I push the Touch Sensor (**Start** button) and off it goes. Results? When I configure the MOVE block **Duration** to Unlimited, the bot stops much nearer to the bottle than when I configure it for a **Duration** of one rotation. I also am forced to increase the sensitivity of the Ultrasonic Sensor to 15 inches or less. After testing again, I find these settings are acceptable, and the PushBot is about 12 to 15 inches from the bottle.

Now that the bottle is found, I need to configure the PushBot to push the bottle. My Push-Bot design requires the bot to spin around and move toward the bottle until I tell it to stop. It will then close the cage mechanism I designed and hold the bottle as the bot pushes it forward. The bot will stop when the Light Sensor is triggered by the black pressure plate (obsidian rock). Let's take all of this one step at a time.

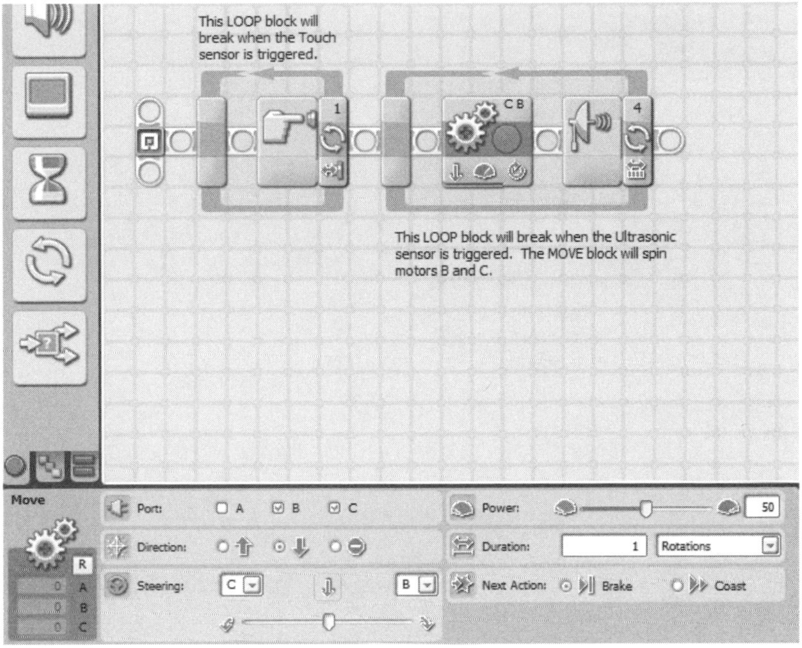

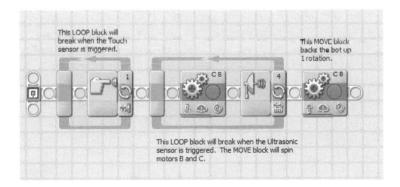

Figure 20-5. *A MOVE block for the PushBot*

First, I need the bot to turn 180 degrees so the cage is facing the bottle. How do I do this? Simple. I first back the bot up to give it room to turn—one rotation of motors B and C should do it. I use a MOVE block to do this, as shown in Figure 20-6.

Figure 20-6. *The PushBot will first back up about 6 inches.*

Next, I will turn ONLY motor B so the bot turns 90 degrees to the left. I will follow this with a MOVE block that turns ONLY motor C so the bot turns 90 degrees to the right. At this point, the PushBot will be facing the reverse direction. This is demonstrated in Figure 20-7.

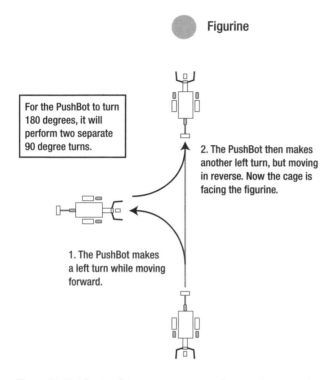

For the PushBot to turn 180 degrees, it will perform two separate 90 degree turns.

2. The PushBot then makes another left turn, but moving in reverse. Now the cage is facing the figurine.

1. The PushBot makes a left turn while moving forward.

Figure 20-7. *The PushBot can turn 180 degrees by a combination of MOVE blocks.*

I used the method described in Chapter 4 for obtaining the correct number of degrees for motors B and C to turn. For my PushBot, the right turn (motor B) made in Figure 20-7 requires 508 degrees. For the left turn (motor C), the motor is configured for –513 degrees (the negative sign simply tells me to configure motor C for 513 degrees but to also change the spin direction). You cannot use a negative number as a duration, so you must enter the same value (513) but select the opposite spin direction. Figure 20-8 shows the MOVE block for the right turn.

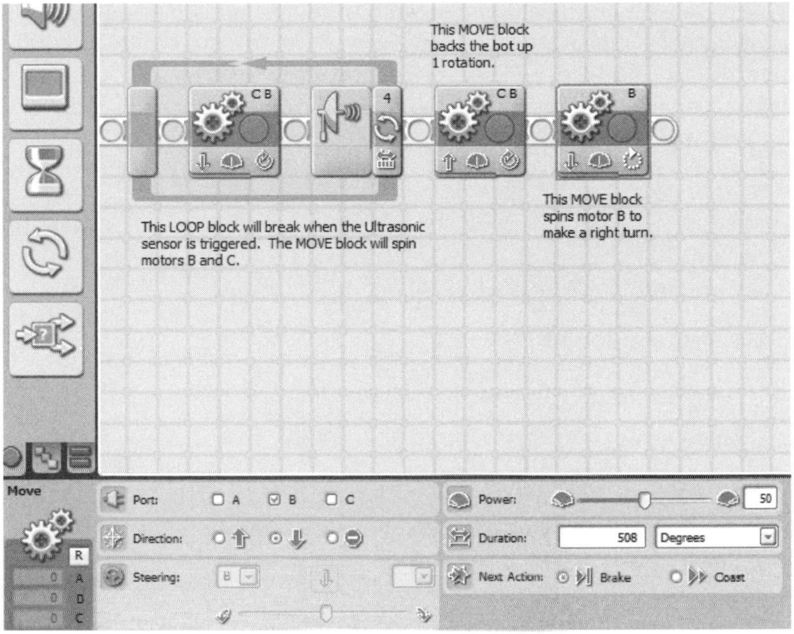

Figure 20-8. *This MOVE block allows the PushBot to make a right turn.*

I follow this with another MOVE block for the left turn in Figure 20-9.

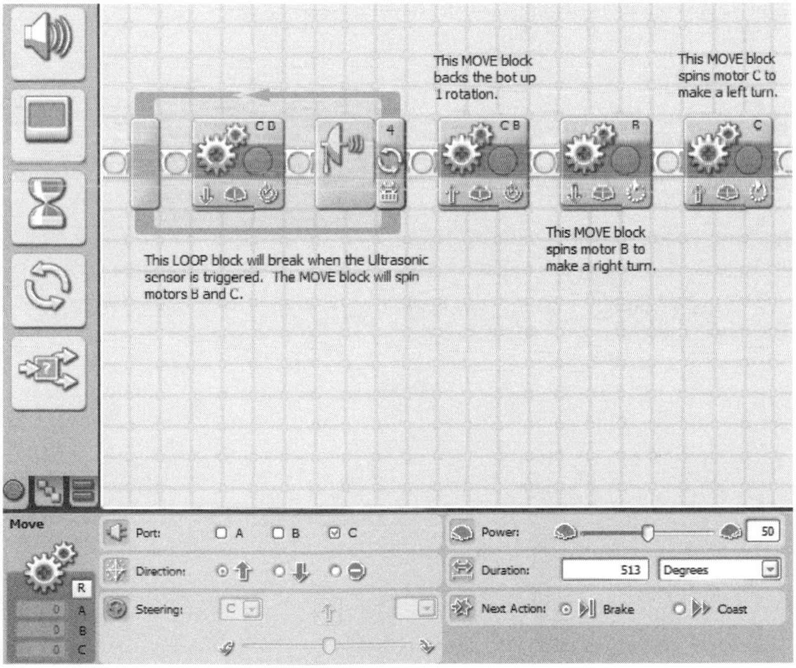

Figure 20-9. *And this MOVE block allows the PushBot to turn left.*

I save and upload the program to my PushBot for testing. After testing, the PushBot is lined up properly with the bottle.

Now, let's pause here for just a minute and look at where my PushBot is located. Currently, the bot has spun around and is facing the first figurine with the cage in the opened position. What happens next? Let me break it down in a small list:

1. Approach figurine 1.

2. Close the cage around figurine 1.

3. Push figurine 1 forward onto pressure plate and stop.

4. Open cage and reverse to starting position.

5. Turn right, move forward a short distance, and then turn left.

6. PushBot is in front of figurine 2.

Do you see the pattern? It will do the exact same steps for figurine 2 and then end up facing figurine 3. It will perform the steps for figurine 3 with the only difference being that after it opens the cage (step 4) and reverses direction, it will need to be directed to the figurine near the ramp.

Because of these repeated steps, I'm going to use a LOOP block that will allow me to perform the preceding steps three times, once for each of the first three figurines.

Positioning Three Figurines

Before my bot locates and begins pushing the final figurine up the ramp, I'll need it to be stopped in front of figurine 3. Knowing this information will help me to determine what I should place inside the LOOP block I'm going to add for the actions needed to push figurines 1, 2, and 3 into position.

But first, I'll drop in the LOOP block (see Figure 20-10) and configure it to execute any blocks placed inside it one time. (I'll later change this to three times after testing so it will perform the same actions for three bottles.)

Now, the first thing I need the PushBot to do is move slowly toward the figurine and stop when the Sound Sensor detects my voice. I'll use another LOOP block and configure it to break when the Sound Sensor is triggered (see Figure 20-11). During testing I'll fine-tune the sensitivity of the Sound Sensor, but for now I'm setting it to detect any sound greater than 50.

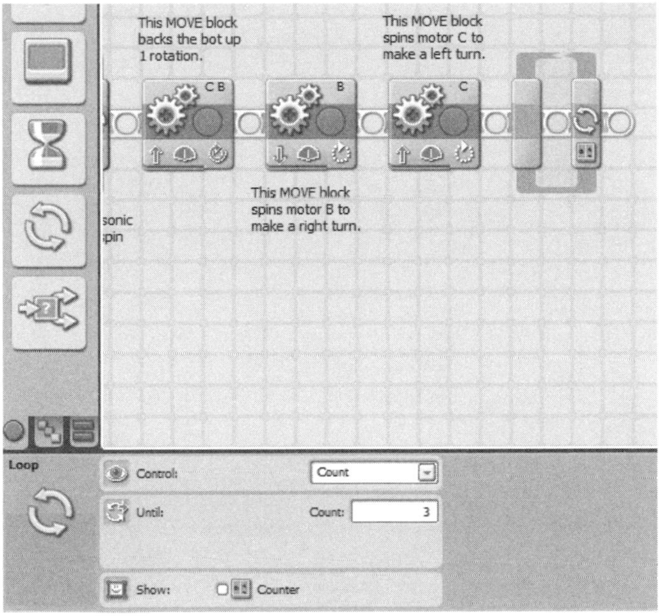

Figure 20-10. *The LOOP block for positioning the first three figurines*

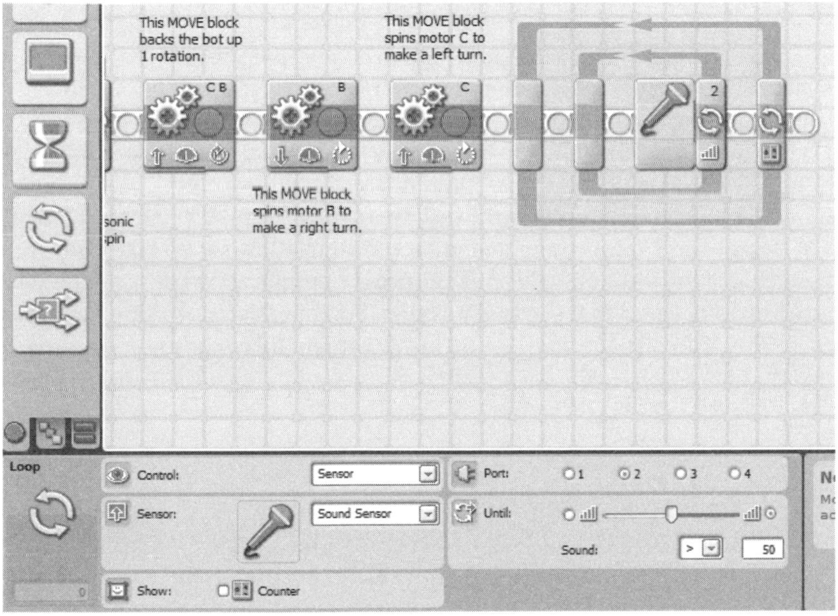

Figure 20-11. *This inner LOOP block will break when the Sound Sensor is triggered.*

I'll add in a MOVE block that will slowly move the bot toward the bottle. Figure 20-12 shows that I've configured it to spin motors B and C .25 rotation (a quarter rotation).

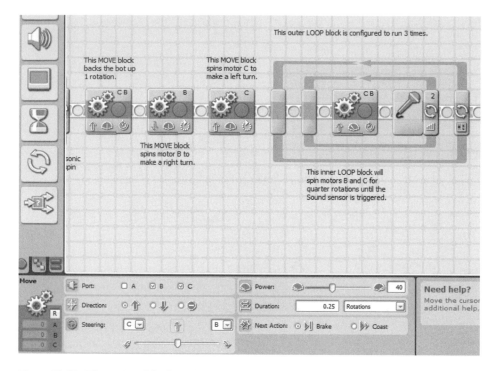

This outer LOOP block is configured to run 3 times.

This MOVE block backs the bot up 1 rotation.

This MOVE block spins motor C to make a left turn.

This MOVE block spins motor B to make a right turn.

This inner LOOP block will spin motors B and C for quarter rotations until the Sound sensor is triggered.

Figure 20-12. *The MOVE block will spin motors B and C in quarter rotations.*

Now it's time to upload the program and test it. I had to change the sensitivity of the Sound Sensor to a value of 70; normal noises around my house were setting off the sensor.

The bot did a perfect turn and approached the bottle slowly until the Sound Sensor triggered. Now I want the cage to close and hold the bottle. This is done with a MOVE block as shown in Figure 20-13.

I configured the MOVE block to spin motor A –65 degrees. In Figure 20-13, I enter a value of **65** for the number of **Degrees** and I also configure motor A to spin in reverse (to take into account the negative value of the rotation). This was the proper number of degrees required to move the cage from an open position to the closed position. I obtain this value using the **View** option on the Brick; refer to Chapter 4 for a review on how to obtain this reading.

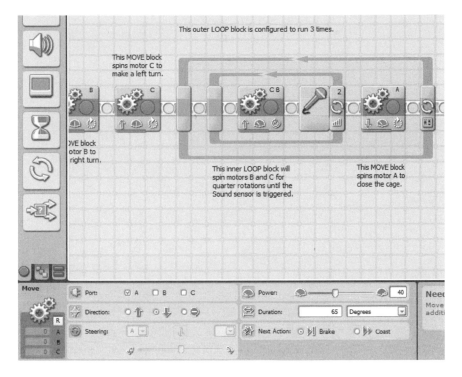

Figure 20-13. *The MOVE block stops motor A to save battery power.*

After the cage closes, I've added in another MOVE block that turns off the power to motor A (see Figure 20-14), saving battery power.

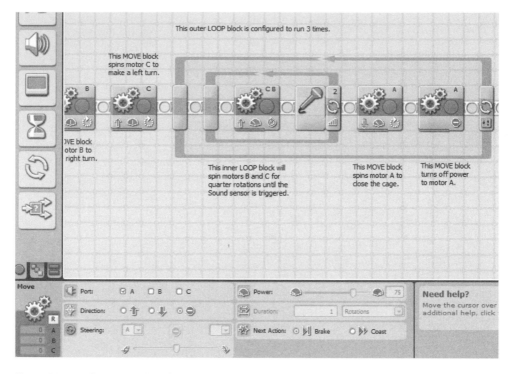

Figure 20-14. *This MOVE block turns off power to motor A.*

Now that the cage is closed, I need the bot to slowly begin pushing the figurine (bottle) until it detects the black obsidian rock floor. For testing, I've taped a black square of paper to the floor behind the bottle. I'll use a LOOP block that will break when the Light Sensor is triggered (see Figure 20-15). Once again, I test the Light Sensor on the black paper to obtain the correct setting (using the instructions in Chapter 4 to use the **View** option on the Brick). The black paper gives me a value of 3; the floor gives me a value of 12. I will set the Light Sensor to trigger if the value drops below 5. Your values may differ, so testing is absolutely required.

I need to drop in a MOVE block to perform the pushing action (see Figure 20-16). I'll have it push forward 3.5 inches at a time (half a rotation).

■Note Notice that motors B and C are frequently changing spin direction. In some instances you might think your robot will move forward, but it moves backward. When I had the PushBot spin around 180 degrees, everything changed! Now when I want motors B and C to spin forward, I have to configure their direction differently. It can get confusing, but that's why we test.

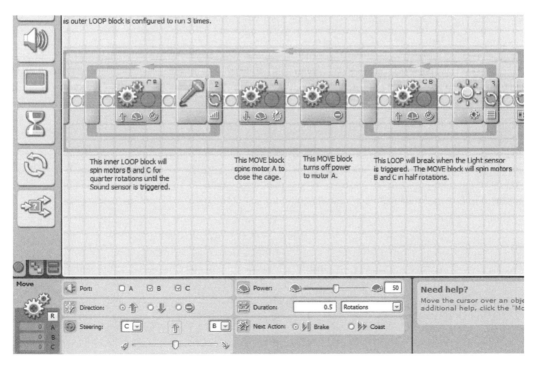

is outer LOOP block is configured to run 3 times.

This inner LOOP block will spin motors B and C for quarter rotations until the Sound sensor is triggered.

This MOVE block spins motor A to close the cage.

This MOVE block turns off power to motor A.

Loop

Control: Sensor

Sensor: Light Sensor

Show: Counter

Port: ○1 ○2 ◉3 ○4

Until:

Light: < ▼   5

Function: ☑ Generate light

Loop Block
Use this block to repeat condition that will end the repetitions, a logic signal loop to go on forever.

Figure 20-15. *The LOOP block will break when the Light Sensor is triggered.*

is outer LOOP block is configured to run 3 times.

This inner LOOP block will spin motors B and C for quarter rotations until the Sound sensor is triggered.

This MOVE block spins motor A to close the cage.

This MOVE block turns off power to motor A.

This LOOP will break when the Light sensor is triggered. The MOVE block will spin motors B and C in half rotations.

Move

Port: ○ A ☑ B ☑ C

Direction: ◉ ↑ ○ ↓ ○ ○

Steering: C ▼   B ▼

Power: 50

Duration: 0.5   Rotations ▼

Next Action: ◉ ▶| Brake   ○ ▶▶ Coast

Need help?
Move the cursor over an obje additional help, click the "Mo

Figure 20-16. *The MOVE block pushes the figurine forward in half rotations.*

Now it's time to upload and test. If everything works as planned, my bot should approach the bottle, stop when the bottle is detected, back up a bit and then spin around, approach the bottle until I tell it to stop, close the cage, and then push the bottle forward until the Light Sensor is triggered.

Does it work? Not perfectly. That's the great thing about testing frequently. I don't reach the end of my program only to find that I made a mistake very early in the program. The problem is easy to fix. Motor A spins 65 degrees, but sometimes it doesn't spin all the way closed. The motor stalls and the program doesn't continue until motor A finishes its movement and closes the cage completely. My fix is to simply have motor A spin for 1 second. I'll leave the MOVE block in that stops motor A, just in case I later decide to switch back to closing it a specified number of degrees or rotations. Other than that, the PushBot works well.

It pushes the bottle onto the black paper (pressure plate) and stops. Now I just need to get it to open the cage, back up a reasonable distance, and perform a couple of movements to put it in front of figurine 2.

First, I'll open the cage by placing a MOVE block (see Figure 20-17).

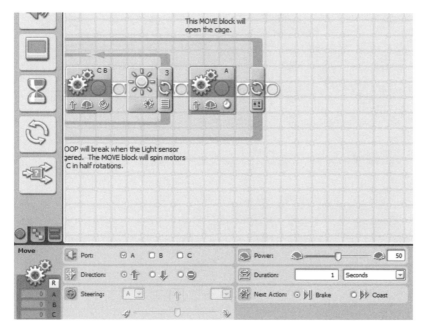

Figure 20-17. *This MOVE block opens the cage.*

Next, I'll get the PushBot to reverse direction a reasonable distance. Referring back to Figure 17-2, I think a safe distance for the bot to pull back would be about 3 feet. I'll test it and tweak that value if I find the bot isn't pulling back far enough. Figure 20-18 shows the MOVE block I've added. (To configure the distance, I've converted 3 feet to 36 inches. I divide that by 7 inches—the circumference of the tires—and I get a value of approximately 5 rotations.)

The last few items I need to take care of will get the PushBot in front of the next figurine. The bot needs to turn right, move forward a small distance (about 2 feet), and then turn left. This will position it facing the next figurine.

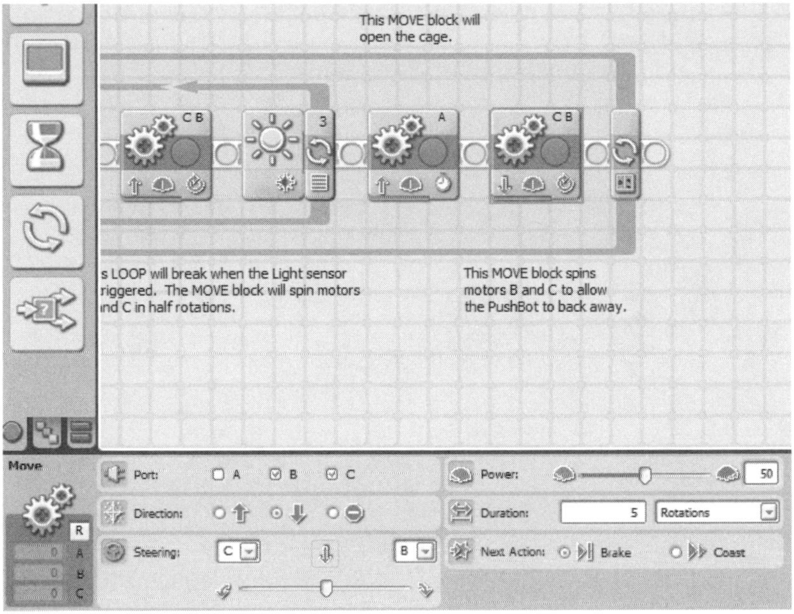

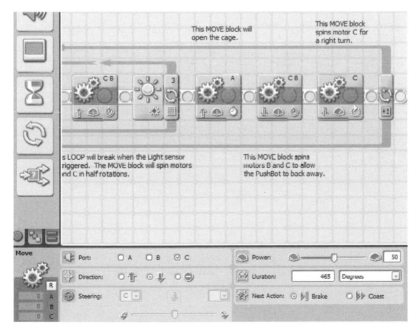

Figure 20-18. *This MOVE block will allow the PushBot to move away from the figurine.*

First, I'll have the bot make a right turn (see Figure 20-19).

Figure 20-19. *This MOVE block allows the PushBot to turn right.*

Next, Figure 20-20 shows the MOVE block needed so the PushBot moves forward 2 feet. Keep in mind that this is one of those configurations that might need to be changed; you won't know until you test your bot with three figurines properly placed.

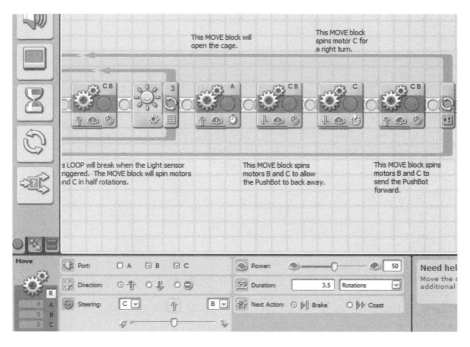

Figure 20-20. *This MOVE block sends the PushBot forward approximately 2 feet.*

And, finally, I need the bot to spin to the left (see Figure 20-21).

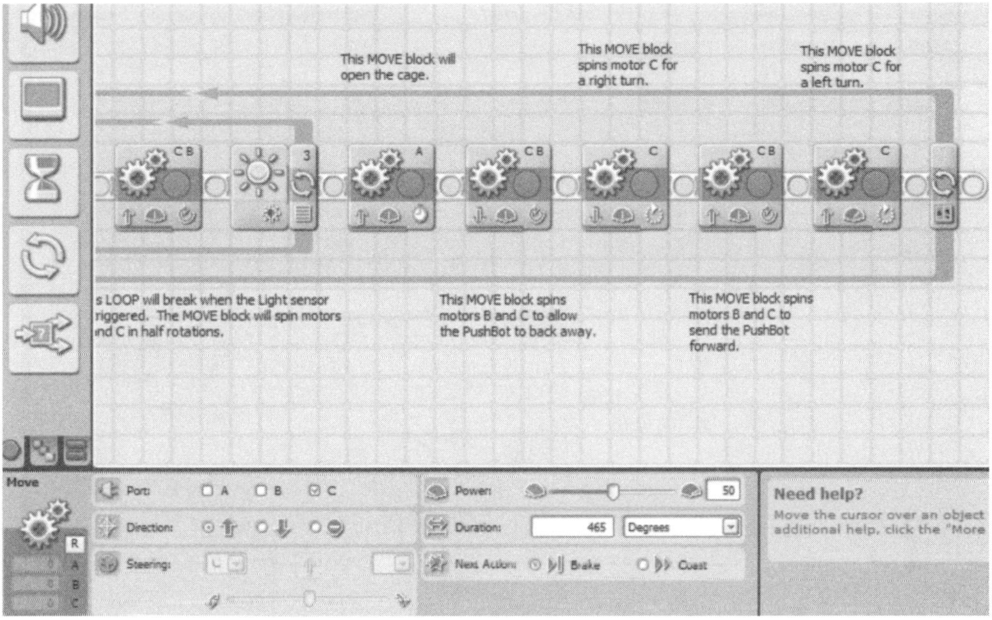

Figure 20-21. *This MOVE block allows the PushBot to turn left.*

Time to test; let me describe my testing environment. I place three water bottles 4 feet from a wall in my living room. Each water bottle is 2 feet apart as well. I then place three squares of black paper about 4 inches behind each bottle (the paper is taped down so it can't be pushed along with the bottle). I then place my PushBot about 9 feet away from the first bottle, pointing directly at the bottle with the Ultrasonic Sensor and with the cage fully open. And here's what happens.

I have success on the first figurine, but overshoot the second figurine by about 6 inches. I fix this by reducing the number of durations motors B and C spin (in Figure 20-20) from 5 to 4. I also have a problem with the cage closing properly but opening too wide, and the arms rub the tires. I reduce the time for the cage to open from 1 second to .5 seconds (half a second). On the second test, I have perfect success—all three figurines are located and pushed to their proper locations without tipping over.

At this point, I'd like to remind you that your settings will probably be different. Motors and sensors all have varying sensitivity, so testing is an absolute requirement at this point. Don't stress about this part of building robots; this is how you improve your skills and gain insight into the way robots work in different environments.

Figure 20-22 shows the approximate location of the PushBot at this point. I've got to get it moving so it can push the fourth figurine up the ramp and onto the sarcophagus.

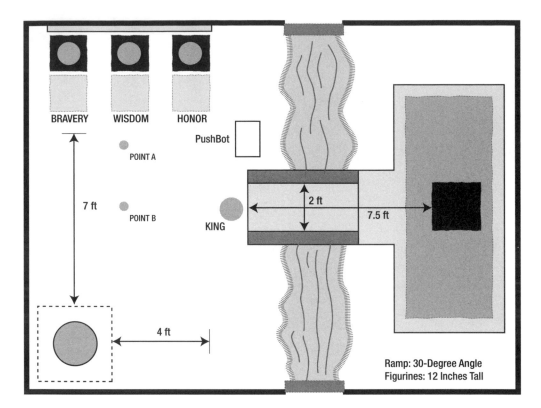

Figure 20-22. *The PushBot should be located here.*

The Final Figurine

Now to what I consider the easy part. Okay, maybe not easy, but definitely easier than trying to push three figurines onto pressure plates. I have some rough distances to work with from Figure 20-22, so I'll use these measurements, along with the Sound Sensor, to help me position the PushBot for its final task.

First, I've got to reorient the bot. Since it is pointing away from the fourth figurine, I'm first going to have the bot spin to the right and then move to Point A in Figure 20-22. The cage will be pointing in the direction of the sarcophagus when it reaches Point A. I'll drop a MOVE block in for the turn to the right (see Figure 20-23).

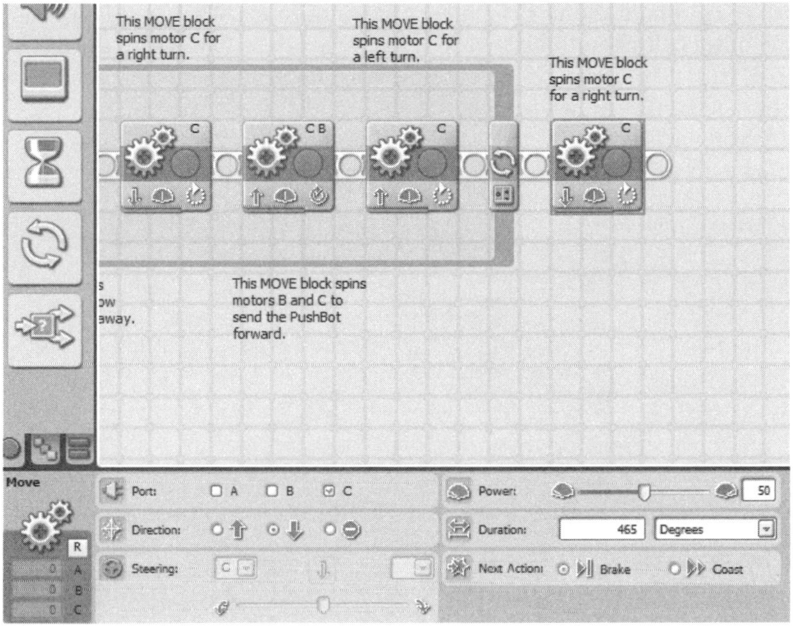

Figure 20-23. *This MOVE block will spin the bot to the right in a clockwise direction.*

Next I'll add another MOVE block that will force the bot to move to Point A—approximately 4 feet (see Figure 20-24).

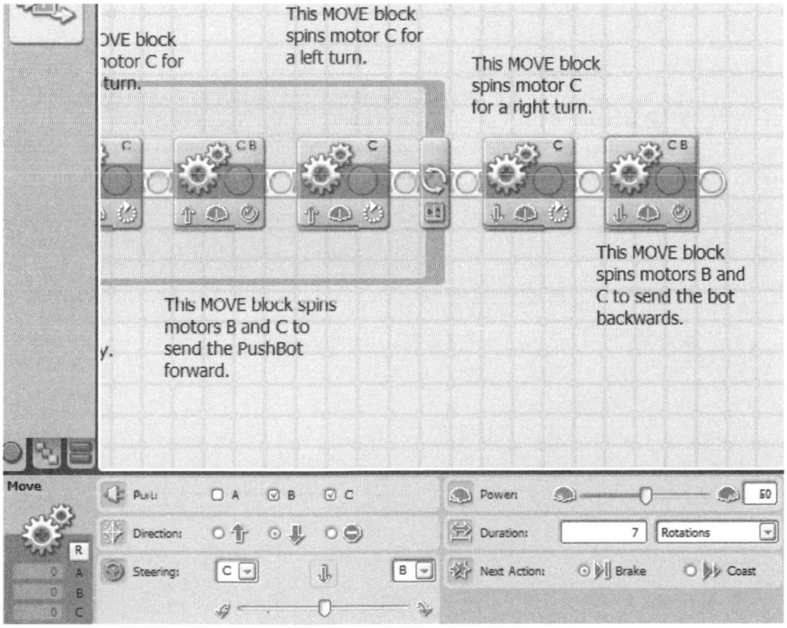

Figure 20-24. *This MOVE block moves the bot backward to Point A.*

My bot moves back seven rotations (approximately 4 feet) and stops. It's now at Point A and I'm ready to get it to point B. It's important for me to have the bot centered with the figurine and the ramp. To do this, I'll perform plenty of tests using the Sound Sensor to get it to stop and turn at precisely the right point where I want it.

I drop in another MOVE block (see Figure 20-25) to get the bot to turn right (the bot's cage will be facing away from the first three figurines).

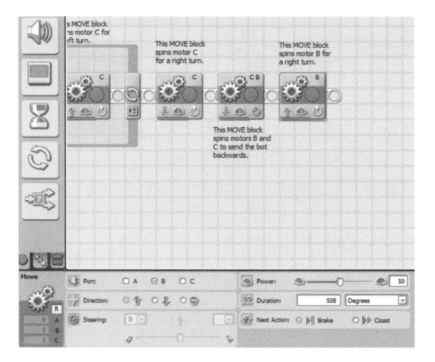

Figure 20-25. *This MOVE block turns the PushBot toward Point B.*

And now I want the bot to slowly move down to Point B. I say slowly because I'm going to watch it and trigger the Sound Sensor to stop the bot when it reaches the center point. Again, this will take some practice to determine exactly where the bot should be when I yell "Stop!" I'll add a LOOP block as shown in Figure 20-26 that will break when the Sound Sensor is triggered.

I add in the MOVE block that will slowly spin motors B and C and a WAIT block configured for 2 seconds to give me time to watch as it approaches Point B (see Figure 20-27).

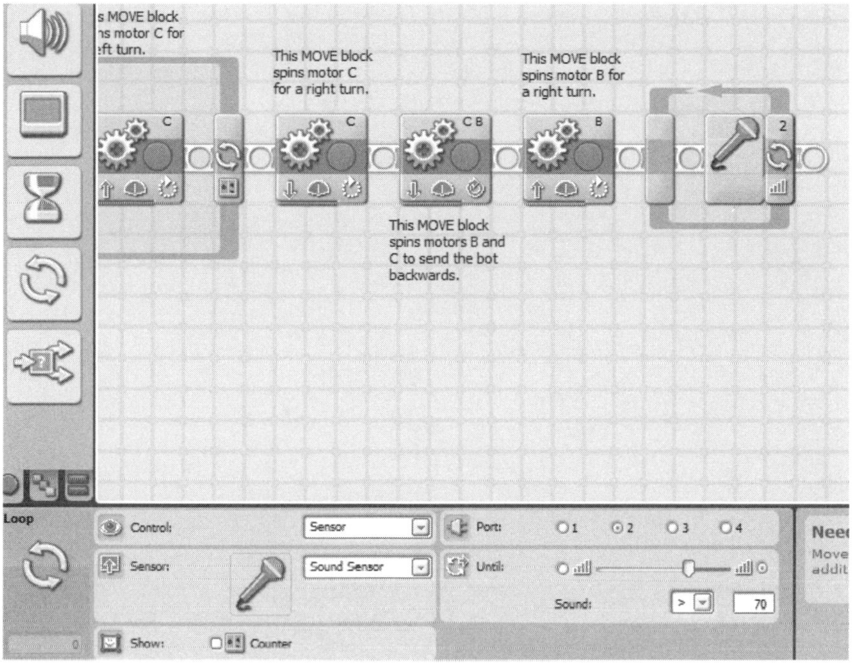

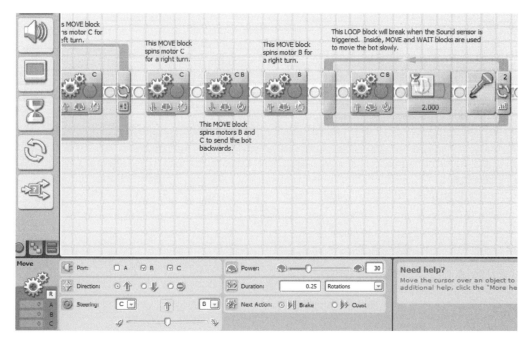

Figure 20-26. *This LOOP block will break when the Sound Sensor is triggered.*

Figure 20-27. *MOVE and WAIT blocks are added to move the bot to Point B.*

Once it reaches Point B, it needs to make a left turn (cage facing figurine 4). I add in a MOVE block for this left turn (see Figure 20-28).

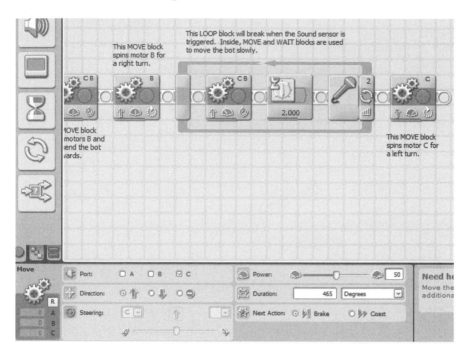

Figure 20-28. *This MOVE block turns the bot to the left with the cage facing the figurine.*

And now I need the bot to move (slowly) toward the fourth figurine. Once again, I'll use the Sound Sensor to tell the bot when to stop and close the cage. I add in a LOOP that is configured to break when the Sound Sensor is triggered (see Figure 20-29).

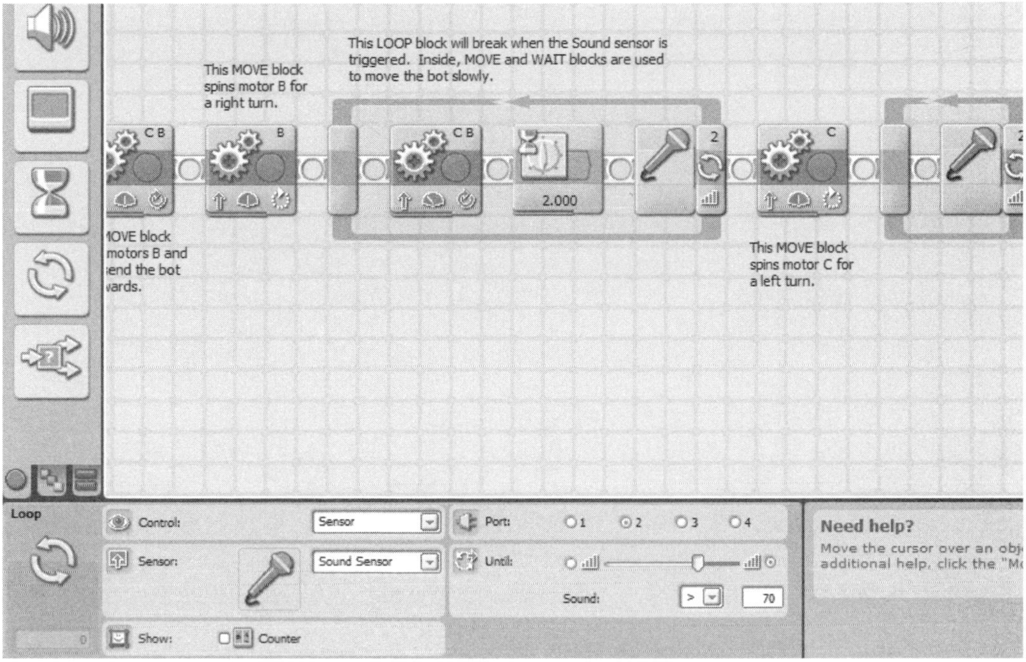

Figure 20-29. *This LOOP block will break when the Sound Sensor is triggered.*

A MOVE block is added inside the LOOP block to move the bot toward the figurine in quarter rotations (see Figure 20-30).

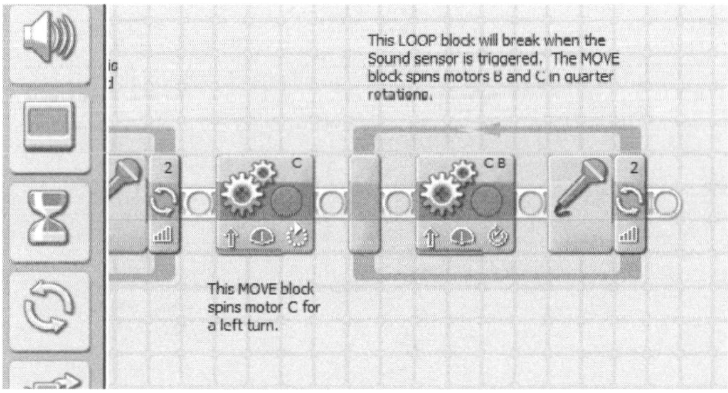

Figure 20-30. *This MOVE block moves the bot toward the final figurine.*

When the Sound Sensor is triggered, a MOVE block will close the cage on the final figurine (see Figure 20-31).

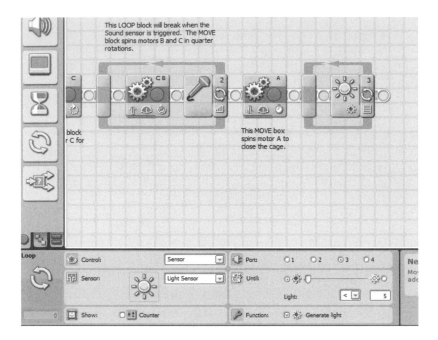

Figure 20-31. *This MOVE block closes the cage on the final figurine.*

I add in a final LOOP that will break when the Light Sensor is triggered by the black pressure plate on top of the sarcophagus (see Figure 20-32).

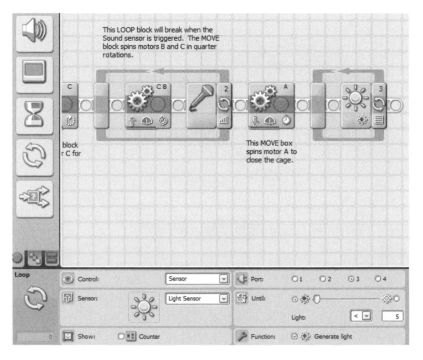

Figure 20-32. *This final LOOP block breaks when the Light Sensor is triggered.*

This last MOVE block will spin motors B and C in half rotations until the Light Sensor is triggered and the bot stops (see Figure 20-33).

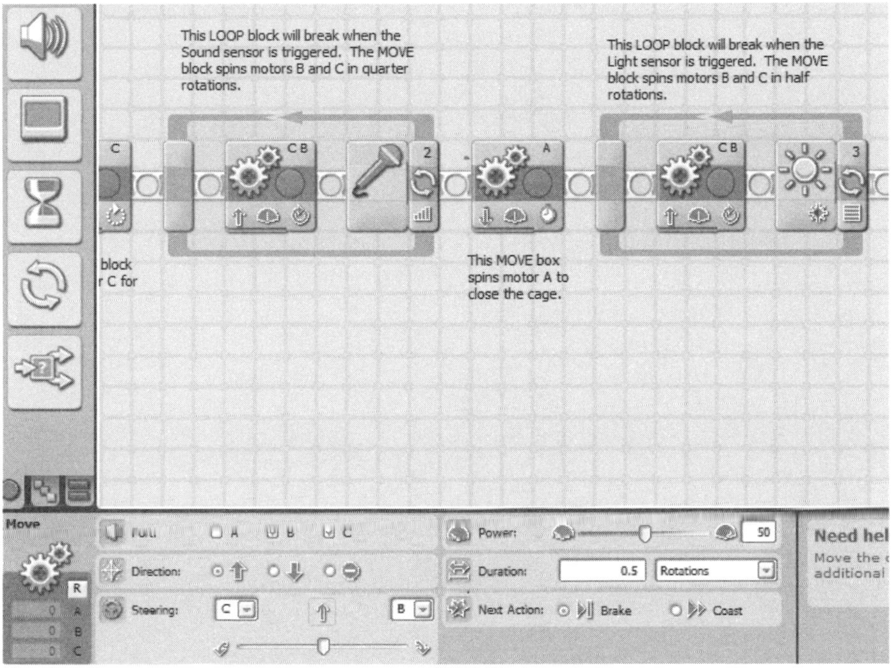

Figure 20-33. *This MOVE block stops spinning when the Light Sensor triggers.*

When the PushBot reaches the black pressure plate, the Light Sensor triggers the bot to stop moving. At this point, the final figurine should be resting on top of the sarcophagus.

If your robot's program succeeded, congratulations! If not, you'll need to test your bot quite a few times to make certain it works as expected. Set up your test environment and run as many as you can. When you're confident of your bot's abilities, run it one more time. If the bot accomplishes all the tasks, pat yourself on the back and get ready . . .

. . . It's time to investigate King Ixtua's burial chamber.

Story concludes in Chapter 21 . . .

CHAPTER 21

■ ■ ■

Discovery, Secret, and Home

Location: Southwest Guatemala

Weather Conditions: 86 degrees Fahrenheit, Humidity 45%, Rain 50%

Day 7: Base Camp, King Ixtua's Tomb, 11:05 AM

The past few days had been a flurry of activity, with Evan assisting Uncle Phillip, Max, and Grace to take pictures and measurements, draw sketches, and weigh artifacts. Evan had never had this much fun in his life. He had taken part in opening King Ixtua's tomb and discovering the king's burial chamber.

Evan sat enjoying a cold drink in the tent and stared at the massive collection of photographs that had been pinned up on every imaginable surface. Uncle Phillip sat across from him, enjoying a drink and a break from the heat.

"Well, Evan, have you enjoyed your time here?" asked Uncle Phillip.

Evan looked at his uncle with a shocked look on his face. "Are you *kidding*?" he replied. "All I want to know is where do we find another tomb?"

Uncle Phillip laughed. "I wish it were that easy. But I do have something you might find interesting," he said.

Evan watched as his uncle placed a small scroll on the table and nodded for Evan to take a look.

Evan picked up the scroll and unrolled it. The small surface was covered with a small number of Mayan glyphs. "What is this? What does it say?" asked Evan.

"That is a scroll that we found inside King Ixtua's sarcophagus. The fact that it wasn't in the king's library makes it something special. Grace has the better translation skills, so I've asked her to come and join us, but if that scroll contains what I think it does, you may get your wish," replied Uncle Phillip.

Evan stared back at the scroll. He carefully rolled it back up and placed it on the table.

"Uncle Phillip, this has been the best summer I've ever had," said Evan. "I don't think I've told you yet, but thanks for inviting me."

The tent flap separated and Grace entered carrying some books and a camera.

Uncle Phillip smiled. "Evan, you're welcome. But I have to say, if you had *not* come along, I don't honestly know if we would have been able to continue. So let me thank you for making the trip."

Grace nodded and set the items on the table. "Yeah, Evan. Max and I are really happy you came along, too. None of us has the proper skills to train a monkey," she said with a smile.

"Have a seat, Grace," said Uncle Phillip. "Evan and I were just talking about this little scroll here. Can you take a look?"

Grace unrolled the scroll and studied it for a moment. She opened one of the books on the table and spent a few more seconds searching for something. She flipped a few more pages and then suddenly stood up. "This is unbelievable!" she yelled.

Uncle Phillip laughed out loud. "I thought so!" he replied.

"What is it?" asked Evan. Grace and Uncle Phillip were laughing together. Evan found himself laughing with the group.

Max stuck his head in the tent. "What's all the noise in here?" he asked, looking at Evan.

Evan shrugged. "I have no idea."

"Sit down, Max. I'll let Grace explain," said Uncle Phillip.

Max and Grace both sat down and Evan looked over at Grace. She held up the scroll and pointed at a small glyph. "I know we were laughing, but this is not the punch line to a joke," she said. "This symbol right here is 'quetz'la'ki,' which translates to king's treasure."

Max looked at Grace and then at Uncle Phillip. "Let me get this straight. Are you telling me that's a treasure map?"

Uncle Phillip nodded with a smile. "I wasn't certain until Grace translated, but I do recognize the other symbols as measurements and natural landmarks," he said.

Grace pointed at some more symbols. "This scroll contains directions from this tomb to the location of King Ixtua's treasure repository."

"Are we all going to be rich?" asked Evan.

Uncle Phillip patted Evan on the back. "Not a chance, Evan. Anything we find belongs to the government of Guatemala. And that's assuming this repository hasn't already been found and looted," he replied.

"But if it hasn't?" Max asked.

"Well, as the team that discovered its location, the Guatemalan government will give us complete access and allow us to catalogue anything we find. But remember, the historical data from the scrolls and artifacts in King Ixtua's tomb is going to keep us busy for years," said Uncle Phillip.

Evan looked at his uncle, a little confused. "I have a question. Do you think the repository has traps like the king's tomb?"

"I'm absolutely certain of it," replied Grace. "This scroll matches the ones we have that were written by Tupaxu. Knowing Tupaxu, the repository probably has even more complex traps."

"Well, I have to go back in a few days and start school," said Evan. "I'll be happy to leave my robotics kit, but I don't think I'll have time to explain everything about it."

Uncle Phillip leaned forward and looked at Evan. "We probably won't be able to start looking for this repository for five or six months. And we have another six months' of paperwork to fill out for the Guatemalan government for King Ixtua's tomb. Trust me, Evan. We won't be able to tackle the repository for at least a year," he said.

Evan smiled. "Are you saying what I think you're saying?"

"Yes, Evan," said Uncle Phillip. "I think it's a safe bet that we might need your expertise again next summer if we find King Ixtua's treasure room. Think you might be interested?"

"Are you serious?" yelled Evan. "The only problem I can think of is all my friends will want to come along. I have two friends, Jeff and Katelyn, who have robotics kits, too."

"Well, let's take it one step at a time. You've got school and we've got a lot of paperwork to complete and reports to write. We'll stay in touch with you during the year, and if everything works out, maybe you can join us next summer if we find the repository," said Uncle Phillip, standing up. "Now, how about we have a nice lunch together and talk more about this treasure room."

Max, Grace, and Evan all nodded.

"Okay, then," said Uncle Phillip. "Lunch is on me. Grilled vegetables and lemonade in the next tent. Let's go."

Evan stood with the team, his mind racing with images of what kinds of traps and challenges the king's treasure room would contain. He also had a new idea for a bot that he planned on designing on the flight home. It was going to be a busy school year. He made a promise to himself to study more for his history class and walked out of the tent.

THE END?

APPENDIX A

■■■

Online Reference and Support

You should have received an *Instruction Guide* and a *Quick Start Guide* with your Lego Mindstorms NXT kit. Thankfully, that's not the end of the reference material available for your robotics kit. The great news is that the amount of information available online is already substantial and growing fast.

There is no way for me to include everything available for your NXT reading pleasure— there are new Web sites, blogs, and training materials popping up every day. From videos to pictures to new operating systems and software, the Mindstorms NXT world has enough to keep you busy for quite a while.

Web Sites

When it comes to Web sites, there are plenty. The Web sites I'm including here have proven to be kid-friendly:

- http://www.mindstorms.com: The official Web site of the Lego Mindstorms NXT. This site offers videos, building instructions, plenty of cool downloads, interviews with NXT designers and demos of their designs, links to blogs and other Web sites, and access to online forums. The site is always changing, so check in frequently to see what's new.

- http://www.legoeducation.com: The companion Web site for Lego Education. This Web site has interesting articles to read (a good source for future bot ideas) and offers up challenges that will improve your robot design skills.

- http://mynxt.matthiaspaulscholz.eu: Matthias Paul Scholz lives in Germany and has worked with me on many NXT projects, including The NXT Step blog (see "Blogs" below). His Web site includes videos, pictures, and instructions for many strange and unusual bots that he's designed. He also provides links to other Web sites and blogs.

- http://www.firstlegoleague.org/: FIRST LEGO League is a series of robotic competitions for students ages 9 to 14. There are local competitions that culminate in an annual international competition, with teams from around the world coming together to display some excellent robotic design and programming skills.

- http://www.philohome.com/nxt.htm: Phillipe Hurbain's Web site covers some fairly advanced robotic subjects, but it's always fun to visit. Philo (his nickname) likes to take his Bricks apart, so don't try and copy anything he does—it could damage your NXT.

There are *plenty* more Web sites that focus on the NXT, and new ones are popping up all the time. You might want to even consider starting your own Web site on the NXT!

Blogs

Blogs have been growing in popularity for a few years now—and the number of blogs related to the NXT continues to increase. The following are some frequently updated and popular blogs that are focused on the Lego Mindstorms NXT robotics kit and related products and news:

- `http://thenxtstep.blogspot.com`: I contribute to this blog with a handful of NXT colleagues. We cover news and products related to the NXT and more. It's a good place to check for updates on new products as well as information on new Web sites, forums, and blogs.

- `http://www.legoeducation.info/nxt`: This blog focuses on the Mindstorms Education NXT kit and includes news and updates pertaining to Mindstorms NXT and the classroom.

As with Web sites, there are many more blogs out there dedicated to the Mindstorms NXT kit. You might want to consider even starting your own; visit `http://www.blogger.com` or `http://wordpress.com` to learn how to create your own blog, absolutely free. Post news of your NXT bot designs with pictures and video and you may find yourself developing a growing base of fans who visit your blog often.

Forums and Message Boards

Forums and message boards are popular places for you to share your comments, questions, and robot designs with other NXT fans. Be aware that most forums require you to register with a username and a password to use the site. Be sure to read the rules for what you can post and what you cannot post—violating the rules can get you banned from using the forum in the future.

Three of the most popular forums right now are the following:

- `http://club.lego.com/messageboards/home/`: After registering at this site, you can post comments and questions on the official Lego forum. The forum is divided into categories, so look for the Mindstorms NXT category to view discussions on the NXT robotics kit.

- `http://news.lugnet.com/robotics/nxt/`: Lugnet has been around for a long time, allowing Lego fans to communicate and share news and everything else imaginable. This new forum has been created just for the NXT. It's also a great place to post questions! The questions do tend to be from more experienced users, but you can learn a lot from reading and participating in the discussions. You will have to register with this site, too, in order to post on the forum.

- `http://www.nxtasy.org`: This blog includes a forum and is building a collection of NXT-related articles (submitted by NXT fans). It maintains some excellent discussions on beginner and advanced topics.

■ ■ ■

Building Instructions for Bots

If you build a unique bot of some sort, someone with a Mindstorms NXT kit might ask you for instructions on building a duplicate. There are numerous methods for demonstrating how to build a robot that you have designed. One easy method is to simply digitally record yourself building it, talking as you go and showing to the camera the pieces you are using and where you place them. I'd like to also introduce to you something called CAD (computer-aided design) software. This type of software allows you to create accurate drawings of your robot designs as well as step-by-step instructions that can be printed or viewed on a computer screen; examples of CAD programs used for Lego creations include LDraw (http://www.ldraw.org) and MLCad (http://www.lm-software.com/mlcad).

For this book, I've been using photographs taken with a digital camera. With the digital camera, I can immediately upload the photo to my computer (a laptop in this case) and view the image. If it's blurry or doesn't show quite what I wanted to capture, I can delete it and take another.

This appendix is a short tutorial containing some tips and suggestions I want to pass along—I've learned a lot from photographing this book's bots and I'm hoping some of my experiences can help you if you choose to create building instructions (BI) from photos of your own bots.

Background

One of the biggest mistakes I made early on was to photograph the construction of my bots against a white background. After converting the photos to black-and-white images, what I found was that the colors of most of the Mindstorms NXT parts (off-white, light gray, dark gray) just didn't show up very well when I placed a white posterboard under the parts. Take a look at Figure B-1. On the left is a collection of parts against a white background, and on the right is the same collection of parts against a yellow background. After converting the photograph to a black-and-white image, which do you think looks better?

Figure B-1. *The background can make all the difference.*

I also tried photos using blue, green, red, and gray posterboard. What I found was that yellow or light-blue posterboard worked best. Whether you convert the pictures to black-and-white or not, photographing your bot's assembly against a colored background instead of white works much better. Even better is to use a colored background with some texture.

Step by Step

I'll jump straight to the secret for taking great BI photographs: Build your bot *first*—get it perfect, the way you like, and make sure it works—and then start taking pictures as you take the bot apart.

You're right, this is not a big secret. You'll photograph the bot as it's disassembled and then reverse the photographs. Simple. But I do have a couple of suggestions for you:

Your first photograph should be of the completed bot: When you are done, you'll reverse the picture order, so this will actually be your last building instruction photo. Whatever angle you use to take a picture, that is the angle you need to keep for the next photo.

Without moving the bot, remove a part and set it down close to the bot: Take the photograph (from the same angle as the first) so that it shows the bot and the removed part, and make sure that where the part was removed is visible in the new photograph. Look at Figure B-2. On the right side is the final bot, and on the left you can see that a part has been removed. You should be able to determine from the photo on the right where the part on the left will be placed. Good building instructions always show you a part in one step that you'll use in the next step (which is why the photo on the right has two parts next to it).

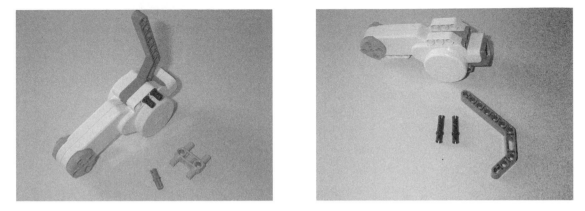

Figure B-2. *Look at the image on the right to determine the placement of the part on the left.*

Remove multiple parts if they are all visible in the most recent photograph: If you have three 15-hole beams and two small black connectors that can be immediately removed and are not hidden by other pieces, feel free to take all of them off. Place them in an organized fashion near the bot (or what's left of it) and take a picture. As long as the locations of all the parts you are removing are visible in the previous photo you took, everything should be fine.

As you take more and more photographs, you'll find even better methods for taking photographs and discover things to avoid. For example, you can't remove a part on a nonvisible side of the bot that you just photographed. If you take off a nonvisible part, place it next to the bot, and then photograph it, how will others using your instructions know where to place the part? They'll see the new part to add, but when they look at the next photograph, the part you removed will not be visible.

▨Note If at all possible, photograph in strong, indirect light. The built-in flash on most cameras tends to "flatten" the image, removing or reducing depth cues. If you can use a strong, even light source from a different direction than the camera, you have much more control over the lighting and depth cues in the picture.

After taking the picture, inspect it closely in the LCD screen of the camera . . . and delete any picture that is not in sharp focus or doesn't clearly show what you want to show. It's digital, so you can always take another picture, but the model will never be at this particular step again, so *check now*, and don't regret it later.

After you've completely disassembled your bot, take the pictures and put them in reverse order. If you used a digital camera and uploaded the photos to your computer, rename the images Step 1, Step 2, etc. The first image will show the first piece (or first few pieces) of your bot being placed or connected together.

Now, use your new building instructions and try to build your bot. If you took good photographs, you should be able to build your bot again. If anything is confusing, take a picture to
capture the proper placement of a part or two where you found the problem. You can give the
picture a name such as Step 3b if it fits between Steps 3 and 4.

When you are happy with your building instructions, you can use image editing software
to add text to your pictures if you like. Then, burn the images to a CD or print them out and
share them with others. You can also post your steps to NXTLOG (see Appendix C). And now
your bot design can be re-created anytime.

APPENDIX C

■ ■ ■

NXTLOG

Lego has created a powerful tool for you to share your robotic creations with the world! It's a Web site called NXTLOG, which I know you're going to love. This is an official Lego Web site, so it's totally safe for kids. NXTLOG is constantly growing and changing, so some features may or may not be available when you visit. But you'll enjoy seeing all the other robots that people are submitting, and hopefully you'll start submitting your own. Now, let me give you a brief overview of how it works.

User Account

First, you create a Lego Club user account (if you haven't already) so that you can access the NXTLOG site. Visit http://club.lego.com and click the Sign-Up button, shown in Figure C-1 (note that the background image on the button changes every few seconds).

Figure C-1. *Create a user account on Lego's Web site.*

If you are already a member, enter your username ("nickname") and password and click **Enter**. If you're not a member yet, click the **Sign Up Now** button at the bottom of the screen. Read the Lego Club Terms of Service, click **Accept**, and fill out the Registration page. After you've created your account, visit http://mindstorms.lego.com and log in to the NXTLOG tool.

Tools

When you are logged in to the NXTLOG site, you should see a page similar to Figure C-2.

Figure C-2. *The NXTLOG My Projects screen*

The following are a few things that you can do from this page:

- *View your projects*: You can view projects you have uploaded, and other club members can provide comments and reviews of your designs. You can also choose a picture for each of your projects and read comments others have left for you.

- *Upload a new project*: You can upload pictures, videos, and notes about your robotic creations. Share your new robots with the world and give others a chance to test your designs.

- *View projects from other members*: If you're looking for design ideas, you'll have plenty of robots to examine. The "Community" of robot designers is growing every day, so you'll need to check back often to see what's new.

Now, if you're wondering how you add steps to your projects, let me give you a small glimpse of how this works. In Figure C-2, if you click the **Edit** button, you are given the ability to upload building instruction photos for your robots, one at a time. If you post building instructions, other members will be able to build and test your designs—and maybe suggest improvements or upgrades!

Clicking the "**add a new project**" link allows you to also upload a new design.

■**Note** Since you are posting your designs on the Internet, don't be worried or upset if others take your designs and modify them. That's just good robot design—and you should do the same! Take a design and change it, add new sensors or more motors, and definitely provide feedback on the NXTLOG site for the original designer and other members.

NXTLOG is a great way for you to work with robot fans from around the world. Think about how much fun you'll have working on a robot project with friends from Europe, Japan, Australia, or other countries. You'll find teams of robot designers discussing project ideas and then submitting their designs. You'll be able to participate in competitions (such as "Design an NXT robot that can change a lightbulb") and even create your own.

The NXT robotics community is going to give you plenty of ideas, and you'll never run out of robots to experiment with and program and test.

Have fun!

APPENDIX D

■ ■ ■

HiTechnic NXT Compass Sensor

A new sensor from HiTechnic Products is available for your NXT robots. This sensor does not come with the basic NXT kit, but you can purchase it directly from the online Lego Store, http://shop.lego.com, or from the HiTechnic Products Web site, http://www.hitechnic.com.

This is a fun sensor to play with and can give your robots a good sense of direction—pun intended. If you are considering purchasing a new sensor for your robots, this would be a good one to start off using. This appendix provides some details about the HiTechnic NXT Compass Sensor.

North, West, East, and South

The Compass Sensor provides digital feedback to your NXT Brick in the form of an integer value in the range of 0 to 359. It does not return negative values for directional headings. So, for example, if your bot is heading east, you will get a return value of 90. Take a look at Figure D-1 for a better understanding of how compass points (North, West, East, South) correspond to numeric values (0 to 360).

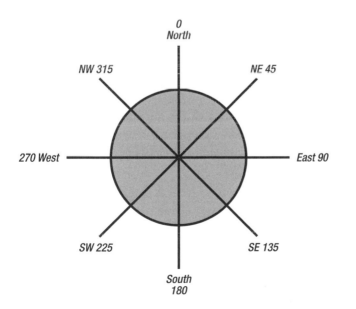

Figure D-1. *A compass with standard North, West, East, and South headings*

When using the HiTechnic NXT Compass Sensor, it is helpful to know that some of the values the sensor returns to the NXT Brick match up to directions such as north, south, east, and west. You can also get rough estimates for northwest, northeast, southwest, and southeast. Simply put, the sensor returns the magnetic bearing.

Using the Compass Sensor

Figure D-2 shows the NXT-G programming block used to configure the Compass Sensor.

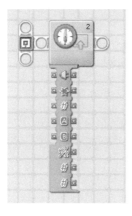 

Figure D-2. *The Compass Sensor programming block*

The Compass Sensor block is on the left side of the small program, and you can see that it works just like other NXT-G blocks. It has a configuration panel as well as a data hub that can send and receive data using data wires.

In the **Port** section, you can select the port number to use when attaching the Compass Sensor.

The **Action** section has a drop-down menu that gives you three options:

- *Absolute Reading*: Returns a value between 0 and 359, depending on the direction heading.

- *Relative Reading*: Enables you to use the sensor to help your bot maintain a specific direction (such as 90). You set a target heading (for example, 90 degrees, which is a heading of east) and the block returns a value showing the difference between the current absolute heading and the target heading. If your absolute heading is 85, the returned value will be 5 (the difference between the target, 90, and the current absolute heading). If the heading is 95, the returned value will be –5. This scheme allows you to decide which way to turn to get back to your target heading quickly. A negative number means your bot should turn counterclockwise and a positive value means your bot needs to turn clockwise.

- *Calibrate*: Lets you calibrate the sensor in the bot's working environment so that you obtain the best readings possible, allowing the sensor to try to compensate for variations in the magnetic field due to the robot itself.

Other options with the Compass Sensor allow you to define a range of values (for example, between 0 and 359 degrees) that you can use to obtain a TRUE/FALSE = response—this response is useful for keeping your robot moving within a certain direction; if the robot strays outside the range, you could use a condition block such as the SWITCH block to put the bot back on course.

It's a fun sensor to play with, and a robot with a sense of direction can perform some very useful movements with a large degree of accuracy.

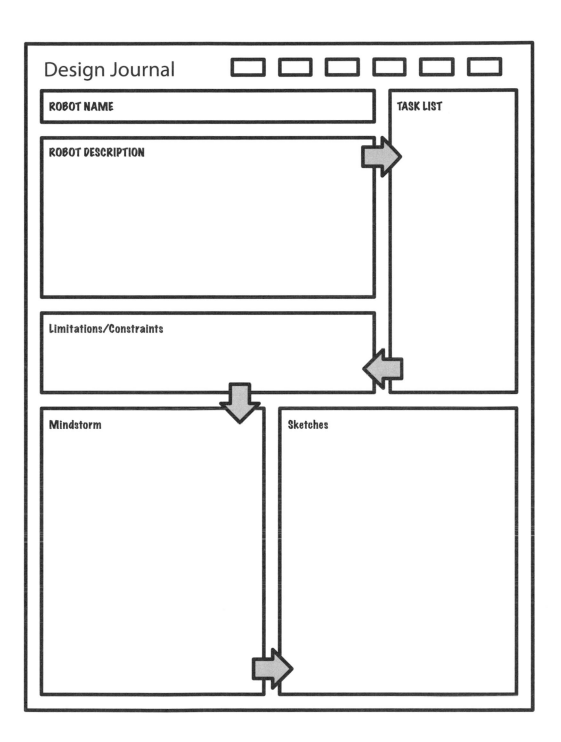

Design Journal

ROBOT NAME

TASK LIST

ROBOT DESCRIPTION

Limitations/Constraints

Mindstorm

Sketches

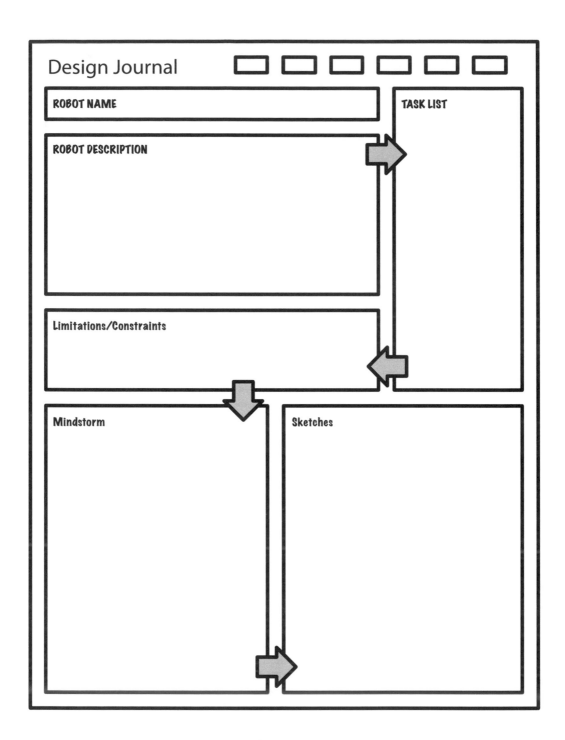

Design Journal

ROBOT NAME

ROBOT DESCRIPTION

TASK LIST

Limitations/Constraints

Mindstorm

Sketches

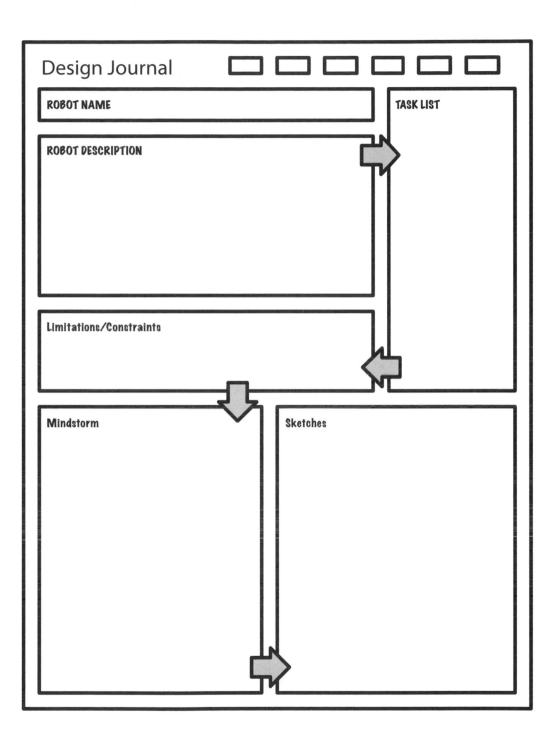

Design Journal

ROBOT NAME

ROBOT DESCRIPTION

TASK LIST

Limitations/Constraints

Mindstorm

Sketches

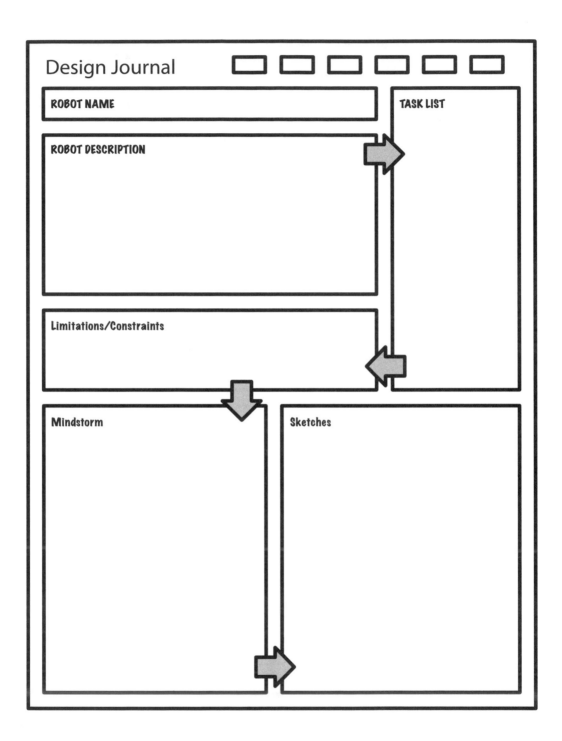

Design Journal

ROBOT NAME

ROBOT DESCRIPTION

TASK LIST

Limitations/Constraints

Mindstorm

Sketches

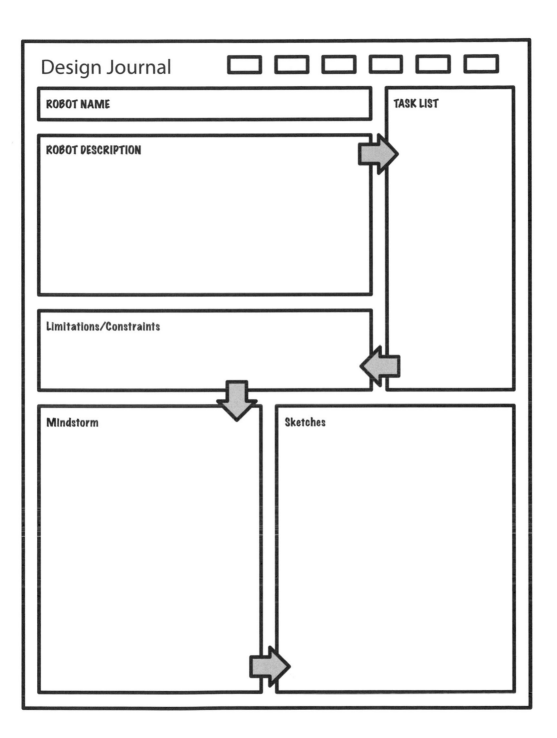

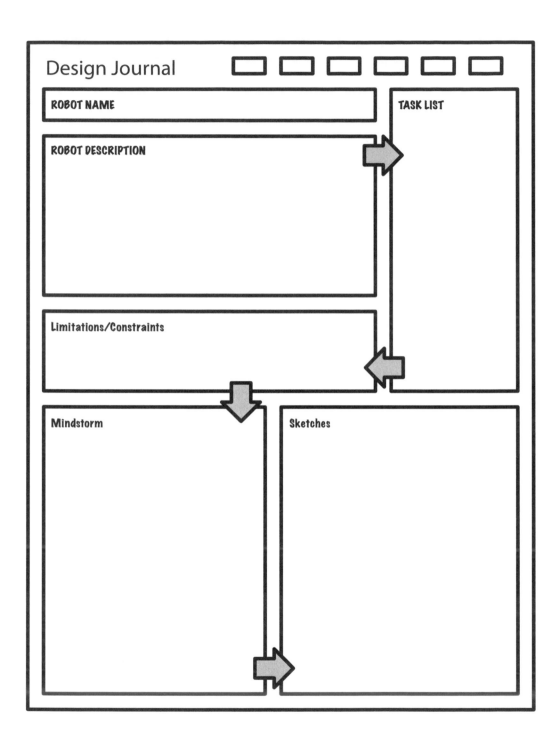

Design Journal

ROBOT NAME

ROBOT DESCRIPTION

TASK LIST

Limitations/Constraints

Mindstorm

Sketches

Index

FIND IT FAST
with the Apress *SuperIndex*™

Quickly Find Out What the Experts Know

Leading by innovation, Apress now offers you its *SuperIndex*™, a turbocharged companion to the fine index in this book. The Apress *SuperIndex*™ is a keyword and phrase-enabled search tool that lets you search through the entire Apress library. Powered by dtSearch™, it delivers results instantly.

Instead of paging through a book or a PDF, you can electronically access the topic of your choice from a vast array of Apress titles. The Apress *SuperIndex*™ is the perfect tool to find critical snippets of code or an obscure reference. The Apress *SuperIndex*™ enables all users to harness essential information and data from the best minds in technology.

No registration is required, and the Apress *SuperIndex*™ is free to use.

❶ Thorough and comprehensive searches of over 300 titles

❷ No registration required

❸ Instantaneous results

❹ A single destination to find what you need

❺ Engineered for speed and accuracy

❻ Will spare your time, application, and anxiety level

Search now: *http://superindex.apress.com*

You Need the Companion eBook

Your purchase of this book entitles you to buy the companion PDF-version eBook for only $10. Take the weightless companion with you anywhere.

We believe this Apress title will prove so indispensable that you'll want to carry it with you everywhere, which is why we are offering the companion eBook (in PDF format) for $10 to customers who purchase this book now. Convenient and fully searchable, the PDF version of any content-rich, page-heavy Apress book makes a valuable addition to your programming library. You can easily find and copy code—or perform examples by quickly toggling between instructions and the application. Even simultaneously tackling a donut, diet soda, and complex code becomes simplified with hands-free eBooks!

Once you purchase your book, getting the $10 companion eBook is simple:

➊ Visit **www.apress.com/promo/tendollars/**.

➋ Complete a basic registration form to receive a randomly generated question about this title.

➌ Answer the question correctly in 60 seconds, and you will receive a promotional code to redeem for the $10.00 eBook.

2560 Ninth Street • Suite 219 • Berkeley, CA 94710

eBookshop   ASP **Today**   Apress®
THE EXPERT'S VOICE™

Offer valid through 6/30/07.